IMAGINE THE SOUND

Imagine the Sound

. . . .

Experimental African American Literature after Civil Rights

Carter Mathes

University of Minnesota Press
Minneapolis
London

Chapter 4 was previously published as "Scratching the Threshold: Textual Sound and Political Form in Toni Cade Bambara's *The Salt Eaters*," *Contemporary Literature* 50, no. 2 (2009): 363–96; reprinted by permission of the University of Wisconsin Press. An earlier version of chapter 5 was published as "'The mind is a strange and terrible vehicle': Fractured Time and Multidimensional Sound in *No Name in the Street*," *African American Review* 46, no. 4 (Winter 2013): 587–604; copyright 2014 Johns Hopkins University Press and Saint Louis University; reprinted with permission.

Published by the University of Minnesota Press
111 Third Avenue South, Suite 290
Minneapolis, MN 55401-2520
http://www.upress.umn.edu

Library of Congress Cataloging-in-Publication Data
Mathes, Carter.
Imagine the sound : experimental African American literature after civil rights / Carter Mathes.
Includes bibliographical references and index.
ISBN 978-0-8166-9305-4 (hc : alk. paper) — ISBN 978-0-8166-9306-1 (pb : alk. paper)
1. American literature—African American authors—History and criticism.
2. American literature—20th century—History and criticism. 3. Literature, Experimental—United States—History and criticism. 4. African Americans—Intellectual life—20th century. I. Title.
PS153.N5M2655 2014

Printed in the United States of America on acid-free paper

The University of Minnesota is an equal-opportunity educator and employer.

20 19 18 17 16 15   10 9 8 7 6 5 4 3 2 1

Contents

The Acoustics of Unfreedom

Resistant Aurality

Assata: An Autobiography recounts Assata Shakur's life and closely focuses on her coming into consciousness as a black revolutionary during the Black Power era. The narrative opens with Shakur's memory of the now legendary May 2, 1973, encounter on the New Jersey Turnpike in which she, Zayd Malik Shakur, and Sundiata Acoli were pulled over by New Jersey state troopers James Harper and Werner Foerster. The events that transpired as a result of this alleged traffic stop left Foerster and Zayd Malik Shakur dead and Assata and Harper wounded, but have never been definitively reconstructed over the course of Shakur's trials for the murder of Foerster and the assault of Harper, or through her autobiographical account.[1] Rather than offering a definitive and authoritative claim regarding the truth of the events, Shakur instead frames the moment through representations of sound that emphasize the immediacy of political conflict.

The first paragraphs of Shakur's text clearly situate the sound of the narrative within a broader tradition of black "fugitive" histories:

There were lights and sirens. Zayd was dead. My mind knew that Zayd was dead. The air was like cold glass. Huge bubbles rose and burst. Each one felt like an explosion in my chest. My mouth tasted like blood and dirt. The car spun around me and then something like sleep overtook me. In the background I could hear what sounded like gunfire. But I was fading and dreaming.

Suddenly, the door flew open and I felt myself being dragged out onto the pavement. Pushed and punched, a foot upside my head, a kick in the stomach. Police were everywhere. One had a gun to my head.

"Which way did they go?" he was shouting. "Bitch, you'd better open your goddamn mouth or I'll blow your goddamn head off!"[2]

She replays the spectacle of domestic-state repression through her recall of the aural texture of the setting, particularly through the way it is suffused with the dominating vocalization projected by the police. Shakur's textual account of the sensory modalities associated with state-sanctioned repression resonates within a tradition of black autobiography that includes the narratives of Harriet Wilson, Frederick Douglass, and Harriet Jacobs. Her recollection of the confrontation between black subject and white power rings all too familiarly as she recalls her shooting, capture, hospitalization, and interrogation with a clear focus on the sensations and sounds of black subjection, containment, and resistance.

The acoustic framework of Shakur's perspective shifts to the wake of the Turnpike shooting, as she is lying wounded in the hospital and awaiting treatment for a serious gunshot wound. She then begins to experience new levels of physical and psychological intimidation by the police. Her account of this torture in all of its sensory depth diagnoses the methods of discipline and punishment that re-inscribe black bodies as threatening to the racial state. Shakur replays the sound of the police as they linger at her bedside, waiting for her to show any visible sign of consciousness:

> "She can talk," one is saying. "The doctor says she can talk. Where were you going? What is your name? Where were you coming from? Who was in the car with you? How many of you were there? I know she can hear me." I keep my eyes closed. One of them leans down real close to me. I feel his breath on my cheek. And smell it. "I know you can hear me and I know you can talk, and if you don't hurry up and start talking, I'm gonna bash your face in for you." My eyes fly open in spite of myself. Immediately they are all in my face, throwing question after question at me. I say nothing. After a while, I close my eyes again. "Oh, she doesn't feel good," one of them says in a sweet, mocking voice. "Where does it hurt? Here? Here? HERE?" With each *here* comes a crash. I look around wildly, but no one is there. More thumps and punches, but none of them hurts as bad as my chest is hurting. I try to scream but I know immediately that that's a mistake. My chest erupts and I think I am gonna die. They go on and on. Questions and bangs. I think they will never stop.[3]

Sound becomes crucial for Assata, not simply as a reflection of the oral dimensions of her confrontations with state power, but more pointedly as a vocalization of black fugitive resistance, a version of what Mladen Dolar terms "a dimension of the voice which runs counter to its self-transparency, sense, and presence: the voice against *logos*, the voice as the other of *logos*, its radical alterity."[4] Dolar's ascription of meaning to what persists outside the phonological linearity of vocal projection and its literal homologizing or analogizing of sound and sense suggests an opening for Shakur's auto-biographical conceptualization of voice and sound to diagnose and disrupt the links between white supremacy and ideas of American law, order, and domestic security.

Shakur's black radical liberation directly confronts the consolidation of state power in the post–Civil Rights era. The brutality enacted against her is inscribed within, and itself helps to inscribe, broader practices of racial governance based on the construction, racialization, and strategic application of categories such as radical, threat, terrorist, and criminal. This process is both visual and phonic; visual in that authoritarian entities of the state wish to depict and sediment a flattened image of black radicalism as a transgressive threat to a constructed idea of American identity, and phonic in the quality of Shakur's resistance to this flattening through her projection of sound that reconstitutes the political along frequencies outside of ocularcentric authoritarian containment. Shakur's ability to project her voice outside the distortion of state and corporate media propaganda is critical to the narrative architecture of the text. Her portrayal of state violence hinges on her manipulation of the sonority and resonance of her voice to signal both the contemporary and historical dimensions of black radical thought. Her conceptualization of sound anticipates and echoes Fred Moten's point that black radical aesthetics resist the primacy of the ocular in favor of embracing the complexities of visual and aural exchange within black cultural production. In the following passage, Moten outlines this problem through the context of the scream as it can be articulated as "always so much more than primal":

> The condition of possibility of such an emergence is the ability critically to think the scream, to offer what the scream demands that is before—which is to say both prior to and past—both interpretation and reading . . . I want to suggest that a quite specific asynchronicity between sound and image marks the spot of a radical intervention. This off-set or off-rhythm animates the audiovisuality (the arrhythmia of its multiple tracks) of the

commodity in general. In this tradition, in spite of whatever powerful voices of disavowal, the man's voice is a woman's voice and the high-pitched truth of the falsetto is the revolutionary tone and content.[5]

Moten defines resistance to the permanence of racialized terror through an embrace of the sonic "asynchronicity" of black radical consciousness, framing the political and critical capacity of sound as an evasion of sedimented or regulated meaning. Shakur approaches this challenge in her text through a focus not only on the actual narrative voice and moments of ambient noise recorded in her account, but also through her imagination of a conceptual field of sound that amplifies the underground, lower frequencies of black radicalism.

Shakur's narration of underground fugitivity, concealment, and flight casts underground existence as a challenge to the policing of blackness by the state, and reveals the complex and multidimensional possibilities for African American life in the face of forms of subjection not solely produced by the force of the law. Shakur explains the increasing amount of repression and dissension that the New York City Black Panther Party faced during the late 1960s, and she points to networks of underground sanctuary, support, and concealment as fluid, organic responses to the attacks that were being levied against black radicals by the police, the FBI, and most urgently, through the multifaceted program of state surveillance and counterinsurgency known as COINTELPRO.[6] Her preconceived notions of "people in some basement, passing through some hidden bookcase door and disappearing into thin air . . . all kinds of elaborate 'I Spy' kinds of hookups, outrageous disguises, stuff right out of 'Mission: Impossible,'"[7] are replaced with a vision of black underground life as a series of movements between visibility and invisibility, and the eventual realization that the underground might represent a new horizon of black organizing from the early 1970s onward, in response to heightened levels of police and state repression.

Concurrently, Assata conveys an awareness of the political efficacy of the underground as a space of clandestine black resistance entangled with the everyday oppressive realities of black working-class life. This entanglement takes shape as Shakur covertly relocates after she has been identified in newspapers and wanted poster photographs throughout the city as a suspect in the machine-gun killing of two policemen on Riverside Drive. When she emerges from hiding and catches the subway in the early morning hours, she notes the parallels between the underground elements of black radical life and the lives of working-class black women in the wake of the Civil Rights movement:

> The subway car has a twilight zone air to it. With the exception of a few white men who look like they are going to factory jobs, the rest are Black women. One has on a nurse's uniform, another looks like she us going to church, hat and all, and the rest of them look more or less like me. I keep staring at them. And it registers. Without one exception, every one of these sisters is wearing a wig. It feels so spooky. I am hiding my beautiful, nappy hair under this wig and hating it, hiding my stuff to save my life. I, who have had to give up my headwraps and my big, beaded earrings, my dungaree jackets, my red, black, and green poncho, and my long African dresses in order to struggle on another level, look out from under my wig at my sisters. Maybe we are all running and hiding. Maybe we are all running from something, all living a clandestine existence. Surely we are all being oppressed and persecuted.[8]

Assata's illustration of the underground speaks to the interlocking forces of political, economic, and cultural repression emerging within the post–Civil Rights era. She juxtaposes the underground as a space of insurgency against racism with a vision of the underground as a condition of life for working-class black women who must hide themselves under wigs in order to survive economically. The wig functions as a floating signifier that bridges the everyday lived struggles of black women with the formations of political critique and praxis deployed by Assata.

The sound of Shakur's reflection on black underground life does not merely resonate through the acoustics of her narrative voice on the page; her rendering of the underground also reverberates as a transgressive articulation of black consciousness. She conceptualizes her sound as an epistemological shift that simultaneously avoids a simplistic acceptance of conventional ideas of racial progress and an unquestioning reliance on armed struggle. In the pages following her subway meditation on the idea of the underground, she elaborates on the multidimensional orientation toward resistance that she comes to appreciate through the efforts of underground black revolutionary movements like the Black Liberation Army. Arguing against consolidation, centralization, and waging a "do-or-die battle with

the power structure in Amerika," Shakur suggests that the quest for liberation is more of an ephemeral and improvisational process than a fixed goal.
Her thoughts challenge caricatured notions of black revolution as a sim-
plistically violent pursuit, but more important, they necessitate considering asymmetry as an orientation toward resistance that may look, sound,
and feel tangibly different, yet remains grounded in its commitment to the
organic qualities of black community formation. Her reflections exemplify
the difficulty of pursuing radical methods of engagement while remaining
grounded in communities subject to the attempts of the media to demon-
ize black revolutionary activity as a terrorist threat. This conjuncture between
black political resistance and the sonic dimensions of expressive form offers
an alternate literary rendering of African American political culture during
the post–Civil Rights era.

What is the literary sound of these underground dimensions of black
radical thought in this period of tension and irresolution following the
apogee of the Civil Rights movement? In its broadest configuration, *Imagine the Sound* explores this question by examining the literary creation and
manipulation of sound by writers who seek to expand ideas of African
American cultural and political identity within the post–Civil Rights era.
Conceptualizing the experimental manipulation of sound within and in relationship to African American literature, I examine sonic effects and states
such as dissonance, vibration, and resonance as they bridge the aural, the
literary, and the political, complicating ideas and representations of time,
memory, and narrative perspective within formal literary structures. Taking into account both the acoustic and philosophical elements of sound
in order to, as Jonathan Sterne suggests, "consider sound as a particular
moment in a broader ontological and political field of vibration,"[9] I analyze
the ephemerality of specific sounds and broader configurations of aurality
as they generate both sensory and philosophical meaning. In emphasizing
the sonic as a conceptual field that might facilitate the radical projection of
African American experience, I raise questions regarding ideas of rationality, progress, and liberty as they underwrite the legislated vision of Civil
Rights–era racial equality propagated by the state. *Imagine the Sound* also
contends that the category "black postmodernism," as a formal and literary historical description of much post–World War II experimental black
writing, is not entirely sufficient in its breadth or precision.[10] As other critics have suggested, the economic, cultural, and formal rubrics that have
generally defined postmodernism in a broad sense have far more specific

valences within African American literary history. I turn to the politics of sound in post–Civil Rights African American expressive culture as one way of further delineating the urgency of this critical intervention in African American literary history.

Ideas of sound have been richly and productively interrogated for some time within musicology and critical theory. Predating, anticipating, and to some degree inspiring the contemporary interdisciplinary explosion of sound studies, Jacques Attali, in his theoretical work *Noise: The Political Economy of Music* (1977), analyzes sound as a pre-formative impulse within music that resists the totalizing efforts of the state to control, manipulate, and produce sound by turning itself into "a gigantic, monopolizing noise emitter, and at the same time, a generalized eavesdropping device."[11] Attali, in conceptualizing sound free from the confines of music, attempts to frame this initial sonic impulse as both outside the political economy of the mass production of music and within its potential as prophetic critique of a world increasingly defined by efforts to control the aural environment. He contends that "no theorizing accomplished through language or mathematics can suffice any longer," because these modes are no longer capable "of accounting for what is essential in time—the qualitative and the fluid, threats and violence," essentially arguing that it is necessary to imagine radically new theoretical forms in order to speak to new realities.[12] Building on Attali's attention to the prophetic qualities of sound as largely unheard, unread forms of critical reflections on the systems it is generated within, I consider these deinstitutionalizing properties of sound as nonlinear openings through which black writers can refine the role of the radical imagination within the politics of narrative construction. Providing black writers with an expressive map through the complexities of racial formation and resistance, sound becomes indispensable in exploring intersections of lived experience and the historical constructions of blackness in the United States. The idea of an expressive sonic–literary map of the political for black writers resonates with Fredric Jameson's idea of history as "the experience of Necessity," a formation of the "narrative political unconscious" in which necessity is not "a type of content," but exists as "the inexorable form of events": "History is what hurts, it is what refuses desire and sets inexorable limits to individual as well as collective praxis, which its 'ruses' turn into grisly and ironic reversals of their overt intention. But this History can be apprehended only through its effects, and never directly as some reified force."[13]

Sound in this equation offers a formal category of experience that resists overdetermined perceptions of historical consciousness. The movement between sound and constructions of black consciousness refuses a straightforward internalization of the "hurt" of history, specifically in considering how this movement has been elucidated through the writings of black intellectuals who challenge constructions of white supremacy through critiques of the unfinished nature of racial redress. Sound represents an important intervention for writers through its potential for disrupting narrative processes of state and racial formations, even as those narrative processes seek to distill, capture, and often commodify the eruptions and traces of recognizable form that emerge from what is heard. The expansion of literary form through attention to the aural balances words, ideas, images, and sound.[14] As an aesthetic tool for African American writers, sound offers a fusion of the sensory, and the political, and the possibility of both eluding and challenging the containment of post–Civil Rights era white supremacy.[15]

My analysis frames the sonic as a realm of resistance to and as a critique of an American narrative of black life defined broadly by a movement toward citizenship and racial equality amid the rapid economic, military, and imperial dominance defining the United States as a global superpower.[16] This struggle is set within what David Theo Goldberg refers to as the formation of "racial states." I use the plural here because part of the theoretical precision Goldberg offers in his description of these states is that they exist both in the institutional sense of producing race (and he also points out that the modern governmental states are produced in large part by race) and as sites that reflect the particular realities, struggles, and experiences of specific groups of black subjects—that is, lived states of racialized existence. Sound offers a means for black artists to challenge what Goldberg refers to as the "homogenizing logic of institutions."[17] At once celebratory and colonizing of difference, the state's maintenance of racial hybridity and heterogeneity preserves and intensifies homogeneity through a vexed institutional genealogy based on a shifting deployment of fear, diversity, embrace, and refusal. Goldberg theorizes a paradoxical landscape of racial formation increasingly articulated by the state in order to produce a homogenized, racially exclusive, yet apparently pluralistic society. This vision of a racial state presents an entanglement of freedom and coercion, set within shifting, overlapping contexts of institutional, representational, and lived realities. Rather than seeing race as "simply threaded through the fabric of modern and modernizing racial states," Goldberg explains that states "are drawn into racial frames of reference," and have "acquired their modernity more or less partially through racial assumptions." The landscape of governmentality, modernity, lived experience, and the smooth sedimentation of racial codes and categories that Goldberg depicts makes the clear case for theorizing the movement between "politics as domain and discipline" and "politics as disciplinary practices."[18] Challenging this hegemonic penetration of the quotidian through dominant articulations of the racial state— those that serve the interest of maintaining divisions in service of a national mythology of capitalist progress—might be most effectively done through a sonic formulation of resistance outside the "fashioning" and "presumption" of such a racial state. Another way of phrasing the question would be to ask: What is the sound a racial state might inspire? What sounds does it initiate? How might the experience of existing within such a state attune one to different sonic possibilities?

I situate black literary sound within the intertwined growth of the United States as a racial state, and the historical trajectory of black consciousness that critically assesses this growth. Cedric Robinson explains how American ideas of governance rely largely on representations of black identity defined by the legacy of enslavement, and in doing so perpetuate the narrative foundations and longevity of white supremacy:

> When manufacturing became the most advanced form of production and democratic institutions the most significant political creed, the African was represented as chattel in their economic image. As slaves in their political and social image, as brutish and therefore inaccessible to further development, and finally as Negro, that is without history. And later, during the industrialization of the country's economy, when individuality and manipulative acumen were at a premium, the Black was a pathetic sharecropper, unskilled and unambitious—the "happy darkies" for whom the society possessed a paternalistic obligation. Finally, in our own time, with the development of corporate structures and the myth of the intensely rationalized and rational society, Blacks became the irrational, the violent, criminal, caged beast. The cage was civilization and Western culture, obviously available to Blacks but inexplicably beyond their grasp.[19]

Robinson offers a genealogy of the interwoven nature of subjectivity and subjection, how notions of racial identity become intertwined across the color line, and ultimately erect a "cage" of Western civilization and culture. The idea of resisting such a mythic narrative construction is complex, for although white supremacy is an ideology securing the broad social and economic dominance of white citizens over those deemed nonwhite (both citizen and nonwhite "alien"), it is not only whites who assert its tenets, for the conceptual "cage" of civilization offers forms of internalized security along many refractions of the color line. Thus the complexity of white supremacy exists within its ability to accommodate seemingly racially transcendent ideas of progress while remaining mired within a foundation of racist mythology. To resist this powerful fusion of mythology and governance is itself layered within contradiction, as the most immediate forms of redress challenge racial exclusion based on the negation of blackness. As Robinson puts it, "Black history thus began in the shadow of the national myths and as their dialectical negation."[20]

Building on the insights and implications of Robinson's analysis, I contend that diagnosing and confronting the mythic construction of white supremacy entails shifting the focus from simply the visual dominance of race in the American public sphere to perceiving the interaction between the apparent, and the more ephemeral, but no less definitive dimensions of racial formation. My use of "visual" stretches beyond phenotypical inscriptions of race, additionally pointing to the reliance on a set of narrative conditions envisioning racial identities as they are defined in respect to constructions of white American identity. The political and aesthetic qualities of sound resist these implicit and explicit perpetuations of white supremacy as they are narrated and enacted across the bodies of black Americans. This opposition is both a form of resistance to the political silence imposed on black voices and a struggle against the presumption of realism in American historical documentation and memory construction.

Given this racial and sociohistorical context for intellectual work, the sonic becomes a mode of aesthetic and political resistance against external and internal oppression, one that fashions itself out of the "sublime" bodily knowledge Terry Eagleton describes as the sensuous aspects of material and ideological struggle that signal the inherent political nature of the aesthetic.[21] Literary sound gathers its power from its transformation of the quotidian and spectacular acoustics of black life into narrative struggle and resistance against restrictive forms of racial definition and subjection. The diffuse properties of sound invest African American literature with the potential to critically break from social realist literary form popularized in early to mid-twentieth-century political protest writing and resists the idea that form can be prescribed by a certain predetermined level of political articulation. This imaginative landscape of experimental sonority in African American literature reframes late capitalist racial formation with a particular attention to the reconstitution of domination indicative of the post–Civil Rights era, and an attunement to a historical genealogy of black resistance to white supremacy.

The Resonance of Resistance

African American writers have imagined the power of sound as a form of resistance to racial subjection in the United States from the earliest transcriptions of black experience in the Americas. W. E. B. Du Bois provides a touchstone in this continuum in his early twentieth-century meditation on black sound, "Of the Sorrow Songs," where he explores the sonic dimensions of the failed promise of reconstruction—specifically, the postbellum collapse of political and social redress across the color line. Du Bois notably distinguishes between song and sound, or rather, makes a case for their convergence as exemplary of the critical expressiveness he sees defining black political culture. Du Bois asserts that "the music is far more ancient than words," offering a "sifting of centuries" through the historical memory embedded within black song. The knowledge of what the words of a song passed down through African ancestry may mean are less resonant than the historical consciousness projected through the tonal memory of the music.[22] The acoustic qualities of black historical experience represent a critical force for Du Bois. Sound becomes what Herbert Marcuse, writing in opposition to the political and cultural repression coming to dominate many Western societies after World War II, describes as an aesthetic attempt to fashion "claims . . . for a dimension of fulfillment which can be created only in the struggle against the institutions which, by their very functioning, deny and violate these claims."[23] Marcuse's sense of "aesthetic morality" that "insists on freedom as a biological necessity," offers one way of thinking about Du Bois's conceptualization of sound as an intervention in the noisy dissonance of American constructions of a national racial mythology.[24] Sound animates and reflects the ongoing African American resistance to domination as Du Bois reminds us, both as "the singular spiritual heritage of the nation," and as "the greatest gift of the Negro people" to the nation.

"The Sorrow Songs" presents an occasion for Du Bois to contemplate the place of sound in the historical and expressive continuum of black life, in its extraction from Africa, and through the redemptive, yet also critical, possibilities of its remembrance. Du Bois's opening lines attest to the connections between the historical and aesthetic echoes of sound in the personal and political elements of the Sorrow Songs:

> They that walked in darkness sang songs in the golden days—
> Sorrow Songs—for they were weary at heart. And so before each
> thought that I have written in this book I have set a phrase, a
> haunting echo of these weird old songs in which the soul of the
> black slave spoke to men. Ever since I was a child, these songs have
> stirred me strangely. They came out of the South unknown to me,
> one by one, and yet at once I knew them as of me and of mine.
> Then in after years when I came to Nashville I saw the great
> temple builded of these songs towering over the pale city. To me
> Jubilee Hall seemed ever made of the songs themselves, and its
> bricks were red with the blood and dust of toil. Out of them rose
> for me morning, noon, and night, bursts of wonderful melody, full
> of the voices of the past.[25]

Du Bois imagines the songs moving out of the South, both unknown and recognizable to his senses, suggesting similar dynamics of black cultural identification to be featured within the actual "great migrations" soon to follow, and later, as material for the builders of the "great temple." In this opening paragraph, Du Bois illustrates what song, as a mode of sonic expression, might convey about the historical dimensions of the encounter between Africans and "America," and proposes that this encounter echoes within the structure of his own literary performance through listening to "the soul of the black slave." His critical perspective on the facts of the color line detailed throughout the individual essays in *The Souls of Black Folk* creates its own sound, reflective of the weariness arising in the face of the seeming immutability of American racism, an awareness framed through his closing invocation in the essay "Let Us Cheer the Weary Traveler." Du Bois's investigation of black political culture and historical memory become fields of contestation inscribed within the sonic and political imaginations of post-Emancipation black life. Sound functions in African American literary discourse as a means of historical perception and critique, and also as a formalized "weapon of theory"[26] animating literary representations to suggest levels of black cultural meaning largely imperceptible to the visual registers through which race is constantly being configured in the United States.

Du Bois sonically confronts the ideological construction of "America," framing the depths of racism as not only a tremendous historical force of oppression in its own right, but also as a force closely interwoven within the evolving economic and expansionist policies of the United States (what he terms the "Spanish war interludes and Philippine matinees") between the end of the Civil War and the dawning of the twentieth century.[27] Du Bois's writing in *The Souls of Black Folk*, specifically in "The Sorrow Songs," represents a critical practice both in the attention he pays to the cultural politics of black sound, and through his focus on sound as a critique of the various levels of national complexity and subjection clouding "free" black life in the decades following the Emancipation Proclamation. Throughout his essays in *The Souls of Black Folk*, he suggests that the illusory qualities of Emancipation actually reify many physical and psychological underpinnings of bondage in the post-slavery American Republic. Saidiya Hartman considers this historical narrative of antiblack institutionalized racism in the following way: "Emancipation announced the end of chattel slavery; however, it by no means marked the end of bondage. The free(d) individual was nothing if not burdened, responsible, and obligated. Responsibility entailed accounting for one's actions, dutiful suppliance, contractual obligation, and calculated reciprocity. Fundamentally, to be responsible was to be blameworthy. In this respect, the exercise of free will, quite literally, was inextricable from guilty infractions, criminal misdeeds, punishable transgressions, and an elaborate micropenalty of everyday life. Responsibility made man an end in himself, and as such, the autonomous and intending agent was above all else culpable."[28]

Hartman analyzes the re-inscription of black life within narratives of criminality and self-governance that evolve as equality becomes translated into a responsibility that, if not met, may result in a greater than equal chance to be adversely penalized by the state. Her theorization of racially inscribed obligation as a condition of freedom, created amid the complex, frequently troubled circumstances of an "autonomous and intending agent" of post–Civil War and post-Reconstruction black life, puts precise pressure on the particular sociopolitical dynamics that Du Bois imagined sound might help diagnose. Du Bois writes "The Sorrow Songs" as an exploration of the historical resonance of black sonority and as an indictment of the political entanglement that Hartman theorizes:

> Little of beauty has America given the world save the rude grandeur God himself stamped on her bosom; the human spirit in this new world has expressed itself in vigor and ingenuity rather than in beauty. And so by fateful chance the Negro folksong—the rhythmic cry of the slave—stands to-day not simply as the sole American music, but as the most beautiful expression of human experience born this side the seas. It has been neglected, it has been, and is, half despised, and above all it has been persistently mistaken and misunderstood; but not withstanding, it still remains as the singular spiritual heritage of the nation and the greatest gift of the Negro people.[29]

Here Du Bois frames the African American response to the "rude grandeur" of American identity (read as white) as the context leading to the "fateful" creation of early black music in the United States. Du Bois defines this acoustic dimension of black consciousness as both an unrealized American ideal and as a broader reflection of "human experience." Through this confluence, Du Bois frames Americanism as more of an ideology than an identity, an ideology that, in its self-maintenance, necessitates the expressive response of black sound. Put slightly differently, it has been the American drive for economic dominance that has created the conditions for the emergence of black expressive sound, a sonic condition of possibility that expands this limited vision of national identity but remains largely unrecognized as distinctly American due to the critical edge of its creative force. This roughly dialectical framework of convergences consequently allows Du Bois to assert a vision of "America" that is contingent on, yet largely unrecognized as, the expressive potential emerging from the struggles of those representing the African or black foundation of the nation.

When Du Bois imagines "the rhythmic cry of the slave" he pushes more deeply into and beyond the aural dimensions of such a cry, in order to evoke the historical resonance of this projection. The flexible vantage point of the "rhythmic cry" becomes a space for considering the far-reaching implications of inter- and intra-racial sonic exchange both within the United States and globally, from field hollers to free jazz and hip-hop. When Du Bois speaks of how the "Negro folksong" has been "neglected," "half despised," and "persistently mistaken and misunderstood," he is not only previewing his later commentary on the struggles of the Fisk Jubilee Singers to project their renderings of the spirituals in the face of post–Civil War racism, but he is also prophetically speaking to the fact that the production and reception of these songs represents a stage in a series of complex cultural exchanges that persistently reshape race relations within the United States. Even in the face of its dismissal, according to Du Bois black music "remains as the singular spiritual heritage of the nation and the greatest gift of the Negro people," and "still lives in the hearts of those who have heard them truly sung and in the hearts of the Negro people."[30] The sound of the spirituals, in its derivation from the cries of slaves, emerges as far more than music; its phonic materiality becomes a sonic tableau through which the long historical condition of African American resistance can be considered.

Through the literary acoustics of his critique, Du Bois questions the fact that while enslaved Africans and African Americans have physically established the material structures and cultural fabric of the nation yet remain subjects and unacknowledged as contributing citizens. His closing thoughts in the essay emphasize this understanding:

Your country? How came it yours? Before the Pilgrims landed we were here. Here we have brought our three gifts and mingled them with yours: a gift of story and song—soft, stirring melody in an ill-harmonized and unmelodious land; the gift of sweat and brawn to beat back the wilderness, conquer the soil, and lay the foundation of this vast economic empire two hundred years earlier than your weak hands could have done it; the third, a gift of Spirit. Around us the history of the land has centered for thrice a hundred years; out of the nation's heart we have called all that was best to throttle and subdue all that was worst; fire and blood, prayer and sacrifice, have billowed over this people, and they have found peace only in the altars of the God of Right. Nor has our gift of the Spirit been merely passive. Actively we have woven ourselves with the very warp and woof of this nation,—we fought their battles, shared their sorrow, mingled our blood with theirs, and generation after generation have pleaded with a headstrong, careless people to despise not Justice, Mercy, and Truth, lest the nation be smitten

with a curse. Our song, our toil, our cheer, and warning have been
given to this nation in blood-brotherhood. Are not these gifts
worth the giving? Is not this work and striving? Would America
have been America without her Negro people?

Through these reflections, Du Bois locates the sound of the sorrow songs
as interventions within the logic of U.S. and global white supremacy in
which "the silently growing assumption of this age is that the probation of
races is past, and that the backward races of today are of proven inefficiency
and not worth the saving."[31] Du Bois considers the sorrow songs not simply as musical compositions, but as counter-narrative forces that emerge as
markers of historical experience distinguished by their capacity to both
subtly and overtly project critically layered indictments of white supremacy.

Du Bois's early twentieth-century push to recognize sound as indispensable to African American resistance previews much of my argument
regarding the politics of black sound—that is, how sound becomes a means
of signaling and emphasizing the deeper critical fissures within narratives
of American progress that remain blind to the complexities of African American oppression. His closing meditation on song in "The Sorrow Songs,"
however, hints at the possibility of realizing the inchoate nature of freedom
within the historical and environmental elements that define the foundation of black song. The freedom music Du Bois outlines bridges "the hope
that sang in the songs of my father well sung" with the release of sound:
"Free as yonder fresh young voices welling up to me from the caverns of
brick and mortar below—swelling with song, instinct with life, tremulous
treble and darkening bass."

Writing several decades later in her essay "The Spirituals and the Neo-
spirituals" (1934), Zora Neale Hurston expands on Du Bois's observation
that a freedom impulse exists within the phenomenological breadth of black
music. In describing the spirituals, Hurston avoids a musicological analysis, instead framing the songs as "unceasing variations around a theme" that
"do not remain long in their original form." Her perspective on the specific
expressive and narrative aspects of the music clearly reflects her broad concern with African American cultural distinctiveness. As her essay suggests,
Hurston's ideas of African American cultural distinctiveness (what many
would simply, but perhaps erroneously, term black authenticity) are less
representative of sweeping notions of essentialism than they are illustrative
of the flexible relationships between sound, narration, and temporality.

Her framing of the improvisatory, ephemeral, and asymmetrical qualities of "the harmony and disharmony, the shifting keys and broken time" that shape what she calls "the real spirituals," signals the relationship between African American expressive practices and an alternate orientation toward historical time.[32] She elaborates on the potential for black sonic expression to reflect an appreciation for the malleability and fullness of time:

> To begin with, Negro spirituals are not solo or quartette material. The jagged harmony is what makes it, and it ceases to be what it was when this is absent. Neither can any group be trained to reproduce it. Its truth dies under training like flowers under hot water. The harmony of the true spiritual is not regular. The dissonances are important and not to be ironed out by the trained musician. The various parts break in at any old time. Falsetto often takes the place of regular voices for short periods. Keys change. Moreover, each singing of the piece is a new creation. The congregation is bound by no rules. No two times singing is alike, so that we must consider the rendition of a song not as a final thing, but as a mood. It won't be the same thing next Sunday.[33]

Hurston proposes that the innovative sound of the spirituals becomes diluted outside of the original contexts of their creation. Her claim regarding the inauthenticity of the spirituals reproduced outside of these frameworks is not based on a claim that the spirituals are mystically connected to a premodern context of black expression; rather, Hurston diagnoses an improvisational impulse within the sound that exceeds flattened constructions of race and culture. Her perspective highlights a fusion of sonority, temporality, and narration that has political implications in signaling different orientations toward black historical consciousness. Toni Cade Bambara speaks to this point in her 1981 introduction to the volume of Hurston's nonfictional, ethnographic writings, *The Sanctified Church* (which includes the essay "Spirituals and Neo-spirituals"), when she remarks that Hurston possessed "a lifelong interest in 'alternative,' as they say, channels of intelligence and being." Bambara's observation can be read to suggest that Hurston's exploration of black sound points not only to issues in black cultural representation, but also to the possibilities for understanding the manipulation of sound as a mode of resistance to externally imposed racial definitions.[34]

Hurston understands the precarious nature of innovative black cultural production when faced with simplified categories of interpretation, a problematic represented in her description of the "truth" of "jagged harmony" that "dies under training like flowers under hot water." The spirituals resist simple categorization as forms of slave song, according to Hurston, and instead represent "unceasing variations around a theme" that "do not remain long in their original form" as they travel from "town to town and church to church."[35] Movement is crucial in both a literal and figurative sense for Hurston, as it is through the geographic, phenomenological, and epistemological movement of sound that the aesthetic energy of black culture emerges.

Hurston notes that black sonic space is defined through its tension with an idea of formalization, as the dynamic, spontaneous, and improvisational basis of its creation resists smooth replication and reproduction. She draws a distinction between the "expression of feelings" as the basis for black creative sound rather than what she refers to as "sound effects." Her use of "sound effects" serves as a critique of the containment of sound's improvisational, expressive qualities by replacing them with smoother, more aurally digestible elements aimed to increase their cross-cultural circulation and commodification. When Hurston discusses "chants" and "hums," for example, she highlights the quotidian elements of the spiritual sound that may elude musicological analyses. She notes that "chants and hums are not used indiscriminately as it would appear to a casual listener . . . As indefinite as hums sound, they are formal and can be found unchanged all over the south."[36] Hurston frames the aesthetic and theoretical depth of sound as a formal and political field of possibility that shapes and is shaped by a critical recognition of black culture on its own terms of production. Both Hurston and Du Bois demonstrate how sound can exceed the field of musical study and can help diagnose and resist the power relations underlining racial formation in the United States.

Attending to the sonic aspects of African American culture, I turn to the specific importance of this trajectory of black expressive practice within what I refer to as the long Black Arts Movement era, specifically focusing on the element of sound within this historical period stretching from 1965 through the late 1970s. In the post–Civil Rights era (1965–80), an inclination existed among certain African American experimental writers to conceptualize their work through critical understandings of sound. This approach to sonic narration reflected a desire to imagine alternate configurations of subjectivity and resistance outside the frameworks for social transformation that had generally been reflected in the linearity and hyper-visibility of the Civil Right and Black Power movements. I consider the work of writers including Amiri Baraka, Henry Dumas, Larry Neal, James Baldwin, Toni Cade Bambara, and Gayl Jones in relationship to expansive ideas of sound proposed by free jazz experimental musicians and contemporary theorists of sonic culture. Framing this intellectual convergence of literary artistry, experimental music, and sound theory, *Imagine the Sound* highlights the role of sound in furthering their approaches to artistic resistance within a rapidly transforming political and racial landscape.

This study offers a critical framework for further rethinking the cultural and aesthetic politics of the Black Arts Movement in respect to the broader trajectory of the post–Civil Rights era. According to the dominant inter-pretations of the Black Arts Movement within African American literary history, the movement served a rather straightforward purpose of militantly politicizing black artists in dichotomous terms that were most clearly identifiable through their rigid opposition to whiteness and Western cul-ture. Despite the recent critical interventions by scholars such as Kimberly Benston, James Smethurst, Mike Sell, and Amy Abugo Ongiri, interventions that challenge the cultural, historical, and aesthetic aspects of this inter-pretive line, a critical inclination persists in which the movement is gen-erally understood as a marker of the negative excesses of black cultural nationalism. I challenge this approach to the period by focusing on the central role of aurality in construing ideas of subjectivity, historical mem-ory, and political ideology, in ways that both exceed and overlap with more recognizable modes of black cultural nationalist representation and political affiliation. Framing sound and race in this capacity, I explore the relationship between the expressive and political dimensions of racial consciousness. Rather than reducing the idea of black consciousness emerging in the mid to late 1960s to a flat or one-dimensional formation in which resistance is framed as narrowly oppositional, the following chapters analyze the capac-ity of sound to convey the indeterminacy of this historical moment as it is contemplated and depicted within experimental literary work of the period.

Imagine the Sound begins by establishing and interrogating ideas of black consciousness and musical experimentation that were shaping the con-texts of political and artistic resistance during the late 1960s. Chapter 1, "The Sonic Field of Resistance," examines the 1960s free jazz break with traditional ideas of musical form and conceptualizations of sound, paying particular attention to how the aural qualities of this break relate to the broader context of post–Civil Rights African American cultural expression. This chapter, which begins with a consideration of John Coltrane's final live performance in April 1967 at the Olatunji Center for African Culture in Harlem, argues that Coltrane's combination of sonic and metaphysical expansion in these last years of his work exemplifies an open creative orientation toward black aesthetics that becomes a viable practice of artistic resistance. While it is not an unusual claim to assert a correspondence between free jazz and black nationalism, my argument here is more precisely that the methods of sonic innovation within the music come to feed into the confluence of aesthetic and political thought defining the more radical practices of artistic resistance during the post–Civil Rights era. I put pressure on this point as I conclude the chapter with a series of thoughts on the interplay between sound, race, and black literary form through a close reading of Amiri Baraka's poem "Black Art," as it is projected across a free jazz soundscape. My focus on black experimental music continues in chapter 2, "Apocalyptic Soundscapes: Listening to Henry Dumas's Short Fiction," as I analyze literary depictions of sound in a selection of short stories of the Black Arts Movement–era writer Henry Dumas. I theorize his use of literary sound as an example of the more layered and complex formations of black radical critique that existed within the Black Arts Movement. Dumas's composition of soundscapes, I argue, frame eruptions of musical and environmental noise as alternate means through which African American writers might reimagine relationships between historical memory and the materiality of his political present.

Imagine the Sound continues to expand and deepen the literary history of the Black Arts Movement, as my third chapter, "Peering into the Maw: Larry Neal's Aesthetic Universe," analyzes the centrality of sound to Neal's critical engagement with black aesthetics. I argue that Neal uses ideas of sound to expand articulations of black radical thought by opening up what he refers to as a "new space" for the reconfiguration of black cultural nationalism in the wake of Malcolm X's 1965 assassination. Considering Neal's critical interventions in connection with Raymond Williams's notion of "structures of feeling," I closely read Neal's theorizations and creative representations of sound as both black vernacular expression and as phenomenological presences that bleed into inchoate formations of the political.

I bring together several aspects of the book's argument in chapter 4, "Sonic Futurity in Toni Cade Bambara's *The Salt Eaters*," as I continue to explore the relationship between sound and inchoate formations of political resistance within Bambara's 1980 novel. Thematically, Bambara's framing of the dialectical relationship between hope, defeat, and resistance through the ambivalent post–Civil Rights era perspective of veteran activist Velma Henry, vividly represents the historical and sociopolitical complexity *Imagine the Sound* sets out to interrogate. Formally, my reading of the novel extends my focus on literary soundscapes framed earlier in chapter 2, as I contend that the eruptions of sound in *The Salt Eaters*, be they comprised of music, voices, drumming, or environmental noise, allow Bambara to create and relate ideas at a more fluid, functional, and expansive level than might be possible through linear conceptions of temporality and historical narration. In its critical formulation, the chapter asks, what if the conditions of historical possibility in the text might be extended as an un-formalized aural vocabulary of politically connected resonant images? I consider the formal and political implications of this question in the final chapter, "The Radical Tonality of James Baldwin's Post–Civil Rights Blues." Returning to focus on the aurality of primarily nonfictional poetics, a focus largely undertaken within my examination of Larry Neal's writings in chapter 3, I explore how Baldwin's formal use of sound heightens the ability of his prose to express a "universal blues," pushing beyond empirical definitions of racial experience to instead convey the more ephemeral complexities of black consciousness arising within the turbulence and indeterminacy of the Civil Rights and Black Power periods. The chapter picks up on the preceding chapter's consideration of the interrelationship between sound, image, memory, and ideology, as I frame Baldwin's appreciation of the interstices between dissonance, remembrance, and futurity as a narrative conjuncture that critically relates known pasts and a sense of the unknown future through his aesthetic crafting of literary vignettes that trouble these temporal and historical relationships. I conclude with an Epilogue that proposes how we might consider the continuing, unending legacy of the post–civil rights period through more contemporary African American literary and sonic forms that offer critical perspectives on the evolving racial state.

    In sum, the goal of *Imagine the Sound* is impressionistically evoked in the words of the experimental pianist, composer, and writer Cecil Taylor, as he poetically renders in a passage of his liner notes (suggestively titled "Sound Structure of Subculture Becoming Major Breath/Naked Fire Gesture") the multidirectional freedom of the sound he creates with his ensemble on the 1966 *Unit Structures* recording: "Joint energy dispersal in parts of singular feelings. A recharge; group chain reaction. Acceleration result succession of multiple time compression areas. Sliding elision/beat here is physical commitment to earth force. Rude insistence of tough meeting at vertical centers. Time strata thru panels joined sequence a continuum (movements) across nerve centers. Total immersion."[37] Taylor's projection of sound through the active energy of his syntax reflects his understanding of sonic space as an "unknown totality" marked by "memory which has identified sensory images resulting social response."[38] His free interplay between words and ideas of sound challenges the point reportedly made by composer and saxophonist Charles Lloyd in response to an interviewer's question about his music: "Words don't go there."[39] *Imagine the Sound* is not only about music and words, however. The book addresses Lloyd's provocation by analyzing the interplay of music, sound, narration, and the black radical imagination. The rejection of the conventional that characterizes the form and sound of this continuum signals the enlarged sense of Black Power that *Imagine the Sound* reveals. In his essay "And Shine Swam On," the afterword to *Black Fire* (1968), the centerpiece volume of the movement, Larry Neal writes that Black Power is "a synthesis of all of the nationalistic ideas embedded within the double-consciousness of Black America." Yet it is a synthesis, he notes, that evades "one *specific* meaning," reflecting instead the ephemerality of "a kind of feeling—a kind of emotional response to one's history."[40] Neal looks to the interaction between black political thought and cultural expression as a bridge toward new ways of envisioning black identity across changing historical contexts of sociopolitical struggle. It is music's "surging new sound," and the "vital newness of its energy," Neal contends, that ultimately undergird this bridge.[41] Rereading Neal's pronouncement with respect to ideas of experimental sound frames the central question of this book: What is the relationship between black aesthetics, sound, and experimentation? And, in what ways might the presence of sound within experimental black expression be heard and read as political, but in ways outside the term's more expected designation?

CHAPTER 1

The Sonic Field of Resistance

Free Jazz and the Horizon of Black Aesthetic Expansion

We have to accept the limits of history but not the limits imposed by the societies where we are living.

—Amilcar Cabral

John Coltrane's Scream

On April 23, 1967, only months before his death, John Coltrane performed at the Olatunji Center of African Culture in Harlem, initiating the "Roots of Africa" series of community cultural events organized by the famed Nigerian percussionist and founder of the center, Babatunde Olatunji. Coltrane performed two sets with his final and perhaps farthest-reaching arrangement of musicians, a quintet comprising himself, Pharoah Sanders (tenor saxophone), Alice Coltrane (piano), Jimmy Garrison (bass), and Rashied Ali (drums). Bernard Drayton, the engineer Coltrane asked to record the first of the two sessions, recalled the sound of the first set as "music beyond what we conceive music to be."[1] Drayton's recollection of Coltrane's expansive, experimental sound at the Olatunji concert attests to the challenging aural context of Coltrane's later musical development and his exploration of spiritually transcendent sonic territory during the final years of his life. Coltrane's drive toward innovation was reflective of a broader free jazz impulse, and was assessed by many in connection with the broader debates that listeners were having about the emerging sounds of this new music and their signaling of a revolutionary turn in black musical and sonic culture. The more conservative voices within the jazz critical establishment felt that this new direction negatively and recklessly refuted the canonical foundations of the music. But at the same time, a growing chorus of listeners identified the experimental sound as a productive challenge to the limitations of the American mainstream. Coltrane's final recorded performance remains a testament to his desire and commitment to explore the furthest reaches of sound. I begin this chapter with a critical rehearing of the expressive and conceptual breadth of his sound and of black experimental music more broadly, as a foundation for contemplating the sonic innovations in literary form taken up across the subsequent chapters. Understanding these sonic interventions as conceptual expansions within black art begins to situate them as aesthetic and political approaches to refashioning African American literary form during the post–Civil Rights era.

The formation of Coltrane's late sound, developed roughly between Coltrane's 1965 release of the eleven-piece collective free improvisation, *Ascension*, and his death only two years later marked a period of intense experimental evolution within his music and the free jazz continuum more broadly. This shift toward engaging with sound as a distinct expressive possibility reflects the desires and designs of black musicians, writers, critics, and artists who were formulating a notion of black aesthetic and political indivisibility. In attempting to fuse aesthetics and politics, however, artists and theorists were quite aware of the potential for black art to be measured exclusively on either its political intent or its aesthetic qualities. John Coltrane's later experimental work at the Olatunji Center offers an aural suturing of the breaks between these positions, as the sound of the performance is embedded in an expansion of artistic ideas that can only be imagined in a flexible relationship to the political contexts and imperatives that motivate them.

Coltrane's approach to free jazz is most overtly marked by its multidirectional pulse, shifting temporality, and destabilization of harmony. These disruptive acoustic and compositional features resonate with a post–Civil Rights era understanding of the unevenness of historical change emerging in the wake of the passage of the Civil Rights Act of 1965, as the retrenchment against the legislative gains gathered steam and the assassinations and attacks on black leaders and activists increased. Considering the interaction between experimental sound and black historical consciousness offers the possibility for imagining resistance outside of more constraining and coercive forms of black cultural nationalism. Rather than proposing a straightforward reaction to racist violence and debasement, the sound of this music compels artists and listeners to conceptualize resistance through the qualities of the sound that suggest a convergence of formal and political alterity. The sensory expansion of free jazz was generated through the projection of its innovative sound, which offered new space for imagining radical ideas of black identity.

The idea of black radicalism is frequently invoked to describe formations of political consciousness that defy conventional ideas of political
participation, which emerge from an understanding of black historical experience as constantly in struggle with evolving forms of white supremacy.
Articulating an identity, consciousness, and critical standpoint on the margins has an inherent degree of indeterminacy, as it is often constructed as
antagonistic to the progressive nature of Western modernity—which itself
is, of course, a construct.[2] This ideological dissonance animating the black
radical tradition is outlined by Anthony Bogues through his delineation of
"two major streams of black radical intellectual production—the heretic
and the prophetic."[3] For Bogues, a tradition of heretical *"epistemic displacement"* is articulated by black intellectuals who seek to resolve, "the tensions
and disjuncture created by 'double consciousness' and the enchantment of
the Western intellectual tradition." He also points to a more radical *redemptive prophetic* approach that questions the validity of a socially removed
intellectual position (even as one might espouse radical ideas from such a
location), and proposes new forms of subaltern irrationality; "a politics of
the world upside down, which eschews the standard political forms and
language of political modernity."[4] Coltrane's experimental sound suggests
an approach to formal innovation in line with Bogues's outlining of the
"redemptive prophetic" quality of black radical thought as it expands creative possibilities, demands new modes of perception, and suggests the need
for more expansive ideas of racial consciousness that can more adequately
diagnose historical and political complexity. John Coltrane's late sound at
the Olatunji Center engages with this configuration of experimental black
expression and post–Civil Rights black consciousness through both the
sonic innovation marking the performance and the resonance of this experimental sound aurally and epistemologically reverberating within and against
the sociopolitical context of black life in the late 1960s.

Coltrane exemplifies the open, elongated, emergent, and contingent qualities of his late sound, and emphasizes the thin line between communion
and rupture that is central to his aesthetic vision in his version of "My
Favorite Things," performed at the Olatunji Center. One of Coltrane's best-
known compositions, he first reworked this Broadway show tune in the early
1960s. For the remaining years of his career, he returned to the composition at different times, with different personnel, generally edging his initial
improvisation on Rodgers and Hammerstein increasingly away from the
source. When he turned to the piece again at the Olatunji Center, the original

compositional framework had become explosively refigured as a dramatically expanded tapestry of sound, and his audience was confronted with something that was barely recognizable. The massive, sweeping breadth of compositional sound arising from this thirty-four-minute version exemplifies a remarkably different sonic orientation, a style of playing in which the elongation, volume, and shifting nature of the sound itself, rather than its projection within more clearly scripted notation, becomes the basis for a narrative movement that troubles tonal and temporal expectations. The idea of musical or sonic narration is an important conceptual principle within *Imagine the Sound*. Although I distinguish my engagement with this possibility for narration from the efforts of musicologists who provide semiotic frameworks for analyzing musical signs and signification, I do see the usefulness of working expansively with an idea of narration that builds on Kofi Agawu's recognition that "some musicians prefer to dispense with such ostensibly superficial analogies between verbal and musical narrative" in order to better consider the impressionistic dimensions of the imagination.[5] It is this less patterned, more potentially open-ended field of narrative possibilities that experimental music may offer (and that the Coltrane quintet's performance at the Olatunji Center exemplifies) to ideas of black expression, that marks the convergence of the literary and sonic at stake in this study.

Jimmy Garrison opens the composition with a seven-minute bass solo that builds toward a glimmer of recognition of the earlier sound of Coltrane's soprano saxophone. But the dissonance and speed of the playing shatter the recognizable bits of the original sound of "My Favorite Things," for this version of the composition has been dramatically intensified, fractured, and bled together. Hearing Coltrane's soprano sound in this context is both familiar and disquieting. A sound that helped to indelibly shape the history of modern jazz seems to reappear here only briefly before receding into a momentum of sound rupturing the quintessential quality of one of Coltrane's earlier career statements. The slightly strained, penetrating pitch of his soprano and the fullness of Sanders's tenor revolve around each other, creating a pulsing sonic wave that only hints through its crashes, frayed edges, and splayed open center, at the form of the original rendition. In particular, the performance features elongated passages in which the notes are generally sustained, allowing the tempo to unfold in a more deliberate fashion, only to be ruptured through the turbulent rhythms that build, in each case, toward a series of crescendos.

Regarding the density of Coltrane's late sound, Billy Taylor, who introduced the quintet at the Olatunji concert, points to this level of tonal exploration as a central impulse in Coltrane's late music:

> His music was always so passionate at that period that I had to digest it. There was so much going on. The volume in that room was much higher than I was accustomed to. But I enjoyed it. The difference between John Coltrane screaming and doing some of the kinds of things he was doing in that period—it took me years to realize that he had learned how to do that in rhythm-and-blues bands, and he was using that kind of cry, that kind of utterance on the saxophone, in a totally different way, than many guys who came along after and said, "Oh, physically he's doing this to make that sound."[6]

Taylor's account reveals how density might exist on both an acoustic and an epistemological level, as he describes the indivisibility of Coltrane's experimentation from a broader continuum of black musical expression. He points to the "cry" and the "scream" being firmly rooted in black musical traditions and simultaneously extending avant-garde technique. Taylor reads Coltrane's innovation, his drive to create and inhabit new sonic territory, as continuing a dialogue with tradition, even as such a dialogue facilitates an experimental, transformational spreading outward into new territory that may at first seem unrecognizable. Tradition becomes contingent on a sense of both inward and outward growth, and this dialectical relationship is amplified as Coltrane confronts listeners with the force of phonic disruption against commonly held sensibilities of musical listening.

The story of how John Coltrane and Babatunde Olatunji became acquainted and furthered their relationship during the 1960s, leading up to the 1967 performance at the Olatunji Center, frames a significant interplay between African diasporic creativity and critical resistance that affected the performance's aesthetic and political contours. According to Olatunji in his written reflections, "John Coltrane: My Impressions and Recollections," Coltrane and Olatunji first became acquainted in the early 1960s when Coltrane would take in Olatunji's sessions at Birdland and the Village Gate with musicians Yusef Lateef, Chris White, and Rudy Collins.[7] During this period, building on the success of his 1959 album *Drums of Passion*, Olatunji was playing in sessions and dates with jazz luminaries including Lateef, Cannonball Adderley, Herbie Mann, Max Roach, Clark Terry, Randy Weston, and Quincy Jones. By the mid-1960s, *Drums of Passion* was viewed as a musical touchstone for the recentering of African culture within expressions of revolutionary black consciousness taking shape in 1960s African American thought. In his autobiography, *The Beat of My Drum*, Olatunji offers his perspective on this moment within his meteoric rise to prominence in 1960s black musical culture: "*Drums of Passion* became the talk of New York, and from there the talk of the nation. *Drums of Passion* became so popular in the 1960s that Murray the K on WNEW would open his daily radio show with the song 'Akiwowo.' He would play it and say, 'The chief is here today. Change is coming. Look out you guys.' Students on college campuses, both black and white, were listening to *Drums of Passion*. I was given credit for the cultural awareness that increasing [*sic*], among African Americans and among all young people black and white."[8]

Coltrane was inspired by Olatunji's African polyrhythmic sensibilities and his commitment to using music as a force of social change. He often took in Olatunji's performances in New York City, sharing billing alternately with Olatunji and Art Blakey's Jazz Messengers in late August of 1961, and Coltrane also dedicated a song to him, "Tunji," on his 1962 self-titled studio album. Olatunji recalls Coltrane's admiration for his approach to music, as well as his desire to collaborate with the Nigerian percussionist: "He told me in no uncertain terms, 'I really admire what you've been doing. Every chance I get, I come to see and hear you. And when I do, I listen close to every move you make, everything you play. So one day I want to come a little nearer and learn something from you.'"[9]

Coltrane's relationship with Olatunji grew through the sixties as both men committed themselves to pursuing new possibilities for the production, performance, and reception of black music. Olatunji's ideas regarding African music as a creative "source" from which forms of black music evolve have a clear correspondence to the engagements with African and non-Western musical traditions around which many free jazz musicians were building their compositional and sonic ideas. Olatunji elaborates on this idea of African music as a flexible source: "All music is one, anyway, when you go back to the source. Rhythm is the source of all music, the rhythm we find in nature, in the universe . . . in the sounds we hear all the time around us."[10] Archie Shepp offers an additional assessment of Coltrane's "fundamentally non-Western" approach, noting the fact that "his use of field hollers in his sound really connotes a thorough and passionate understanding of tradition."[11]

Coltrane's musical aesthetics featured in the Olatunji Center performance, cultivated in part through his understanding of African musical sources, are also marked by the centrality of the drone and the groove to his late sound. Due to the absence of prearranged chord progressions, identifiable key centers, and a regulated rhythmic beat, Coltrane's droning, groove-oriented elaborations of Olatunji's ideas of polytonal and polyrhythmic composition take the form of "sequences [that] almost always rise, and very rarely fall."[12] These "sequences" persist in their accumulation of dissonant sounds, becoming projected within registers that build and maintain a focused sonic idea and feeling amid seemingly tremendous cacophony. Coltrane's late compositions and performances are orchestrated with an ear for this sequenced, grooving energy. His inclination heightens the music as a form of communion in which the sites of performance and audition seek to expand the consciousness of those listeners willing to transfer the expectation of relating to the music into a more interactive phenomenological state—one in which the bodily and the cognitive dimensions of subjectivity are brought together through a refocused application of new sounds. Coltrane's formulation of free jazz sound structures elongates temporal spaces, allowing the grooves of the music to create a psychic, phenomenological gravitational state that "pulls and draws you, through participatory discrepancies, into itself, and gives you that participation consciousness."[13] Listening to Olatunji's work on *Drums of Passion* and *Zungo! Afro Percussion*, and taking into account the fact of Sun Ra and his Afro Infinity Arkestra's performance of a twenty-minute composition, "Atlantis," also at the Olatunji Center in 1967, we can begin to understand the presence of a groove-based energy music within the Olatunji Center that Coltrane's performance builds upon.[14] The Olatunji Center performance can be heard and understood as part of a broader configuration in which the music is creating new phenomenological possibilities for inter-subjective communication.

By challenging the ears and the body of the listener, the levels of noise and dissonance situated within the groove of the sound also challenge the commodification of listening practices engendered by a music industry that sublimates the contemplative, creative energy of music to the quest for corporate profit. Indeed, this interplay between innovative sound and the contested socioeconomic field of its production was central to the establishing of the Olatunji Center. Olatunji writes that in 1965, Coltrane began supporting his efforts to open the Olatunji Center, pledging his financial assistance after attending Olatunji's show at the African Pavilion of the 1964–65

World's Fair in New York City. Olatunji paraphrases a conversation with Coltrane regarding his unhappiness in the face of the economic power structures dictating the terms of musical production:

> Tunji, I am tired of being taken and exploited by managers, club owners and concert promoters. I worked too hard to get where I am today and still don't get adequately compensated for my talent. I hate to see promoters manipulating one artist after another . . . They don't really care about you, your music, what you are trying to accomplish artistically, nor do they give a damn if you are up today and down tomorrow because they know they will soon discover another victim!
>
> Look, Tunji, we need to sponsor our own concerts, promote them and perform in them. This way we will not only learn how to take a risk but will not have to accept the dictates of anybody about how long you should play, what to play and what you get. What else can any right thinking black musicians say to that—but, "Amen! Amen! Amen!"[15]

Coltrane and Olatunji joined with multi-instrumentalist and composer Yusef Lateef in order to create an informal organization dedicated to furthering the economic and creative self-determination of black music. In a 2006 interview, Lateef elaborates on his recollections of the brief yet groundbreaking work and plans that he, Coltrane, and Olatunji were involved in, as they planned a concert series at Lincoln Center that would present "an anthology of our music, starting in Africa, the Americas, its development."[16] Both Lateef and Billy Taylor explain that Coltrane's connection with Olatunji reflected a shared concern with creating new spaces for black art, essentially an atmospheric ethics of space connected to black expression. As Lateef recalls, Coltrane was in search of a new type of performance space, "without whiskey, without alcohol . . . so children could come and hear the music." Taylor includes Coltrane as representative of an ethical movement among black musicians "who had serious intent for their music and for the community," and speaks to the specific concern Coltrane and other musicians had regarding the need to create and perform music "where the cash register is not making all this noise."[17]

Coltrane himself provided a critical perspective regarding the forces of mass consumption and commercialization exercised by the music industry in a 1966 interview with Frank Kofsky, in which he directly addresses his drive toward innovation in sound as a form of resistance. He conceptualizes artistic form as "an expression of higher ideals" based on a communal ethic and posed in opposition to the destructive forces of war:

> I can truthfully say that in music I make or I have tried to make a conscious attempt to change what I've found, in music. In other words, I've tried to say, "Well, *this* I feel, could be better, in my opinion, so I will try to do this to make it better." This is what I feel that we feel in any situation that we find in our lives, when there's something we think could be better, we must make an effort to try and make it better. So it's the same socially, musically, politically, and in any department of our lives . . . jazz—if you want to call it that; we'll talk about that later—to me, it is an expression of music; and this music is an expression of higher ideals, to me. So therefore, brotherhood is there; and I believe with brotherhood, there would be no poverty. And also, with brotherhood, there would be no war.[18]

The imbrication of sound and politics within the broader context of the Olatunji performance suggests the need to rehear the experimental sound emanating from free jazz as a refusal of mainstream culture on both aesthetic and cultural terms. This struggle against the containment of form that circulates between the energy and texture of the sound, and the sociopolitical contexts of its creation and transmission, reimagines freedom as a totality that can't be considered through constructs of linear historical time. The new music explores and extends the aesthetic and phenomenological qualities of sound, and its acoustic features become interwoven within evolving notions of black consciousness.

Moreover, we can say that in this account sound becomes an actor of sorts, enabling and encouraging musicians and listeners to reimagine alternate spheres of creative, anticapitalist political activity through transgressive articulations of black cultural nationalism. The artistic horizons of this openness—what many at the time referred to as playing and existing "out"—offer an aural archaeology that gives depth to the expansive, unfolding texture of the sound as an underside of the Black Arts Movement. The dimensions of sound that emphasize a disruption of exceedingly static ideas of masculine, antiwhite, and confrontational black revolutionary identity are described by A. B. Spellman as he reflects on Coltrane's impact on the period being manifested through approaches to black musical tradition on one hand, and the metaphysical possibilities of communion within the more abstract levels of the music on the other. He states that "Coltrane was playing about something consciously black, no matter how abstract his formulation," writes Spellman. And yet the sound was projecting a "culturated spirituality that splices together the artist's nerve ends of the collective nervous system of the audience."[19] This description is particularly noteworthy in his refusal of any divisions between the political density of black identity and the potential alchemy of its formal expression. Recognizing the phenomenological interaction between multiple, fluid, and experimental sound structures and the sociopolitical context of the post–Civil Rights years, Spellman highlights black sonic experimentation as a synesthetic and organic expansion of the movement's social and political critique, in implicit contrast to stricter, more overtly political definitions of black artistic expression. Coltrane's performance at the Olatunji Center accentuates the relationship between sound, aesthetic experimentation, and post–Civil Rights racial formation as an artistic and historical convergence that highlights the changing terms of racial identity, outlines new configurations of culturally emergent expression, and refashions the possibilities for black political critique.

Preceding his extensive reworking of "My Favorite Things," Coltrane's first set at the Olatunji Center opened with an extended version of the composition "Ogunde." First recorded earlier that year, and included as the opening track on the posthumously released 1967 album *Expression* as a three-minute version of an Afro-Brazilian folk song, "Ogunde Varere," this rendition of "Ogunde" is extended into a twenty-eight-minute-long reverberating sonic field marked by the exchanging and converging tenors of Coltrane and Sanders as they alternately screech, honk, and wail across Rashied Ali's relentless percussion, Garrison's understated bass lines, and the cascades of Alice Coltrane's piano.[20] Thematically, "Ogunde" refers to Ogun, generally recognized as "the god of hunting, iron, and warfare" within the Yoruba belief system. As Sandra Barnes explains, although Ogun has taken on a wide array of additional meaning over time, the central issue in assessing the cultural resonance of the deity lies in understanding Ogun's duality: "In the minds of followers, Ogun conventionally presents two images. The one is a terrifying specter: a violent warrior fully armed and laden with frightening charms and medicines to kill his foes. The other is society's ideal male: a leader known for his sexual prowess, who nurtures, protects, and relentlessly pursues truth, equity, and justice. Clearly this figure fits the destroyer/creator archetype. But to assign him a neat label is itself an injustice, for behind the label lies a complex and varied set of notions. As his devotees put it, 'Ogun has many faces.'"[21] By invoking the complex, shifting, multidimensionality of Ogun—through music cast in a space dedicated to the idea of the African diaspora—the Coltrane quintet's performance suggests a convergence of sound and black consciousness emerging through the Olatunji Center set, yet the elongated, cacophonic sonority of the music destabilizes a reductive idea of Pan-African consciousness. The song resonates within Olatunji's Yoruba cosmological grounding, providing a context through which the Coltrane quintet's sound emerges and interacts within an African diasporic epistemological field constituted more as an aural collage of possibility than as a predetermined set of cultural and political identification. Ideas of creative destruction and the magic of possession link the compositional reference point of "Ogunde" and the powerfully haunting expansiveness of the sound.

On a conceptual level the shifting meaning of Ogun travels in diasporic space and time as both spiritual force and cosmological idea, resonating strongly with the principle in free jazz whereby forward inventive movement involves the double move of return and advance. Here, the double move specifically refers to Coltrane articulating a forward push through the music into a new space of black consciousness while calling on a diasporic network that maintains a relationship between this advance and its source. Coltrane's aural invocation of Ogun, we should remember, arises amid a general growth in Black Power consciousness, independence struggles throughout the black world, a questioning of the principles of nonviolent self-defense, and resistance to the imperialism of the Vietnam War. While his invocation of Ogun could reflect martial ferocity and militant resistance dominating domestic and geopolitical experience, in Coltrane's late sound the ambivalence of creative destruction embodied by Ogun reflects a vision of possibility, transformation, and futurity that can be worked toward amid moments of historical uncertainty in the post–Civil Rights period of the late 1960s. Coltrane's late sound troubles the horizons of black artistic expression, expanding aurality by suggesting fluidity, amplification, and convergence as modes that fuse sound and the broader sociopolitical contexts within which it is situated.

An active quality of the music and a sense of its exterior mark the movement between the composition as sonic text and the possibilities for its signification of broader social, historical, and political meaning. Olatunji himself explains the importance of such links between the aural and extra-aural qualities of musical creativity, as he reflects on the connections between possession and Yoruba praise music for the Orishas such as Ogun: "The most important Yoruba rhythms are the ones that communicate with the Orisas, the spirits of the ancestors. . . . Sometimes we make sacrifices at the shrines of Orisas and offer them gifts. Or else we have a feast with drumming and dancing, and as we chant and dance, the master drummers play an ancient trance rhythm that calls the Orisas down into the bodies of the dancers, and some of the people become possessed by the spirit of maybe Ogun or Shango, and are raised to a higher spiritual level."[22] The level of spiritual communication Olatunji describes within the incantatory rhythms of the Yoruba praise songs is strikingly similar to an experiential dimension of Coltrane's sonic approach during the later years of his composition and performance. His wife and musical partner, Alice Coltrane, speaks of this "kinetic" quality of the music as "very powerful." She explains witnessing the interaction between the energy of the sound and the audience: "I've seen listeners do all kinds of things. Sometimes, as soon as the music started, someone in the audience would stand up, their arms upreaching, and they would be like that for an hour or more. Their clothing would be soaked with perspiration, and when they finally sat down, they practically fell down. The music just took people out of the whole material world; it lifted them up." The mystical, interactive sound of "Ogunde" reflects an attunement both to the African diasporic cultural context of the composition and to the later developments in Coltrane's sonic awareness, as, in the words of Alice Coltrane, he sought to "take us beyond ordinary human perceptions, so that we can see we're more than just limited human beings, that our spirits, our souls, are much higher, much larger, much grander."[23]

The point at which free jazz and broader configurations of the avant-garde meet moves within and against both avant-garde modernism and black cultural nationalism, as the composers and musicians creating these soundscapes blend the intentions of renewal and innovation with tradition, a continual process of forward-moving recovery in which tradition is refigured within a fluidly changing present.[24] The sonic dimensions of the Coltrane performance arise from this matrix of blackness, modernist innovation, and historical tradition situated within formations of African American experience and collective memory. Rather than reduce lived experience, historical subjection, and resistance to a compressed sense of consciousness, the engagements with sound in the music suggest an idea of black con-sciousness based on a commitment to refashioning ideas of time, memory, and perception. In the Coltrane quintet's performance, one of the promi-nent aesthetic features troubling the show's temporality unfolds through the interactive creation of sound structures between Coltrane and Phar-oah Sanders and the interminable drumming of Rashied Ali. This sonic interaction clearly exceeds the limits of music as it would be commonly rec-ognized, as the movement between the pulsing, screeching, and honking sound of the instrumentation creates an elongated sense of crescendo that maintains itself through sudden starts and stops amid brief openings, frag-ments, or suggestions of melodic passages that move into yet more disso-nance. The sense of duration created in the performance, both through the length of the compositional selections, and through the specific elongated instrumental features I've mentioned above, as well as through notable lon-ger solos by Alice Coltrane on piano and Jimmy Garrison on bass, becomes a crucial factor positioning the performance within a broader continuum of free jazz experimentation.

Coltrane's attempt to create new relationships between time, sound, and the sensory as conduits linking composition and audience impels form out-side of simply music, as time is unfolded within, yet also outside the compo-sitional space. Reflecting on his approach to playing (with) time in a series of drum and saxophone duets with Coltrane recorded in February 1967 and released posthumously in 1974 as *Interstellar Space*, Rashied Ali describes how the duets created a destabilization and re-articulation of musical tem-porality through an ephemeral idea of what the beat might feel like and what this idea of musical feeling might convey in a compositional frame-work: "If you listen to *Interstellar Space*, you can hear that something's going on that's holding the whole thing together. I'm not playing regular time, but the feeling of regular time is there. I'm thinking in time. We'd start out in three or four; five-eight or six-eight, whatever. I would anchor it in my mind, but play everything not on it, but against it. I'm hearing the beat and I'm feeling the beat, but I'm not playing it. It's there, but it's not there."[25] Ali reconfigures time through maintaining a refracted, shifting sense of the beat. His approach represents a deeper intervention than simply a structural reor-ganization of musical composition as the fleeting contingency of his "feel-ing" of time and the beat become determining factors of the compositional frameworks. Thinking slightly beyond the specificity of music, Ali's recalibra-tion of time in order to generate alternate aesthetic and phenomenological possibilities presents an expressive method that pushes against formal demarcations of the structure and narrative movement of a work of art. In exploring the flexible relationships between playing regular time and creating the experience or feeling of it, Ali helped Coltrane create new sonic space to communicate with listeners beyond the limits of more familiar musical language.

Sound, time, and the social converge through a relationship between the experimental energy of the concert and the migration of a "Coltrane crowd" to Harlem. Billy Taylor and Bernard Drayton have both spoken of the specificity of a "Coltrane crowd" during this late period of his career, and particularly in relationship to the Olatunji performance, as multiracial, and constituted of people "who wanted to hear something different."[26] This social formation, cohering around Coltrane's particular experimental approaches to extending and unfolding sound, critically underlines Coltrane's aesthetic pursuit of spatial and temporal openings within his music. The formation of a specific listening community in connection with Coltrane's late sound reflects a calibration between his experimental re-formation of sound, the spiritual and ethical beliefs of Coltrane that emerged late in his career, and a shared desire among Coltrane, his fellow musicians, and their audiences, for a musical performance that offered a space of communion within a sonic refutation of continuous harmony and recognizable musical time.[27]

Opening up compositional sound and space to achieve more profound levels of connection with listeners, what Coltrane terms as "the life side of the music," has its roots in Coltrane's early 1960s collaborative efforts with multi-instrumentalist Eric Dolphy, a collaboration that raised the ire of established jazz critics such as John Tynan and Leonard Feather, who felt that the impact of Dolphy's proclivity for dissonance, lyrical unpredictability, and altered tonality was basically stripping Coltrane's classic sound of its musical merit. In a November 1961 issue of *Downbeat*, Tynan characterized the new sound of Coltrane and Dolphy as "a horrifying demonstration of what appears to be a growing anti-jazz trend exemplified by these foremost proponents [Coltrane and Dolphy] of what is termed avant-garde music."[28] Responding to these charges roughly six months later, in a reflective interview with Don DeMichael, Coltrane and Dolphy explain the relationship between their new directions in the form and structure of the music in accordance with their desire to forge new connections with audiences. Coltrane elaborates:

I think the main thing a musician would like to do is to give a picture to the listener of the many wonderful things he knows of and senses in the universe. That's what music is to me—it's just another way of saying this is a big, beautiful universe we live in, that's been given to us, and here's an example of just how magnificent and encompassing it is. That's what I would like to do. I think that's one of the greatest things you can do in life, and we all try to do it in some way. The musician's is through his music.[29]

Through Coltrane's comments, above, as well as Dolphy's proposal that "music is a reflection of everything," that it interacts with "the vibrations from the people," it is clear that the disturbing break Feather and Tynan feel in Coltrane and Dolphy's music is in respect to the realignment of its formal priorities to speak and respond to deeper levels of communication with the audience rather than having them reflect the dimensions of a "clean" tune devoid of extramusical effects.[30] While the comments of Coltrane and Dolphy are not based on overt expressions of radical politics, their use of sound as a method of creating deeper bonds with their listeners, even posing the basis of such connection in terms of a sweeping idea of universalism, nonetheless suggests alternate modes of expanding the sound as the sociohistorical contexts in which Coltrane operates become increasingly tense and politically charged.

Coltrane's flexible relationship to sound refigures ideas of political engagement through the aesthetic dimensions of the imagination. The openness of Coltrane's communicative, relational aesthetics demands a renewed understanding of the interaction between black cultural politics and the aurality of black experimentation. Notably, his use of experimental sound as a transformative tool avoids the determinism that much black political and cultural discourse often adopted during the 1960s. The exploratory sound of his music questions and transcends reductive ideas of black struggle and black political consciousness frequently demarcating the Civil Rights and Black Power eras.

The Consonance of Dissonance

The Coltrane quintet's performance at the Olatunji Center features the discordant elongation of sound as an expansive, shifting field of expression and spiritual communion. By exploring new sonic territory, Coltrane and

other black experimental musicians envisioned the purposeful manipulation of dissonance as an interactive, often ecstatic process through which
new concepts of transformation might emerge. Theorizing the defamiliar-
izing yet productive interaction of dissonance and black consciousness at
the Olatunji concert stresses the relationship between hegemonic ideas of
revolutionary black consciousness and the relational space of black alterity
that James Stewart, writing in the 1971 collection of essays *The Black Aesthetic*, refers to as "the inner dynamic of the new black music." This quality
of the sound, the "revolutionary political implications of the music," is not,
Stewart contends, solely determined by "explicitly political" rhetorical signification, but rather through the inner workings of the music that offers a
sense of the political as "implicit in practice." This innovative edge of black
musical practice represents an important formal break within the history
of African American music that, for Stewart, complicates what it means for
black art to be "vanguardist in a political sense." Stewart hears in the revolutionary sound "a totally new vision of aesthetic reality" that, through its
sonority, critiques the logic of capitalist production and the connected indi-
vidualist virtuosity that had affected the music by the 1940s and 1950s.[31]
Free jazz refused virtuosity in favor of a more communal approach to musical performance and musical experience. Stewart hears the aural fracturing
of the music as a politically radical attempt to rupture the relations of musical production and consumption. Free jazz musical expansion has its genesis in a set of epistemological and political interventions that reconfigure
approaches to critical thought and resistance by destabilizing harmony, melody, and temporality.

The critical inclination toward bending and at times completely breaking with established compositional frameworks and refashioning the con-
stitutive sounds of black music into new aural configurations reflects a larger,
historically tectonic set of implications for black acoustic creativity within
Western culture. The outline of this philosophical and theoretical problematic also emerges in relationship to the concept of repetition—its sonic
possibilities, economic implications, and epistemological meaning. Jacques
Attali, in a later section of his influential text *Noise: The Political Economy
of Music* (1985 [1977]), directly addresses the potential of free jazz to inter-
rupt the repetitive economic and political orders of U.S. late capitalism. In
Attali's schema, "The organized and often consensual theft of black American music provoked the emergence of free jazz, a profound attempt to win
creative autonomy, to effect a cultural–economic re-appropriation of music

by the people for whom it has a meaning." Attali's view of free jazz and its sonorous utopian possibility in the face of authoritarian attempts to delimit social life, may signify an "attempt to express in economic terms the refusal of the cultural alienation inherent in repetition," but ultimately he views free jazz's "inability to construct a truly new mode of production" as the lesson to be drawn from what he represents as an ultimately unsuccessful experiment in cultural resistance.[32] Yet he relies on a strictly structural analysis of the production, distribution, and consumption process that cannot account for the depth of free jazz's intervention within networks of repetition. Rather than measuring success or failure based on the proposition that free jazz begins with a desire to completely break outside of repetitive cycles, I argue that the creative impulse at work within black experimental music was never based on such a sharply defined sense of rupture and reconfiguration, but was contingent on exploring complex models of historical and cultural repetition as the basis for conceptual and epistemological expansion.

Attali is right to focus on the crucial contestations over the economic and epistemological meaning of cultural production that free jazz invoked, but his idea of repetition does not take into account the importance of the "cut," which James Snead notes as a particular creative and critical decision to break away from teleological lines of "accumulation and growth." The cut, Snead proposes, is defined by an asymmetrical attunement to spontaneity and improvisation. The black cultural "cutting" of cycles of repetition has both an aesthetic and a political impact, as it signals a level of critical resistance through its formal operation. As Snead explains, "Black culture, in the 'cut,' builds 'accidents' into its *coverage*, almost as if to control their unpredictability. Itself a kind of cultural *coverage*, this magic of the 'cut' attempts to confront accident and rupture not by covering them over, but by making room for them inside the system itself."[33] The sound of the cut is manifested in both its tempo and its timbre. In discussing examples of black music and literature from artists including James Brown, Toni Morrison, Ishmael Reed, and John Coltrane, Snead suggests that repetition reflects a conceptual complexity regarding linear order that has receded and is now being returned to European creative work and social thought. Snead's schema suggests a vision of the avant-garde with black creativity at the center, the implication being that forms of aesthetic abstraction associated with European modernism and surrealism are generated in large part through modes of repetition with a difference, modes that emerge as fundamental to creative realms of African diasporic consciousness. Read through the lens of repetition that Snead provides, dissonance operates not simply as abstraction in black music, but as a critical and epistemological challenge to practices of social division.

In a 1967 *Jazz Monthly* article, Keith Knox examines the relationship between dissonance and "the flickering, fleeting parts of the subconscious which are always active," suggesting that the political possibilities of the musical experimentation within free jazz hinge on the ability of musicians to use "musical techniques to represent struggle" by reworking the sound of the music, "not to represent any one single experience directly, but rather an abstraction, an idealization, a distillation of a certain aspect of his experience."[34] Knox, and others who were contemplating these experimental possibilities, understood the critical meeting point of audition, signification, and listening, a conjuncture revealed and reshaped through the tonal aspects of free jazz. In Knox's conceptualization of free jazz dissonance and tonal expansion, the ability of the sound to convey meaning and to directly communicate with the listener depends on the calibration of sound and what Nathaniel Mackey, quoting Anthony Braxton, has referred to as its "vibrational affinities." In Mackey's epistolary fiction, *Bedouin Hornbook*, the main character and narrative voice, N., seeks to explain to his ethereal muse, Angel of Dust, the relationship between the intense feelings of loss and "bottomless hurt" he experienced in a recent dream about his brother, and a recording of N.'s band, the Mystic Horn Society, that N. includes with his letter to the Angel of Dust:

> But you're probably wondering what this has to do with the tape I'm sending. Well, isn't the pathos, the ache we hear in certain music a longing for kin? Isn't that what Braxton means by "vibrational affinities," that no sound exists of itself but as a leaning towards others? I see that some time ago I even copied words to that effect, from a book I came across called *Sound and Symbol*, into my journal: "The dynamic quality of a tone is a statement of its incompleteness, its will to completion. To hear a tone as dynamic quality, as a direction, a pointing, means hearing at the same time beyond it, beyond it in the direction of its will, and going toward the expected next tone. Listening to music, we are not first *in* one tone, then in the next, and so forth. We are always *between* the tones, *on the way* from tone to tone; our

hearing does not remain with the tone, it reaches through it and beyond it."[35]

Mackey's description of an acoustics of longing plays with time in important ways, aligning the duration of a deeply felt aching with the contingent, interconnected, and liminal framing of tonality that N. records from the pages of Victor Zuckerkandl's *Sound and Symbol*.[36] Mackey's voicing of N.'s critical thoughts asks us to understand listening as a practice that may bend, fall between, and penetrate discrete systems of tonality.

Thinking through sound in terms of its external features, those ephemeral qualities that cannot be explained solely through aurality, the dissonance of "My Favorite Things" performed by the Coltrane quintet at the Olatunji concert highlights the acoustic field of interaction between listeners and the music, blurring the cyclical progressions of the early 1960s version of the song with the dramatic expansion and fracturing of that patterned structure six years later at the Olatunji Center. Coltrane's transformation of the composition from an improvisational reformatting of a tune into an impressionistic field of sound expresses the often counter-cyclical movements of historical progression, regression, and uncertainty marking the social, political, and racial transformations occurring through the transition between the Civil Rights and the post–Civil Rights era. His manipulation of dissonance not only questions assumptions regarding musical form through the formal texture of his music; Coltrane also encourages and supports a critical resistance to social, racial, and ideological containment.[37] Jonathan Sterne defines this convergence of the formal and the political as "sound's exteriority," the interdependent, suffusive ability of the sonic to be "shaped by and through its exteriors, even as it acts on and within them." Both compositionally and contextually, sound reflects a field of possibilities rather than simply echoing its own cultivated and categorized aural stability, an echoing which, Sterne cautions us, may too conveniently and uncritically attest to the idealization of a subject centered "voice of the one."[38] The resituating of political and social agency through a sense of the relational, rather than discrete properties of sonic communication, demands an attunement to the relationship between sound and the conditions of its emergence. The exterior dimensions of black experimental sound necessitate practices of differential listening that question the seeming stability of identity formation. Dissonant sound, as it might analogize or amplify what it means to exist both inside and in contradistinction to a hierarchy of racial identity construction, becomes an important political tool for the critical refiguring of post–Civil Rights era racial equality. The Coltrane quintet's performance at the Olatunji Center resonates with the political potential of this dissonant exteriority. While the projection of the show's sound indelibly marks the moment of its live performance, it is the resonance, the acoustic reverberation that works through overlapping qualities of duration, fidelity, and echo, that suggests the ways in which the sonic dynamics and contextual elements of this performance create exterior levels of social and political (as well as aesthetic) meaning. In this context, resonance is not solely sonic; it becomes a concept that decenters and enlarges possibilities for interpretation between processes of listening, cognition, and political formation.

The experience of absorbing Coltrane's asymmetrical sound involves what Jean-Luc Nancy calls a "straining toward possible meaning . . . that is not immediately accessible." Nancy's framing of the liminality of sound offers a sense of this in-between-ness as a critical, interpretive edge: "To be listening is always to be on the edge of meaning, or in an edgy meaning of extremity, and as if the sound were precisely nothing else than this edge, this fringe, this margin—at least the sound that is musically listened to, that is gathered and scrutinized for itself, not, however, as an acoustic phenomenon (or not merely as one) but as a resonant meaning, a meaning whose *sense* is to be found in resonance, and only in resonance." For Nancy, resonance lies in the density of significance projected within the ineffability of the cutting, splicing movement of sound, suggesting an inchoate unfolding of meaning that is disclosed through the sonic quality of timbre, "the very resonance of the sonorous," a quality eluding notational measurement and granting sound a rich representational possibility. Nancy explains that "timbre is communication of the incommunicable: provided it is understood that the incommunicable is nothing other, in a perfectly logical way, than communication itself, that thing by which a subject makes an echo— of self, of the other, it's all one—it's all one in the plural."[39] The intentional slipperiness of Nancy's elaboration of what is generally described as tone-color, provides a philosophical lens through which the simultaneously expanding and constricting, opening and closing, multidirectional properties of experimental sound might be heard both with a deep attention to its aurality, and through a simultaneous consideration of the extra-sonic dynamics which emanate from the sound. In this way, the term resonance also suggests an ulterior quality to the sound, as it is situated and fluidly interacting within a specific sociohistorical and creative continuum, the present and lingering meanings of its phonic qualities critically indexing and containing much of the aesthetic force of late 1960s black radical thought.

The Political Contours of Black Aurality

By 1965, John Coltrane had made a substantive, and—as it appeared to many of those in the hierarchy of mainstream jazz criticism—devastatingly anarchic break away from the sense of tradition that granted jazz its institutional and cultural legitimacy. Coltrane's pursuit of expressive and formal freedom exemplified the multiple epistemological breaks at play in this decadelong surge of free jazz. For not only were the innovations that Coltrane and others pushed forward redefining musical possibilities, they also implicitly, and at times, explicitly, demanded experiential groundings outside of what was considered to be the mainstream. In the early summer of the year, Coltrane began posing these possibilities through *Ascension*, a groundbreaking recording for which he assembled a group of ten, mostly younger avant-garde musicians to record two takes of a roughly thirty-minute-long collective improvisation. The recording presents a watershed moment in the arc of Coltrane's late sound through the ensemble's exploration of, and collective improvisation upon, a compositional idea as it is being formulated, and through Coltrane's desire to carry out the project through the efforts of the newest voices on the free jazz scene. Two of these young practitioners, Archie Shepp and Marion Brown, are quoted extensively by A. B. Spellman in the liner notes to *Ascension*, expanding on Spellman's contention that the album "is truly modern; it is as advanced as the most advanced contemporary jazz is . . . the kind of event which *Ascension* is will be unfamiliar to anyone who has not made it a serious avocation to search out and understand the new jazz." The comments of Shepp and Brown render the detail and nuance of Coltrane's approach to narrative, compositional innovation:

> Archie said, "The idea is very similar to what the action painters
> do in that it creates various surfaces of color which push into each
> other, creates tensions and countertensions and various fields
> of energy." Marion Brown approached it another way, "In the
> ensemble sections you get a different idea of what harmony is, or
> can be. Certain chords were used, but they were stretched out and

orchestrated." Which has been the basis of John Coltrane's solo work in the years since he left Miles Davis.

[Again quoting Shepp] "The ensemble passages were based on chords, but these chords were optional. What Trane did was to relate or juxtapose tonally centered ideas and atonal statements along with melodic and non-melodic elements. In those descending chords there is a definite tonal center, like a B-flat minor. But there are different roads to that center. [Archie added] "The emphasis was on textures rather than the making of an organizational entity. There was unity, but it was a unity of sounds and textures rather than like an ABA approach. You can hear, in the saxophones especially, a reaching for sound and an exploration of the possibilities of sound."[40]

Shepp and Brown portray a rhizomatic sound structure as the shifting foundation that allows for the unpatterned unfolding of Coltrane's experimental work. Their comments suggest that his approach to formal innovation was being shaped by the broader context he was helping to fashion, for he was becoming both an example and a collaborator within the younger cadre of avant-garde jazz musicians including Archie Shepp, Marion Brown, Pharoah Sanders, and Albert Ayler. For many of these artists, Coltrane presented a model of revolutionary creativity, constantly pushing forward as a pioneer of new music, while consciously linking the aesthetic search for new and extended forms, to a spiritual, ethical, and ultimately political awareness. Understood in these terms, Coltrane became an example of how to simultaneously probe the horizons of sonic innovation while also striving to redefine aspects of black political and cultural identity. A reflection from tenor saxophonist, Frank Lowe, included in Valerie Wilmer's indispensable history of black avant-garde music, *As Serious as Your Life*, speaks to Coltrane's influence and impact: "In the beginning I wanted to be a 'hip jazz musician.' But Coltrane changed all that . . . the musicians have always been a part of the community from Buddy Bolden on down. But Coltrane re-emphasized this. He took it out from being a 'hip' musician and into being a musician of value or worth to the community. A musician to inform, a musician to relate to, a musician to raise kids by."[41] For Lowe, Coltrane's readiness to explore sound outside of fixed compositional spaces exemplifies a link between ethics and sonic experimentation that builds off of and supports the innovative ability of younger musicians such as Albert Ayler and Pharoah Sanders to explore narration, temporality, and tonality outside of the confines of prearranged scales, notes, time signatures, and harmonic expectations. In a telling comment from an interview with Frank Kofsky, Coltrane questions the assumption that he might have influenced the up-and-coming saxophonist Ayler by stating, "Not necessarily; I think what he's doing, it seems to be moving music into even higher frequencies. Maybe where I left off, maybe where he started, or something."[42] Sanders, who began playing regularly with Coltrane in 1965, explains his disavowal of playing solely on chord changes as a process predating, but extended through his time with Coltrane: "I stopped playing on changes a long time ago, long before I started playing with Coltrane. They limited me in expressing my feelings and rhythms. I don't live in chord changes. They're not expanded enough to hold everything that I live and that comes out of my music." Sanders's refusal of the sonic regulation of patterned chord changes furthers his efforts to recalibrate his sound outside the "very restricting" context of "that whole business thing," reflected in "those 30, 40 minute sets in clubs," instead suggesting a creative process that is generated through translating sonic energy into expressive moments that narrate what "can't be put into words."[43]

As these perspectives indicate, Coltrane was part of a collective inquiry into black sonic expression based on an idea of freeing sound from the confines of compositional form, an approach that became generally considered a foundation within the genre of free jazz in the wake of the late 1950s music of pianist Cecil Taylor and after the 1961 release of Ornette Coleman's groundbreaking album *Free Jazz*. The conceptual basis of free jazz, it should be remembered, emerged from a longer continuum of collective improvisation and the use of nonstructured sonic enactments marking the early history of African American performance and vernacular practices.[44] Free jazz represents a watershed within African American experimental thought, magnifying ideas of compositional flexibility, and presenting multiple, shifting, intersecting, but texturally distinct narrative lines as working in constant tension with harmonic expectations. In her reconstruction of a conversation between Ornette Coleman and drummer Ed Blackwell, Valerie Wilmer captures Coleman making this point to Blackwell in regard to the importance of "play[ing] out the phrase rather than sticking to the form." The implications of Coleman's point suggest a focus on improvisational sound over fixed harmonic structure, a choice allowing for the expansion of narrative space and time by calibrating musical invention and performance with respect to the quality and quantity of melodic sounds rather than harmonic chord progressions. Innovators such as Coleman, Coltrane, Ayler, Sanders, Taylor, Brown, Sun Ra, and many others during the 1960s, set about challenging the authority of patterned musical structures through the power of the sound itself. Coleman continues, offering a succinct take on the capaciousness of his sound as it relates to the exteriority of broader social and historical fields: "When you hear me, you probably hear everything I've heard since from when I was a kid. In fact, it's a glorified folk music."[45]

Coleman's attention to the circulation of sound, lived experience, and cultural tradition frames sonority as a contingent auditory field. Philosopher and sound theorist Don Ihde describes such an "existential possibility" of sound as multidirectional, indefinite, penetrating, and all encompassing.[46] The enveloping, invasive, and unremitting qualities of sound invoked through Ihde's idea of an auditory field provide a means for considering the totality of sound within free jazz as a point of expansion within black aesthetics, suggesting the emergence of the political through a modulation of sensory experience and historical memory. For Ihde, sound's enigmatic character is reflected in a physicality that is both directional and physically pervasive: "Here an enigma of the auditory field emerges from these two dimensions of field spatiality; for the global, encompassing surroundability of sound . . . and the often quite precise and definite directionality of sound presence . . . are both constantly co-present. This double-dimensionality of auditory field characteristics is at once the source of much ambiguity and of a specific richness which subtly pervades the auditory dimension of existence."[47] Ihde's notion of "double dimensionality" reflects a theoretical and experiential dynamism within the way sound is shaped as a structure of meaning and feeling, outlining the central elements of sonic architecture and deployment that are explored in the free jazz quest for new musical, spiritual, and political space. Although free jazz musicians were not necessarily envisioning a direct correlation between their musical production and recognizable political action (although this was the case for some), their expressive work takes on a political dimension through the metaphysical alterations enacted across their various temporal and spatial engagements with the auditory field. Playing out, feeling out, and living out represent an inchoate and open trajectory of black cultural nationalism that supplants the equation of outness with a distinctive, recognizable construction of black radical identity.

Resisting prescriptive correlations between sound and politics, improvisers such as Coltrane were instead focused on construing new phenomenological connections with the minds and bodies of listeners. The refashioning of sound structures pushes listeners to realize the connections between sound and political existence on a level not simply reducible to progressive sequences. The experimental bridging of sound and politics exceeds a mimetic correspondence, as the sound structures possess an internal political valence projected through the multidirectional, indefinite, penetrating, enveloping, and unremitting qualities of the music. Coltrane understood and engaged with these transformational possibilities being charted through free jazz; and in accordance with these ideas, his musical innovations in the last years of his life suggested new structures of political meaning and feeling emerging within black aesthetics.

As experimental musician Anthony Braxton explains, Coltrane's music underlines the "vibrational situation of black people in the sixties"; a situation marked in part by an awareness of "the confusion that naturally results when the essence of a given culture's moral and ethical position is exposed as either not relevant or in decay."[48] Braxton's use of the term "vibrational" (signaled earlier in this chapter through my quotation of Nathaniel Mackey regarding Braxton's "vibrational affinities") moves beyond simply the oscillation of phonic matter into a broader concept reflecting the multidimensional possibilities that shape both individual experience and collective historical consciousness. The vibrational represents the interdependent, accumulating, and composite nature of a perspective or orientation as a site of personal, historical, and/or collective belonging and meaning. In the following exchange, Graham Locke captures Braxton's illumination of this point as he asks Braxton about the "distinctions in his use of the words spiritual, vibrational, and mystical":

B: I make distinctions. By spiritual, I'm talking with respect to God; but for the person who'd say, "wait a minute, I don't believe in God," then it's OK to say vibrational—it serves the same purpose (*laughs*). What was the other word?

L: Mystical.

B: Well, mystical would have to do with the same area, but by mystical I'd be talking more in terms of forces, spiritual forces at work, when you're asleep (*laughs*). And when you're awake! (*Laughs.*)[49]

Braxton's notion of vibration as a mode of mediation between the sonic, scientific, and cosmological is central to the conceptual architecture of his aesthetic and social theory that animates much of his three-volume treatise on music and philosophy, *Tri-axium Writings*. For Braxton, Coltrane's vibrational impact can be understood in listening to Coltrane's late work as a break with the Enlightenment-inflected "vibrational dynamics of progressionalism," instead offering a sonic pronouncement on "the reality and vibrational position of black people in America and in Africa."[50] Braxton's understanding of the interactions between the physical properties of sound and transformations in black consciousness represents an important reconfiguring of political meaning in this sociohistorical and aesthetic context, and draws attention to ideas of liberation emerging from the sonic dimensions of the music that overlapped with, yet were also at variance with formations of Black Arts Movement cultural nationalism more strictly defined along ideological lines. As Braxton points out, Coltrane's "alternative functionalism" opens a chain of critical reflections on the political complexities of black life during the 1960s. His fusion of and inflections on musical composition, spiritual practice, and Western culture writ large, offers a broader framework of shifting influence and meaning that marks the relationship between ideas of the West and black expression.[51] Western culture in this configuration of Braxton's is both hegemonic and contested, and for Braxton it is the contestations of sonic improvisers that represent a rupture in the ability of Western culture to assume its province as "(1) more advanced than any other culture group that ever existed," or "(2) that its methodology—and criteria—was necessarily relevant to every culture group, regardless of whether that group agreed with its interpretations or western culture's right to impose their definitions on nonwestern focuses."[52] In Braxton's view, Coltrane's music, with its progressive approach to sound and harmonics within the context of shifting cultural and social dynamics, bridges specific phenomenological aspects of sound with ideas of identity formation, consciousness, and critical theory. Echoing the intentions of Coltrane and others within this creative continuum of black aesthetic innovation, Braxton situates vibration as a force within black aesthetics that enables engagements with sound to create possibilities for epistemological expansion across expressive forms. Braxton's writings explore the breadth of sound as a simultaneous expansion of black experimental and critical thought. For Braxton, sound's latitude creates new possibilities for reflecting creatively and critically on the convergence of aesthetics, politics, and black historical consciousness.

Notable here is the attempt of black musicians to offer descriptions of the broader expressive totality of their experimental music. Writing about the function of sound within their creative visions, free jazz musicians like Braxton cultivate ideas of black experimental expression through understandings of sound that expand ideas of aurality and fashion alternate possibilities for sociopolitical critique. The synergy between sound and words offers a conjuncture through which the transcendent potential of aurality can more fully emerge. This conjuncture emphasizes the sonic as a fluid realm of creative and critical thought. Braxton's interdisciplinary, multidimensional consideration of sound locates experimental sonic composition as an intellectual practice that involves multiple spheres of sensory expression and critical thought. His approach to sound as a critical force is paralleled by the work of free jazz musician and composer Marion Brown, who also recognizes sound as a tool that may bend and stretch narrative capacities and phenomenological possibilities. As a collaborator with Coltrane on *Ascension* (and with Braxton, on Brown's 1970 recording *Afternoon of a Georgia Faun*—about which I'll have more to say below), a close associate of Black Arts Movement figures such as Amiri Baraka and A. B. Spellman, an explorer of African musical and cosmological ideas as they relate to expressive forms, and a forerunner among musicians interested in exploring the acoustic and phenomenological possibilities in musical experimentation, Brown's artistic and critical contributions question the established categories of black cultural identity and critical thought. His interdisciplinary work during this historical moment situates the flexibility of sound as a central and defining element of the intersecting possibilities for social, political, and artistic transformation.

Marion Brown's perspectives on the relationship between his music, the physical architecture and spatiality of his environment, and the sensory impact of these surroundings are featured in the 1967 short 16mm film *You See What I'm Trying to Say*.[53] Director Henry English conceived and undertook the film project while participating in New York University's Summer Motion Picture Workshop. English recalls that his intention was to have the film "*embody* Marion rather than be *about* him," as English intended to have the film's "conception and realization rooted in the subject itself as opposed to adhering to a standard aesthetic or genre."[54] The roughly eight-minute black-and-white production opens with a brief reflection of Brown's, in which he somewhat deceptively states, "A musician's music is only what it is, music." The deception, or indirection (unintended or not) behind Brown's words becomes clear when just over a minute into the film, he adds, "What I see, more than what I hear, I imagine I try to translate into music. Or it becomes my music."[55] The line within the film's construction between biography and autobiography is troubled, as Brown's aesthetic and ethical approach to sound becomes the basis of the film's movement and meaning. As English states in response to a question about the degree to which the sound and structure of Brown's music affected the texture and form of the film, "Well, it all began with his statement, in the course of the recorded interview I did with him, that the source of his musical inspiration was visual experience. When asked to elaborate, Marion drew the contrast between midtown with its verticals and horizontals and the browns, grays, and dark blues of people's clothes, etc., and the vitality and color of the Lower East Side. We tried to interpret that with our cameras in the editing. We wanted the film to cinematically personify Marion through the synthesis of his music and the inspiration behind it."[56] The shots of these various visual sites emphasize the synesthetic movement between visual and auditory dimensions, as they are set within a broader tapestry of experimental music performed by Brown, Dave Burrell (piano), Norris Jones (bass), and Bobby Kapp (drums). Shifting between a brief section of Marion Brown in his Williamsburg apartment exercising and then walking through different parts of the city, footage of the band performing the composition that the film is set to, and an impressionistic collage of people, spaces, structures, and words scrawled on walls depicting political sentiments of the time, the sense of narrative movement feels derived from the energy and sound of the music. Brown's presence guides the film through the interaction between his words, images of New York City, and the sound of his music, creating both a reflection on Braxton's framing of the relationship between sonic and social vibration, and at the same time, through the vehicle of English's film, suggesting the role of sound as a flexible narrative force.

Brown's sense of the expanding narrative possibilities of sound is further detailed in his critical essays, "Improvisation and the Aural Tradition" and "The Relationship between Language and Texts and Language and Music in Afro-American Songs."[57] Taken together, these contributions articulate a broad framework of aurality in contradistinction to what he feels is an ocular-centric tendency within Western culture. For Brown, "the special kind of rhythmical and tonal vitality" of black speech and song facilitates practices of aural improvisation that not only reflect approaches to sonic expression beyond musical notation, but that also feature a more compressed sense of temporality in which "immediacy is expressed through spontaneous responses to particular musical stimuli."[58] Brown understands the creation of improvisatory moments and exchanges to be projected through a musician's distinctive sound as it is marked by the intersection of a desire for phonic rearrangement and the interaction of individual historical consciousness.

The issue of existing and creating "outside" bridges the work of Brown and Coltrane in several ways—certainly through Brown's participation in the watershed 1965 *Ascension* recording, but also in Brown's study of the mystical and spiritual qualities that became central to Coltrane's music in an increasingly revolutionary fashion from 1957 through his death in 1967. In Brown's essay "A Love Supreme: The Spiritual Awakening of John Coltrane," ideas of sonic expansion, black consciousness, and a philosophy of the aesthetic converge as Brown suggests that the formal features emerging in Coltrane's music during the 1960s, such as "the use of modes, chanting, the use of 'atonal,' or 'free' harmonies, and rhythmic patterns that are characterized by an absence of 'regular' meter," arise through Coltrane's understanding and refashioning of religious mysticism within the sound of his music. Brown quotes from religious philosopher Rudolph Otto to explain that the extramusical, mystical qualities of Coltrane's music "express feelings and emotions quite beyond the sphere of the usual" and emerge "quite outside the limits of the canny." Brown points to the sublime, or what he terms "ineffable," by way of noting William James's use of the term in *Varieties of Religious Experience* as an aesthetic and experiential state that is both a formal and ethical presence in Coltrane's work. This ineffability arises through the supplanting of a predetermined, intellectually configured musical path—what Brown terms a "nonintellectual mode of consciousness."[59] Brown's attunement to the layers of meaning within Coltrane's sound hinges on his awareness of meaning within the sound that pushes beyond its own phonic materiality. For Brown, going beyond the threshold of what we imagine music to be entails recognizing and summoning experiences and sensations outside the range of familiarity that marks musical and social convention, as these convergences of the experiential and the sensory move through time, space, bodies, and levels of consciousness. The texture of sound is central to his musical approach, as he points out to interviewers Terence Beedle and Juergen Abi Schmitt: "It's about sound. Everything is about sound. . . . I surround people with sound. I try to think of myself as wrapping them in velvet, nice fur; I like Sound!"[60]

Brown was also attuned to the ways in which this orientation to sound as radically exterior to the mainstream was reflected in his migratory experience as an "outcast" free jazz performer moving from Atlanta to New York City in the early 1960s. Brown explains this free jazz migratory phenomenon as signaling the necessity for alternative sociopolitical formations:

> One of the odd things about new jazz music was that the players developed individuality in many different parts of the country and when they came together they already knew what they were doing. There was no Minton's. There was no Storyville for this music! In other words, a site where people could come together and make it, put their ideas together. All the people playing free jazz and things like that, when they were doing it they were freaks in different cities and places. The people didn't like the way they were playing, telling them it was not music. It was like that with me in Atlanta, Georgia. When I read music that was on paper, I was right there with everybody. But like, when it came time to play an improvisation or solos, my concept of everything like time, melody and all was so strange— I won't say concept because I had no concept—my ability, let's say, was so strange it didn't fit. So, I was constantly being insulted by my friends. One day I heard Ornette Coleman on the radio, and I said, there it is! I am not by myself!—and when I went to New York then, in the Sixties, all the people started to come from different places, playing free jazz. But they'd all come from a similar situation in their hometowns of being outcasts. They didn't fit.[61]

Brown describes sound as a broader refashioning of identity, calibrating its transgressive and ephemeral potential with the acknowledgment of one's status as marginalized within an already marginalized identity. The density of experimental energy converging around black sonic expression during this period creates a context in which the creation of new sounds signals and sustains radical ideas of freedom through black artistic innovation. Brown acknowledges that the radical edge of experimental sonic expression is formed outside of, or at least in great tension with, the constraints of mainstream American culture. His music and writings explore the space and possibility of sound's conceptual breadth, beyond simply its tonality.

His landmark recording of the two-part-extended improvisation *Afternoon of a Georgia Faun* exemplifies this inclination toward reimagining the possibilities for sonic expression. He elaborates in an interview with John Turner included in the collection of reflections on the album, "Views & Reviews," published several years after the album's 1970 release. In Brown's estimation, "the uniqueness of it [*Afternoon of a Georgia Faun*] is not so much the music, how it sounds; but, how it was organized. It is structured in such a way, and played at such a level of understanding by the musicians that it defies classification." The fact that Brown, among black free jazz musicians, tended to describe in some detail his creative process, offers one avenue for understanding the narrative conceptualization of sound that was a distinct and telling aspect of the broader free jazz creative continuum. By "narrative conceptualization of sound," I mean to draw attention to what Brown might call sound's contingency. It matters to Brown that his process of sonic creativity is interactive between composer and players, but also within the creative consciousness of the composer. Brown provides an example of sound's conceptual flexibility in describing the opening of the title track through the interactions between his technical conceptualization of a sound, its phonic qualities, and his narrative description of the sound's effects. Responding to an interviewer's question as to whether Brown thought of the track's opening sounds of wooden blocks as representations of raindrops before or after the recording, Brown replies, "After. I conceive the sounds first, and name them afterwards, when I have heard them back. I did not realize they were wooden raindrops until I heard the tapes and felt the unreal quality of imagination. They were wood-blocks. But, for me, they became, in my mind's ears, the sound of wooden raindrops, a figment of my imagination."[62]

In detailing his process of imagining sound, Brown frames recording technology and the ability to rehear his composition of sounds as central to his creative process. His notion of hearing outside the time of performance creates a new space through which he can access the "unreal quality of imagination." This distinctive temporal relationship to sound revolves around Brown's consideration of improvisation as an alternate modality of formal composition, one occurring both as a method within the structure of the performance and within Brown's practice of subsequently listening to and reflecting on the sound. His contemplation of the structural and compositional qualities of sound through its resonance allows him to reconfigure sound as a narrative framework, situating acoustics and audition as flexible concepts that mark the sonic realm as one in which projection and listening are never quite stable or fixed processes. This instability generates new possibilities for narrative composition through flexible alignments of sound and text. Brown's theorization of the relationship between sound and black narration expands the possibilities not only for musical composition, but for black literary innovation as well. His engagements with experimental narrative form anticipate the connected methods writers were fashioning that brought together the energy of experimental sound and the compositional possibilities that unfold when words and ideas are set in relationship to the unharnessed quality of this sonic energy. Brown's intellectual exchanges with experimental sound, often within the social context of the Black Arts Movement, are provocatively distilled in a comment he makes regarding his artistic community in New York when he first arrived in the early 1960s: "The writers who listened to me and liked my playing, they inspired me to be better and I inspired them to keep listening. LeRoi Jones opened the door for me, he introduced me to the world. . . . We used to practice at 27 Cooper Square, and he lived in that building on the top floor. Archie Shepp lived on the second floor. So he knew what we were doing all along, because he was upstairs listening."[63] Brown and other experimental black artists working across generic forms were increasingly conceptualizing innovation through ideas of sound that often exceeded music as they searched for additional levels of meaning in this surplus of aural expressivity. Baraka's "listening in," as Brown puts it, is an important critical opening or conduit bridging the experimental possibilities moving between sonic and literary expression and emphasizing the experimental underside of black cultural nationalist expression during the Black Arts Movement.

Black Art

Few black artists and intellectuals have invested more time and thought into contemplating the convergence of experimental music and black expression during the Black Arts Movement period than Amiri Baraka. From his 1963 social history of black music, *Blues People*, to his late 1960s collection of essays and concert reviews, *Black Music*, and his recent volume *Digging*, Baraka's writings explore and are in dialogue with black music as a conduit between sonic expression, black cultural production, and, perhaps most crucially for Baraka, the possibility of radical political thought. Central to Baraka's understanding of post-bebop black sonic creativity, what he refers to as the New Black Music rather than the more common referent "free jazz," is the unsettling nature of Albert Ayler's groundbreaking, overwhelming, and sound-altering explorations of the saxophone. The rupture that Ayler's sound presented to the mid-1960s jazz world inspired Baraka through the fusion of beauty and terror projected through his sonic disruption of tonality. In an essay accompanying *Holy Ghost*, the massive box set of Albert Ayler material released in 2004, Baraka recalls encountering Ayler between late 1964 and early 1965, when "the gauze of old bebop chords and concept had been lost and a space had been 'newed' apart." Baraka explains, "Albert came to see me, I guess, because my name had been associated with the new music—as publicist, critic, as poet expressing the new consciousness. 'You think it's about you?' His favorite question. A challenge more than an inquiry. In other words, is it about the music or about possession, ego trip, getting over, and employment, something superficial? It was also a challenge to my definitions, analysis, evaluation, and hierarchy of artists. 'You think it's about you?'"[64] Ayler's conceptual challenge to Baraka underscores the distinctively enigmatic nature of the "new music" and conveys Ayler's desire for the music beyond simply as a means of furthering personal and political agendas imposed on it. Ayler's sense of sonic autonomy within black experimental music that, nonetheless, organically supports ideas of struggle, resistance, and liberation, reflects an important aspect of the tension and interplay between experimental sound and black aesthetics. Baraka's reflection on Ayler, taken alongside Baraka's 1966 performance of the poem "Black Art," with the instrumental accompaniment of Ayler, Sonny Murray, Henry Grimes, and Louis Worrell, offers the chance to delve more deeply into the convergence of sound, poetics, and ideology that offered new possibilities for aesthetic and political expansion to writers during the Black Arts Movement.

The recorded performance of the poem provides an example of Black Arts Movement cultural nationalism intersecting with new black musical expression in complicated and intellectually productive ways. The recording aurally confronts the term "free jazz" as a description of 1960s black (and) American musical history, tonally projecting the ambivalence many of the innovators felt and continue to feel toward this categorization through the enigmatic quality of the sound. Baraka, in both his creative and critical work, anticipates the perspectives of recent critics such as Fred Moten, George Lewis, Nathaniel Mackey, Aldon Nielsen, and Kimberly Benston, in his skepticism regarding the efforts to fit black cultural expression into easily classifiable labels. As he points out, once the music is encountered through an already fixed critical framework, its ability to be understood as a deeper intervention within black American consciousness and intellectual thought becomes too easily overlooked. Baraka makes this contention in his formative Black Arts Movement essay on black musical and sonic culture, "The Changing Same (R&B and the New Black Music)," defining the "New Black Music" as "expression, and expression of reflection as well." This inherent, fluid instability of the music offers "a consciously proposed learning experience" through "the *unknown, the mystical*."[65]

Baraka's composition and reading of the poem reflects and projects his attunement to these revolutionary possibilities of sonic innovation through his interplay with the music of Sonny Murray, Albert Ayler, Don Cherry, Henry Grimes, and Louis Worrell. Rather than mere accompaniment, however, the sound of the instrumentation is more of a provocation to the supposed solidity of the poem's charting of black cultural nationalist possibility. In both its performed aural projection, then, and in the way its sonority converges with a more textually produced set of representational and ideological contingencies, his reading troubles matters of form, voice, and sound in black nationalist poetics. In doing so, Baraka suggests that the Black Arts Movement, black radical thought, and artistic representations might be propelled through the strangeness of experimental sound—the strangeness itself symbolizing a revolutionary break, yet simultaneously troubling the definitive violence of that break through its own instability.

The opening of the composition feels rushed, as if the listener has been thrust into a scene's frantic climax. This beginning, largely defined by the brightness of Cherry's trumpet, sounds like an ending, as a shrill, six-note progression becomes a phrase repeated several times in the first half-minute, almost inverting the structure of the music as the phrasing moves both backward and forward toward Baraka's delivery of the title and opening line. When Baraka begins his reading, after a second or two of soft, almost whispered percussion from Sonny Murray, there is a balance between Baraka's measured verse and a texture to the poetry that exceeds the page through its relationship to the accents of the drums, horns, and bass of Murray's quintet. In contrast to the frenetic noise that many came to associate with this era in black music, this composition is defined instead by a hauntingly minimalist atmosphere. We can clearly hear the influence of Ornette Coleman's angular, non-tempered, spontaneous approach to free improvisation in the quintet's structuring of a compositional framework for Baraka's poem. Freed from the twelve tones of the tempered European scale, the improvisation moves in accordance with the sound being created by the other musicians. Especially noteworthy here is Don Cherry, a co-innovator with Coleman in their particular orientation toward more brightly toned and quickly moving styles of free improvisation. The legacies of new music course through this quintet, with Albert Ayler also representing a new horizon in saxophone freedom, influencing the likes of John Coltrane with his fusion of down-home spirituality and an unrelenting push, as Baraka notes in a 1966 jazz column, "purely into sound."[66] Murray himself reveals another trajectory that takes us to an equally formative yet often overlooked influence within the new music, that of Cecil Taylor, who, as Baraka states in his review of Murray's album *Sonny's Time Now*, is the conduit through which Murray "first got turned on to what freedom was" (177).

Given the particular circuit of experimental practice present in this quintet, how might their presence, and the sound they foster, allow for an understanding of Baraka's revolutionary poetic tract as an exploration of freedom rather than simply the violent diatribe it is usually cast as? Listening to the sound of the quintet surrounding and interacting with Baraka's reading of "Black Art" forces the reader/listener to think more carefully about lines such as "We want 'poems that kill.' / Assassin poems, Poems that shoot / guns. Poems that wrestle cops into alleys / and take their weapons leaving them dead / with tongues pulled out and sent to Ireland." The aggressive tonality of Baraka's verse is consistently troubled by a tension between the almost vaudeville sound of Cherry's muted trumpet bopping along behind and between the words, and the haunting, more elongated structure of Ayler and Murray's interplay of saxophone and drums. "Setting fire and death to / whities ass," "cracking / steel knuckles in a jewlady's mouth," or "scream[ing] poison gas on beasts in green berets": lines such as these imagine something beyond violence in a common-sense understanding of the term; violence becomes pushed beyond the visceral quality of what physically happens to bodies and is instead projected as a reinvention of verse in all its prosodic and sonic capacities.[67] These lines are painting pictures that reflect a role for words and images in the freed, liminal space outside the page. It is not necessarily that the poem is expected to erupt in a Dali-esque surrealistic vision—in which the words enact violence upon actual human bodies—but rather that a rethinking of the role of the poem might create sensibilities that will confront and upend the world as we have come to know it through the freedom of creative destruction.

There are at least two important points to make here, one dealing with black cultural politics and the other with the formal convergence of sound, poetics, and black literary aesthetics. First, I must address the interplay between sound and cultural politics in Baraka's and the Sunny Murray Quintet's performance of the poem. As recent trends in scholarship on this period show, it is necessary to examine specific moments of cultural production in order to consider the multitude of perspectives, postures, ideologies, influences, and antagonisms that marked the late 1960s and early 1970s Black Arts Movement period. Clearly, the performance of Baraka's poem adds more dimensions to the tensions between black consciousness and experimental music that are covered in the recent work of both Benjamin Piekut and Iain Anderson, who partially frame the terms of this relationship between experimental sound and black cultural identity with the understanding, in the case of Anderson, that the promotion of free improvisation during the Black Arts Movement was based on "an Afrocentric, nationalistic, and separatist ideology that claimed free improvisation as the contemporary manifestation of a residual black aesthetic." Piekut, in a similar vein to Fred Moten, analyzes the hypermasculine, heteronormative dimensions of pre- to early Black Arts Movement musical production and criticism, mainly through the tensions over racial authenticity and black revolutionary identity as they emerge between Amiri Baraka and Jazz Composers Guild leader Bill Dixon: "The racial consciousness of the Black Arts writers, critics and musicians around Baraka (Lawrence Neal, Spellman, Shepp, Graves, and others) was characterized by a polarization of positions." Dixon, then, becomes posed between the "separatist and militant impulses" of this group and the "color blindness of white jazz musicians and critics."[68] Although Piekut's study seeks to problematize this polarized context, he also asks us to first accept the truth of the oppositional terms from which Dixon's middle space can be framed. While Piekut is right to point out that while the sound of the music was often being configured along lines of inter- and intraracial masculinity and revolutionary authenticity, we should remember that this disruption occurs not only in relationship to oppositional ideologies, structures, and epistemologies, but also in an ironic way, against a stagnant sense of what militant and/or separatist black nationalism might entail. The movement of the poem from a clear poetic statement of the Black Arts Movement, occupying the center of the movement's primary anthology, *Black Fire*, into a less stable and more contingent realm of spoken and instrumental performance complicates the poem's masculine energy. The sound suggests a darker space of haunting as the sentiment through which the poem might be felt. In this case, the phonic matter of the music that the recitation is set within gains a level of density that the poem cannot achieve by itself on the page. The density that the words gather through the experimental sound of Murray's quintet is not based on an uncomplicated, celebratory refusal in which the musicians simply project an imagined idea of Baraka's voice to fit the words we see on the page and the images they may foster. The poem is instead deepened through the various projections of feeling emerging from the sparse, hesitant, erratic interaction of sound and text.

In positing a relationship between transformations in racial politics, the manipulation of sound, and experimental literary aesthetics during this period, it is certainly instructive to pay attention to the intersection of several genealogical lines of cultural production that can help us to better imagine the political and aesthetic contours of this moment. This intersection involves, on one hand, considering the meeting points of artistic experimentation and black revolutionary identity, and on the other, situating an idea of sonic resistance within the continuum of Afro-Atlantic cultural production initiated in response to the ruptures of the Middle Passage and systems of chattel slavery in the Americas, and reworked from that point of initiation, moving up to the immediate post–Civil Rights era of the late 1960s and early 1970s. Finally, this work seeks to chart the meaning of a movement beyond form into a sonic field of creation, specifically how it represents not only an artistic project, but also a political strategy of aural and expressive transformation within the Civil Rights and Black Power eras.

I end then, with a series of questions that may also be provocations for the continued, intensified critical rethinking of African American literary history during the time of the Black Arts Movement. What does it mean to conceptualize a soundscape of black freedom through the experimental sounds created by musicians, and, furthermore, through the fusions of those sonic orientations with both spoken and written literary representations? How might we generate new interpretive dimensions of sound studies to account for the relationships between experimental sound structures and the sociopolitical contexts from which they emerge? How do the historical contexts of institution building suggested by the Olatunji–Coltrane relationship offer a framework in which the sounds of black avant-garde performance are cast within formations of community and collectivity that outgrow flattened constructions of blackness as they remain unapologetic in their fealty to black aesthetic practice as a space of constantly unfolding, non-stagnant, irreducible critical energy? Such questions help to complicate the too-often flattened orthodoxies of interpretation that ignore the complexities of black cultural nationalism. The chapters to come will further investigate the specific dimensions of this aesthetic countermove as they become articulated through projections of a longer Black Arts Movement sense of black literary experimentation—one in which relationships between word, sound, and image are refashioned to convey alternative and expansive representations of black critical thought.

· CHAPTER 2 ·

Apocalyptic Soundscapes

Listening to Henry Dumas's Short Fiction

*You got to reach people with all kind of sounds now. Sound, that's what
they need. They got to have sound bodies now (and) sound minds.*

—Sun Ra

Sonic Temporality / Literary Space

In a 1967 letter written to critic Larry Neal and his wife, Evelyn, Henry
Dumas offers an impressionistic overview of his relationship to the bur-
geoning literary scene of the Black Arts Movement. The one-page letter
accompanying the submission of his short story "Fon" to the anthology
Black Fire, which Neal was coediting with LeRoi Jones (Amiri Baraka),
offers a glimpse into the all too brief career of this curiously understudied
Black Arts Movement creative voice. Referencing his journey to the Mid-
west to begin a position as the director of the Upward Bound program at
Hiram College in Ohio (and to subsequently serve as a teacher–counselor
within the Experiment in Higher Education at Southern Illinois University), Dumas explains to Larry and Evelyn Neal that he has "made the trip
out ok" and is "getting [his] feet wet out here." The occasion of the letter
marks an important stage in Dumas's career. He had left what many felt
was the epicenter of the movement in New York City in order to expand
his artistic activism by increasing access and radicalizing approaches to
higher education. His letter, nonetheless, reflects his continued investment
in the happenings of Neal and others back in New York. Dumas asks about
Neal's efforts to independently publish the black music journal *The Cricket*,
comments positively on having seen Neal's outline for a book on jazz, and
generally suggests his desire to remain connected to the dynamic elements
of the movement:

> Too bad we didn't get together for a reading. I had decided last
> year after reading at the Folklore Center that I wasn't going to read

anymore, but after talking with you I think that perhaps I would like to read to a black audience for a change. You must let me know all about your readings and the things you are doing with the mag. I am so interested and would have loved to help you push any-thing. Saw Russell down at Slugs and I told him to get on you and make you get the magazine out. You know it is funny, but there is so much black talent just bursting with fire, but so far the man is able to keep things in the shadows.

Dumas's expressed desire to connect with black audiences, as well as his references to the experimental black poet Russell Atkins and the Lower East Side underground jazz club Slug's Saloon, outline his investment in bridging literary innovation, experimental sound, and black expressive cul-ture. When read closely, this seemingly quotidian letter more deeply reveals Dumas's need to explore the connections between black aesthetics and polit-ical transformation. In order to strengthen the ability of his creative writ-ing to illustrate "what is happening to my people and what we are doing with our precious traditions," Dumas crafts an expansive approach to black cultural nationalism by exploring the aural dimensions of his prose.[1] Dumas's fashioning of a scriptural sound epitomized the Black Arts Movement's ideal of using innovative aesthetic effects to help generate political mean-ings, and in doing so, offered a counter to the more reductive approaches to black artistic representation within the movement.

The tensions between prescriptive and expansive black aesthetics are expressed in Larry Neal's opening to his benchmark essay, "The Black Arts Movement," in which he argues that "Black Art is the aesthetic and spiri-tual sister of the Black Power concept," and it "speaks directly to the needs and aspirations of the Black America" through "a radical reordering of the western cultural aesthetic." Neal conceptualizes innovation as a window into black artistic expression through "the Afro-American's desire for self-determination and nationhood."[2] This aspect of the Black Arts Movement, for some exhibiting a reductive critical position, is also what makes it cen-tral to any serious contemplation of twentieth-century black modernism. The desire to renew and revitalize aesthetic horizons through an idea of black cultural nationalism presents possibilities for a "radical reordering" of ethics and aesthetics that might accommodate new expressions of black revolutionary consciousness. Yet Neal's assertion also reflects a broader modernist inclination to contemplate the aesthetic as a means of reflecting the complexity of human consciousness in relationship to social and political transformation.[3] Henry Dumas's writing reflects Neal's expansive critical framework for Black Arts Movement cultural production, as both Neal and Dumas understand the movement as a space to rupture, and extend categories of artistic expression. In Dumas's case, this inclination was frequently articulated through his philosophical and representational uses of sound. Dumas's short stories seamlessly blend supernatural and realistic elements within musical and environmental contexts that are marked by the presence of sound as an active force, which helps direct the narrative movement of the stories. Through his exploration of sound within particular narrative contexts, Dumas forges connections between the historical immediacy of black cultural nationalism and more ethereal approaches to aesthetic innovation. By translating this experimental energy of sound into literary form, Dumas creates soundscapes that index narrative space through voices, music, or the sounds of various environments in order to unfold the thematic and ideological qualities of his stories.

The concept of the "soundscape" was introduced by R. Murray Schafer's late 1970s environmentally engaged examination of the various physical and spatial sonic contexts shaping our world, *The Soundscape: Our Sonic Environment and the Tuning of the World*. Schafer defines the idea of the soundscape in respect to his focus on acoustic ecology and his concern with the aural impact of technological development and modern industrialization on the environment. Schafer's framing of the barometer of sound is capacious enough, however, to allow for the concept's expansion across the many disciplinary methodologies comprising the rapidly expanding field of sound studies.[4] Schafer explains, "The soundscape is any acoustic field of study. We may speak of a musical composition as a soundscape, or a radio program as a soundscape, or an acoustic environment as a soundscape. We can isolate an acoustic environment as a field of study just as we can study the characteristics of a given landscape. However, it is less easy to formulate an exact impression of a soundscape than of a landscape. There is nothing in sonography corresponding to the instantaneous impression which photography can create."[5] Schafer's idea of an "acoustic field of study" denotes the presence of an aural object or phonic materiality; the soundscape is signified by a sonorous environment or by an acoustically manufactured cultural production. And while a work of literature is not actually materially sonic in this way, the idea of a literary soundscape as a narrative framework might reflect the techniques employed by an author to represent the aurality of an environment that is being phenomenologically construed, imagined, or experienced within a text. Dumas's integration of sound into his literary practice, both conceptually and in terms of the acoustics of his writing, provides an additional means of understanding the aesthetic and ideological braiding of narrative form. In many ways correlative to Fredric Jameson's suggestion that "the aesthetic act is itself ideological, and the production of aesthetic or narrative form is to be seen as an ideological act in its own right," sound provides a method for Dumas to expand his literary practice within a long-standing black cultural and vernacular idiom, while also providing a means of ideological engagement through aesthetic innovation.[6] Dumas articulates sound as a transcendent principle that guides and bridges the formal and thematic qualities of his stories. His short fiction is both attuned to the literary transcription of sound into narrative, and is invested in a more diffuse conceptualization of sound as central to a larger ideological and philosophical framework of black consciousness.

Sound functions not only as an aesthetic device for Dumas, but also offers a visionary approach to cultural and political critique within his short fiction. Dumas fuses the aesthetics and politics of his writing by orchestrating sound to highlight moments of critical resistance in the metaphysical and phenomenological dimensions of particular characters' consciousness. Dumas's rendering of the various rhythms of oppression and resistance is depicted through the vibrational and synesthetic manifestations of sound experienced and conveyed by characters across many of his stories. Through his acoustic narration, Dumas critiques the limitations on black progress that exist beneath the more evident manifestations of structural racism. His stories diagnose racism as a form of alienation that persists beyond contestations over equal access. Sound becomes a force in Dumas's writing through which he frames the epistemological violence underlining racist subjection.

The aesthetic and political breadth of Dumas's writing is well-documented within the 1988 "Henry Dumas Issue" of *Black American Literature Forum*, guest-edited by Dumas's colleague, friend, and eventual literary executor, Eugene Redmond, twenty years after Dumas was mysteriously killed by a New York City policeman in a purported case of mistaken identity.[7] Redmond, having written several introductions to volumes of Dumas's work, compiles an impressive slate of critical and creative reflections on the craft and cultural import of Dumas's work. For example, Gwendolyn Brooks identifies Dumas's "sharp perceptiveness and zeal" in conveying a "*correct*" sense of self-determined historical consciousness, while Margaret Walker cites the musicality of Dumas's language as a window into "the powerful meaning of all our lives," a reflection of "the visual, the auditory, and the feeling/tone of our sacred history."[8] Brooks and Walker both analyze Dumas's writing outside of simply black literary form. They value the relationship Dumas suggests between the prophetic and mythic qualities of his writing and the quotidian elements of experience and struggle marking black life during the post–Civil Rights years. In a similar vein, Amiri Baraka, in his description of Dumas as an "Afro-Surreal expressionist," elaborates on the prophetic level of Dumas's writing as the creation of "an entirely different world organically connected to this one." Although he avoids a succinct definition of the tradition of "African American literary Afro-Surreal Expressionism" within which he places Dumas (along with Zora Neale Hurston, Jean Toomer, and Toni Morrison), Baraka specifically cites Dumas's "language of exquisite metaphorical elegance" as a formal dimension that "*tells* as well as decorates," creating a "broken quality" to the narration.[9] The "broken quality" Baraka identifies in Dumas's writing designates an impressionistic correspondence between language, image, and meaning that reverberates throughout his narration.

Experimental black musicians Joseph Jarman, Famadou Don Moye, and Johnny Dyani capture the evocative and transcendent quality of Dumas's writing on their late 1979 recording of the track "Black Paladins." The poetic recitation and musical composition directly references Henry Dumas's representation of Black Arts Movement revolutionary energy and sound represented roughly fifteen years earlier in his poem, from which the Jarman track takes its name. Jarman's reading of Dumas's one-stanza poem, part of a cycle of works Dumas titled, fully or in part, "Saba," appears on the page and is read by Jarman as follows:[10]

we shall be riding dragons in those days
black unicorns challenging the eagle
    we shall shoot words
    with hooves that kick clouds
    fire eaters from the sun
we shall lay the high white dome to siege
cover screams with holy wings, in those days
    we shall be terrible[11]

The poem builds toward a sense of the "terrible" that confronts the eagle and the dome, symbols central to the construction of the United States as a representation of neoclassical, Western Hemispheric power, and in doing so reinforces a particular convergence of the mythic and apocalyptic aspects of black struggle that mark Dumas's creative–critical universe. The relationship between Dumas's writing of "Black Paladins" and Jarman's re-invocation of it a dozen or so years later revolves around an idea of sonic energy that Dumas and others were applying to the architectonics of Black Arts Movement creative writing. As much as Dumas's poem anticipates, inspires, and facilitates the sound Jarman, Moye, and Dyani create on "Black Paladins," the poem possesses its own textual acoustics, from the imagining of flapping dragons' wings, to shooting words, kicking hooves, and screams covered "with holy wings." Dumas's poem represents a soundscape both in its depiction of the mobilization of sound on the page and through its exploration of the temporal dissonance generated through the poem's narrative arc. He inverts and remixes the possible futurity of "we shall be riding dragons in those days" from the poem's initiation, to the past distance in its concluding phrasing, "in those days / we shall be terrible." The particular space through which Dumas imagines struggle in "Saba: Black Paladins" refuses temporal stability, and in doing so, points to an interminable quality of black struggle. The sonic qualities of the poem expand when Dumas's disruptions of temporality are reconstructed within the sound of Jarman, Moye, and Dyani over a decade later. This relationship, between Dumas's creation of the poem and its later musical arrangement, highlights Dumas's exploration of sound's potential to formally and thematically disturb narrative structures that are based on uncomplicated ideas of progress.

Joseph Jarman explains his desire to channel Dumas's creative energy and revolutionary spirit through exploring his understanding of the relationship between the sound of the music and Dumas's commitment to transformation:

When I discovered Dumas' writing, it became very important for me, because he was carrying on a kind of tradition that I had only found in Black African writers. But here was an Afro-American telling stories about things that I knew about, because although I grew up in Chicago, I was born in Arkansas, and somehow my consciousness still remembers some of that Arkansas wonderfulness. Dumas' poetry and his stories were very close, are very close to me, and became I guess a principal inspiration for me. Not only did this "Black Paladins" become a kind of manifesto for me, but it also generated a whole theatre piece that I had the opportunity to perform, but don't have any music, tape or recording of it at this time.[12]

Jarman, Moye, and Dyani resituate Dumas's words and the expanse of his poetics by fashioning a swinging, almost down-home sound that unfolds after Jarman's recitation of Dumas's poem. The walking bass and steady, lightly kept time of the drums gives way to the somewhat atonal, yet still-swinging saxophone, followed by a more frenetic section of bass and drums that work toward a freedom outside the confines of regulated musical time. When the saxophone returns into the fold, the sound escalates into an aggressively dissonant-free collective improvisation that ultimately recedes in intensity to recapture a slightly fractured and sped-up version of the opening phrasing. The interplay between temporality and free improvisation echoes Dumas's own enfolding of the traditional and the innovative, his attempts to bring together a black cultural orientation steeped in black vernacular epistemologies, while very much open to the new revolution in sound.

The Textual Space of Mythic Sound

Dumas's fusion of the literary and the sonic emerges as a challenge to the reductive categorizations of historical experience and political life that were also being confronted through the mythic, interstellar, and metaphysical extensions of African diasporic consciousness envisioned by the innovative musician and composer Sun Ra.[13] John Szwed, in his biography of Sun Ra, notes that the relationship between Dumas and Sun Ra was particularly strong from 1965 to 1966, when Dumas "hung out at Sun Ra's . . . while he was employed as a social worker in New York City."[14] Critics have increasingly recognized the connections between Henry Dumas and Sun Ra, particularly given the 2001 release of a 1966 conversation between the two, as well as the volume of Dumas's collected short fiction, *Echo Tree: The Collected Short Fiction of Henry Dumas*, which was published in 2003 with the inclusion of a previously unpublished story, "The Metagenesis of Sunra (to Sun Ra and His ARKestra)." Dumas's connections to Sun Ra—both on the page and in conversation—frame his engagements with Sun

Ra's aural and philosophical ideas regarding black sonic expression, and provide a crucial context for interpreting Dumas's attempts to blur the line between the literary, the sonic, within ideas of black consciousness.

Dumas's aural approach to resistance and transformation is heavily indebted to Sun Ra's idea that "space is the place." Sun Ra imagines the sonic as a conceptual field that, through its inchoate and expansive nature, can challenge constructions of rationality, and more precisely, the ways that those general assumptions might delimit a more capacious sense of black identity. Sun Ra's conceptualization of mythic, supernatural, and extraterrestrial black identity is less a reflection of eccentricity than it is a critical construction for questioning the foundations of historical knowledge that underline hegemonic formations of social and political hierarchies. Graham Locke points to this pivotal aspect of Sun Ra's biography as a formative theoretical element within his ideological vision, explaining, "It is as if Sun Ra was deliberately reversing the formal conventions by which the slave narratives claimed to be documented truth, perhaps to signal that he was breaking his historical links (as an African American) with the fact and condition of slavery. Indeed, the point at which many slave narratives end—with the act of renaming—is the point at which Sun Ra's new narrative of mythic identity begins: a shift from history to mystery, past to future, time to space."[15] As Locke's comments suggest, Sun Ra creates narrative, temporal, and spatial breaks through his mythic renaming. Dumas's understanding of Sun Ra's ideologically revolutionary potential, manifested via sound, emerges through a range of connections between the artists as they use creative expression to critically question and move beyond preestablished constructions of racial identity.

In the 1966 conversation at Slug's Saloon subsequently released by Ikef Records, Dumas engages in a dialogue with Sun Ra regarding his philosophy of sound and its relationship to different modes of critical perception, that is, the way that the sensory, cognitive, and sociopolitical realms might intersect. Sun Ra and Dumas discuss these ideas against the backdrop of music from Sun Ra's Myth Science Arkestra's 1963 album *Cosmic Tones for Mental Therapy*.[16] Dumas, in writing the liner notes to this album, frames the mythic, phenomenal, and at times apocalyptic sense of black sound emerging from Sun Ra's music:

TO HEAR THIS MUSIC IS TO HEAR THE SOLAR BAND OF REVE-
LATION, THE TONES REVERBERATING HERE PASS THROUGH

THE TIME SPECTRUM OF THE ARKESTRA'S MIND AND YOU SEE
WITH EAR AND WITH EYE AND YOU BECOME THE METAGEN-
ESIS OF COSMIC ATOMS, AND THIS ALTERNATION IS ALSO AN
ALTERATION WHICH IS THE TRANMOLECULARIZATION OF
MAN'S FUTURE MIND. LIKE THE METAMORPHOSIS OF THE
EARTH AS IT MOVES IN ITS THREE DIRECTIONS AT ONCE IN
ITS THIRD POSITION FROM THE SUN, THIS MUSIC IS THE
VOICE OF THE GALACTIC FATHER–CENTER. AND LIKE STAGES
OF THE TRANMOLECULARIZATION OF THE EARTH, IT CAN BE
HEARD ONLY UNDER THE DRIVING POWER OF THE SUN.

In his exploration of the sound of Sun Ra's music, Dumas represents Sun
Ra's idea of "metagenesis" as an "alternation" and "alteration" outside of more
familiar spatial and temporal dimensions. To conceptualize existence through
the openness of the infinite, as Dumas and Sun Ra discuss in detail during
their conversation at Slug's, is to imagine Sun Ra's sound "painting pictures of another plane of existence . . . something that's so far away that it
seems to be non-existent." Responding to Dumas's query, "How are the
souls called forth?" Sun Ra remarks that the intention of his music is to
correspond to a desire "for that world where nothing is impossible." Reflecting on the line between the possible and the impossible in an almost surrealistic vein, Sun Ra reminds Dumas:

> All the great men on this planet have not yet come close to that
> world. They've tried everything and everybody. But people will
> have to have new mind-cepts. All the old ways will have to pass
> away. When people reach the stage where they can use their
> infinite mind power to concentrate and direct truth in these
> cosmic equations I am talking about, then they will be ready
> for the grand experiment. There will be no more death in the
> next plane of existence. You might say that I am the bridge to
> the next plane of existence. When they reach that stage they will
> be resurrected.

Sound creates an opening into Sun Ra's imagination of blackness as otherworldly. The "mind-cepts" and "infinite mind power" that he cites as necessary means to transition into "the next plane of existence" correspond to
the formal dynamics of his "space music." Sun Ra describes this approach

to sonic expression in a 1968 essay (included in the jazz journal *The Cricket*) as "an introductory prelude to the sound of greater infinity," a transcendent expression of his "natural being and presentation . . . a different order of sounds synchronized to the different order of being."[17]

The relationship between sound and Sun Ra's visionary otherness revolves around the hidden mystery of the present and projects black historical experience and consciousness as critically layered, generative horizons for black expression. In their conversation, Sun Ra elaborates on this existential relationship, responding to a question from Dumas about the role of images and symbols in determining the reality of one's surroundings:

> DUMAS: Is that the reason why you are in this sign of Sun Ra?
>
> SUN RA: Well, everybody have to be what they really are. That's what I really am. Somewhere else. Because I don't consider myself as nothing on this plane of existence because there isn't anything here.
>
> DUMAS: You mean on Earth?
>
> SUN RA: It just looks like it is, but it's not. It's . . . just like you go to a theater and sit up and you look at a beautiful stage. It doesn't stay that way as soon as the next act come in. You got some more scenery and won't look like the same stage after the stagehands get through changing it around.
>
> DUMAS: Well, you're saying the Earth is a stage? What's the next act . . . for planet Earth?
>
> SUN RA: The next act is the finale.
>
> DUMAS: The finale. Will music be a part of this finale?
>
> SUN RA: Well music is going to be the bridge to . . . it's just the finale of the traditional things. The traditional things got some meaning in 'em, but there comes a time when you need something else. You might say you go out, buy some food and cook it. You have to have some pepper and salt, too. You have to have some seasoning.

The "seasoning" of Sun Ra's music creates a tonal bridge between the present and the revolutionary, transformative "finale." If, as Sun Ra states to Dumas, "there isn't anything here," then fashioning an idea of the otherworldly through sound structures might offer a means of destabilizing the transitory facades or "acts" of the present, rational world.

Sun Ra's ideas of musical sound, shaped as they are by the infinite temporality and possibility of space, resonate through the sonic dimensions of the *Cosmic Tones* album. The record is impressionistically construed rather than musically composed, creating vibratory effects that lean heavily on delay, echo, and moments of resounding futuristic reverberation. The vibrations of the log drum and cosmic side drum, blended with the higher registers of the flute, oboe, and clarinet, add an Eastern dimension to the sound. Disquieting and provocative, the album's sounds are more tone than tune, although melody and harmony are not entirely absent. The ambient aurality of Sun Ra and his Arkestra, considered alongside the conversation between Dumas and Sun Ra, Sun Ra's essay, and Dumas's liner notes, reveal Dumas's understanding of Sun Ra's conceptualization of sound as a form of resistance through its ability to access the interior and exterior dimensions of the rational world.

The ideas of sound Dumas develops throughout his relationship with Sun Ra take shape most prominently in his story "The Metagenesis of Sunra (to Sun Ra and His ARKestra)." The lyrically prophetic tonality of Dumas's storytelling initiates the epic tale of mythic creation and supernatural power by establishing the presence of Sun Ra as coming into being, "the way which sound becomes energy and energy becomes sound." The opening pages of the story convey a prophecy, as Dumas elaborates on the origin of Sun Ra's mystical presence, signaling a communal ethos being forged through the phenomenological impact of his sound:

> So you can see that the birth of Sunra is a tradition. It is not a mystery in the sense that its nature is completely unknown, for all people who can radiate wavelengths of variable lengths and distances understand that Sunra's music is his birth and his birth is our music. To know one thing is to know all things. To hear is to feel. To taste is to speak. To exist is to swing as a child from a long umbilical rope on a tree, and from that height the child knows he is a bird. The birth of Sunra is like that.[18]

Dumas's framing of the legend of Sunra's creation within the story and of the practice of storytelling itself rely on an idea of narrative composed of songs being sung or spun. The conclusion of the above passage is followed by the statement "we will play Sunra's birth and message this way:" with the colon leading to the remaining pages of mythic narration that Dumas projects as if it is being relayed orally from Griot to audience, syntactically measured to facilitate a smooth, rhythmic delivery in which the tonality and density of thematic meaning operate symbiotically. Sunra, as the story relays, is one of the Bluepeople ("so black that they were blue"), and his presence reflects a prophetic possibility of salvation, redemption, and re-awakening for the Bluepeople in the face of the white Wof Nyck and the Wofpeople who worship the god of the Kingdom of Ice, heeding his commandment that "the flesh of the painted people should be the food of the Wofpack." Dumas offers a familiar vision of racial division and antagonism, but through his literary invocation of spectacular sound he simultaneously emphasizes Sun Ra's commitment to charting alternate possibilities. This quality of sonic representation and narration is demonstrated through Dumas's rendering of the crux of the story, an early scene of Sunra's birth, an event foretold by a long-held prophecy contained in the songs of the Bluepeople. Dumas portrays Sunra's birth as it is summoned and celebrated in song, and how, at the time of his delivery, the angry and jealous Wof Nyck finds Sunra's mother, Panta, in labor and "swallowed her whole, so anxious was he to destroy her music." Before the music can be vanquished, however, Sunra emerges from his mother's womb and channels her dying sonority into the strength to evacuate himself from the jaws of the Wof, singing Nyck to his death as he pierces the space "where his heart should be."[19]

In the wake of killing Nyck, Sunra becomes celebrated as "the Terrible Child," a prophetic savior, "feared by the enemies of the painted people, loved by their friends," as he manipulates the metaphysical qualities of sound to amplify black historical self-knowledge among his people. Dumas renders the visionary qualities of Sunra in a style that blends the fantastic context of the narrative and the self-fashioned role of Sun Ra in the world outside of the text:

> Sunra began his ministry telling his people that there was to come
> a time in the near future when the Wofpeople would feed upon
> the Blue and Red people no longer. It was written in a prophecy.
> Whenever he spoke this, he would take out his long bluehorn and his
> bonelute and he would attach the bronze cord from his belly to the
> end of the long bone and he would anchor the bone against his thigh,
> and when the pressure was just right, he would pluck the cord and
> the people would hear the music and it taught them. When he had
> another thing to tell them, he would take the bone that he saved from
> his mother and he would place it across the cord and stroke it, and a
> sound would spring up such as the people had never heard, except in

their womb memories, and Sunra would spend days teaching the people thus, and then he would take the omega of the cord, attach it to the alpha of the otherbone and he would shoot himself away like a marksman shooting an arrow. When he was gone to another city, the sun would come out. During these days the people awaited the visits of the child Sunra, for he brought them hope and restored their perceptions for he taught them to believe in the impossible thing. He taught them to believe in death as a dimension of sound.[20]

Dumas's depictions of Sunra's transformative sound, as it is heard and felt among the Bluepeople, connect the revolutionary potential of sound as a form of resistance to Sunra's corporeal and instrumental generation of sound, and to the way that this modulation of sound is contingent on an improvisatory framing of its maternal origin. If, as Hortense Spillers suggests, black maternity "breaks in upon the imagination with a forcefulness that marks both a denial and an 'illegitimacy,'" then Sunra's triumphant, sonorous defeat of Nyck, and his subsequent use of "the bone that he saved from his mother" to produce sounds inspiring powerful "womb memories" among the Bluepeople, can be understood as an attempt to uplift the collective through constructions of sound that are refigured through the body.[21] The radical challenge to the ordering of personhood that Spillers ascribes to the epistemological rupture of black gender reconfiguration is apt for contemplating Dumas's depictions of the dissonant structure and interactive qualities of Sunra's sound. These are qualities that escape attempts to be categorized simply as song and contain the possibility of rebirth, regeneration, and creative destruction.

The dissonance of Sunra's sound is also characterized by Dumas as something that cannot be fully captured on the page. He makes this point by rendering what he calls at one point "the flint of the song":

The lives into it are evils through it
All the pain shall turn to rain
Tears shall flow, wind shall blow
Into it we make mouths that eat into it
All the pain shall melt to rain
Into it the evil lives
Tears shall flow from ice and snow
The lives into it are evil through it

After transcribing the song, Dumas explains that what "you have read or heard is only an attempt to allow you a bit of the feeling of how and what the sounds were saying, for they meant far more than the words, being as you know, *meta-music*." The sound troubles semantic boundaries as Dumas, through extending the capacity of his prose, imagines the wavelengths, energy, and vibrations that define the projection and reception of Sunra's sound. In this way sound is both a weapon and a form of communion. Dumas's literary representation of sound as a ubiquitous force of creative destruction concludes the story as Sunra, playing an "ebony horn" with increasing intensity, and a Blue youth who has "climbed up the side of the drum," engage in a methodical dismantling of Wof society: "Machines died in the air. An electric power plant reversed its power and the plant electrocuted and melted everything in range of it for ten miles. The ice mountain melted and the freezelines dissolved. Icelances faded, and panic went through the Wofpack. But it was too late. Sunra took panic itself and drove it into them."[22] The aural and epistemological dissonance of Sunra's sound suggests a political irruption similar to what Steve Goodman, in considering the example of the Jamaican Maroons resisting British colonial power in the late 1700s, notes as "the power of sound to instill dread."[23] The dreadful projection of "sweet sounds, deadly to the untrained ear" emanating from Sunra's horn provides a prophetic and apocalyptic dimension to Dumas's narrative account, as he contemplates the bridging of the literary and the sonic as a rearticulation of resistance to repression.

The Sound of the "Afro-Horn"

In November 1966, *Negro Digest*, a popular African American periodical featuring creative writing, cultural criticism, and political analysis, published Henry Dumas's short story "Will the Circle Be Unbroken?" The story offers a portrayal of experimental black music as a transformative, revolutionary force. Dumas depicts the mythic and phenomenological energy of sound by setting it within an emergent sense of black cultural nationalism, which is responding to the inability of an integrationist model of Civil Rights struggle to substantively and comprehensively transform the U.S. racial state. Larry Neal, in a 1978 lecture, recounts the publication of Dumas's story as a reflection of the ideological orientation of the Black Arts Movement. Noting Dumas's representation of "music as a force of judgment," Neal reads the story's questioning of white authority as a statement of black artistic and critical independence that epito-mized a dominant political standpoint during the movement: "We didn't want the white critics in there. I think the object was for black people to find out who they were without someone overlooking their shoulder. Black people had a feeling of always being on stage for white folks. It was time, some of us thought, to be in certain contexts, socially, unasham-edly on our own terms without someone else intervening in the defini-tion."[24] Dumas's representation and exploration of black experimental sound, for Neal, parallels the broader pursuit of black political and cultural autonomy pointedly demonstrated, for example, in Amiri Baraka's early 1965 move from Greenwich Village to Harlem in order to establish the Black Arts Repertory Theater and School in the wake of Malcolm X's assassination on February 21, 1965.[25] While Neal's analysis focuses on the more overt political dimensions of sound in "Will the Circle Be Unbro-ken?" within the sociohistorical context of the Black Arts Movement, for Dumas, sound also provides a multidimensional narrative framing of black consciousness. His portrayal of sound's texture and its resonance within and against characters' memories creates an experimental middle space between sonority and textuality. This creative orientation allows Dumas to reimagine racial politics and resistance as fluid, complex structures that are articulated through the aural and metaphorical resonance and reverberation underlining the narrative architecture and aesthetic form of Dumas's story.

Dumas opens "Will the Circle Be Unbroken?" with the description of a mythical afro-horn that is rumored to produce sounds in frequencies and pitches only recognizable to the ears of those most intimately attuned to its cultural, mythic, and metaphysical dimensions. The story opens within the Sound Barrier Club, an underground black cultural space in Harlem, where a legendary musician, Probe, prepares to play:

At the edge of the spiral of musicians Probe sat cross-legged on a blue cloth, his soprano sax resting against his inner knee, his afro-horn linking his ankles like a bridge. The afro-horn was the newest axe to cut the deadwood of the world. But Probe, since his return from exile, had chosen only special times to reveal the new sound . . . Probe's dark full head tilted toward the vibrations of the music as if the ring of sound from the six wailing pieces was tightening, creating a spiraling circle.

The drums took an oblique. Magwa's hands, like the forked
tongue of a dark snake, probed the skins, probed the whole belly
of the coming circle. Beginning to close the circle, Haig's alto arc,
rapid piano incisions, Billy's thin green flute arcs and tangents,
Stace's examinations of his own trumpet discoveries, all fell
separately, yet together, into a blanket which Mojohn had begun
weaving on bass when the set began. The audience breathed, and
Probe moved into the inner ranges of the sax.[26]

The wailing, vibrating, and tightening circle embodies the tension marking the title of the story through the communal sonic experimentation of
the ensemble. Dumas explores the improvisatory nature of the music as
Magwa, the drummer, initiates an "oblique" or indirect probing of the skins
that form his drums, and possibly of the "oblique" muscles defining the "belly
of the coming circle." The sound of Haig's alto sax and Billy's flute form
"arcs" that become parts of the circle as it begins to anticipate the sound of
Probe's afro-horn.

Against this moment of ensemblic possibility the story shifts, focusing
on three white hipsters with complicated relationships to black music and
culture, who wish to enter the club. As they attempt to enter the Sound Barrier Club, Jan, who seems to lead the three, arrogantly dismisses "this new
philosophy the musicians were talking about," for "he had known many
Negro musicians and theirs was no different from any other artist's struggles
to be himself, including his own."[27] Motivated by a vision of assimilation in
which the cultural specificities of black artistic production are dissolved,
Jan downplays the black cultural basis of the experimental music as essentialist rumor. He expresses a desire to erode racial barriers, not in service
of an antiracist vision, but as a means of appropriating the power of "undis-
covered" black sound as a reflection of his own artistic struggles.[28]

Jan is accompanied by a couple, Ron and Tasha, whom he describes as
"two of the hippest ofays in town." Dumas reveals the intentions of the
three through Jan's hope that they will be able to "break the circle of the
Sound Club." He depicts fleeting yet telling constructions of whiteness by
rendering overlapping representations of blackness through the minds of
these three characters. Ron, for example, "was not fully satisfied that he
had found the depth of the black man's psyche," and when he tried unsuc-
cessfully to enter the Sound Barrier before, he "almost carried the result of
one attempt to court." Ron's girlfriend Tasha, "a shapely blonde who had

dyed her hair black . . . a Vassar girl," has written a biography of a cutting-edge black jazz trombonist, Oliver Fullerton. During her writing she was involved in a physically and psychologically destructive relationship with Fullerton that simultaneously catapults her into fame and possibly contributes to Fullerton's descent into heroin addiction. Dumas's blurring of external and internal focalization in his portrayal of Tasha moves from a generalized representation of her as a type into an intimate detailing of her reflections on the descent of Fullerton's career:

> No one knew why. Sometimes Tasha was afraid to think about it. If they had been married, she knew that Oliver would have been able to continue making it. But he had gotten strung out on H. Sometimes she believed her friends who said Oliver was psychopathic. At least when he stopped beating her, she forgave him. And she did not believe it when he was really hooked. She still loved him. It was her own love, protected deep inside her, encased, her little black secret and her passport to the inner world that Oliver had died trying to enter. It would be only a matter of time. She would translate love into an honest appraisal of black music.

Dumas's description allows a deeper glimpse, beyond the archetypical and into the complex, conflicted emotions of Tasha. The disjointed flow of her thoughts bridges the frozen quality of the moment when "three white people were opening the door" to the words of the Sound Barrier Club doorman telling them, "Sessions for Brothers and Sisters only." The statement mystifies Jan, Tasha, and Ron, and causes Jan to challenge the doorman through an unsettling, contrived performance of vernacular authenticity, pushing him to recognize that his whiteness as well as that of his companions does not detract from their connections to the music. First leaning in to the doorway and asking, "What's the matter, baby?" Jan quickly follows his query with a more forceful statement as he holds up his saxophone case: "Man, if you can't recognize a Brother, you better let me have your job . . . We're friends of the Probe . . . Man, what you talking bout . . . Are you blockin Brothers now? I told him I am blood. We friends of the Probe." A bizarre series of actions ensue as the doorman and his two associates who respond to his call for assistance with the situation deliberate in a huddle and emerge from it with a sign stating, "We cannot allow non-Brothers because of the danger involved with extensions." The initial doorman on the scene, Carl, motions for a passing policeman to come and observe the situation: "He wanted a witness to this. He knew what might happen but he had never seen it." As Jan views the sign and dismissively shakes his head, thinking to himself, "It was incredible that all the spades believed this thing about the lethal vibrations from the new sound," Carl reacts by "shoving the sign in their faces" until the policeman arrives and overrules the decision of the doormen, in essence, helping the three to break the sound barrier.[29]

In this scene, Dumas positions dissonance as a force bridging the aural and critical dimensions of the sound. The sound resonates acoustically beyond the walls of the club as Dumas represents the force of its alterity, which affects the interracial dynamics developing on the outside. Because Carl and the other doormen are well aware of the sound's "extensions," their position as guardians of the sound is both flexible and strategic. Rather than articulating a strictly militant posture and excluding Jan, Ron, and Tasha, they remain peaceful and "buddha-like" in the face of "the potential belligerence of the whites," and manipulate the racist policeman into sanctioning and taking responsibility for the entrance of the three into a zone of sound outside their ken. The idea of extensions mentioned on the sign held up by Carl could refer to the practice of adding a note to the structure of a chord in order to deepen and expand its harmonic capacity. Reading the sign in this way adds further depth to the perceptive rather than antagonistic demeanor of the doormen, as their observations of and interactions with Jan, Ron, and Tasha suggest that the three individuals lack the preparation to hear the depth of the sound produced by the afro-horn. Much like Dumas's representation of the sound of the afro-horn in "The Metagenesis of Sunra," the extensions of the music inside the Sound Barrier represent an alternate dimension of metaphysical experience that challenge racialized patterns of consumption and containment. The dissonance between the exterior and interior of the Sound Barrier Club is underlined by the thoughts of the policeman, who cannot imagine any value to the new experimental sound emerging in Harlem: "The Irish cop, not knowing whether he should get angry over what he figured was reverse discrimination, smirked and made a path for the three. He would not go far inside because he didn't think the sounds were worth listening to. If it wasn't Harlem he could see why these people would want to go in, but he had never seen anything worthwhile from niggers in Harlem." The sound of Probe and his ensemble is both fetishized and debased through the perspectives of Jan, Ron, Tasha, and the cop. After being admitted to the club, the three proceed "into the dark cavern which led to the music," moving toward the performance space "in an alien silence." Dumas describes the synesthetic interaction of sound, color, and movement as follows: "The whole circle now, like a bracelet of many-colored lights gyrated under Probe's wisdom." The circle is not only a description of the musicians' positioning, but also marks the sound moving through and manipulating time. As Probe blows his saxophone, "each note fell into the circle like an acrobat on a tight rope stretched radially across the center of the universe."[30] The falling of the note through an infinite space–time continuum of the "center of the universe" creates an impression of suspension and duration through an idea of space music or space sound that Sun Ra and the Arkestra were developing.

Dumas's rendering of this scene depicts the horizons of sound through writing that grapples with its liminal, suggestive capacities, doing so outside of simply an aural context, and significantly enlarging its ephemerality through the lens of the literary. Nathaniel Mackey, writing several decades later in the second installment of his epistolary fictional meditations on black music, *Djbot Baghostus's Run*, provides another example of this inclination within African American literary explorations of sound and temporality through the narrator N.'s account of a drummer, SunStick, who is auditioning for a position in N.'s sextet, the Mystic Horn Society. Recollecting what he has seen and heard of SunStick's playing, N. explains:

> He tends, that is, to pit the bass drum against the cymbal in such a way as to rescind the punctuality of time, exacting a feeling for the tenuous, uninsured continuum the so-called beat thereby allows or is made to admit itself to be. In this, of course, he works the vein opened up by such people as Milford Graves, Sunny Murray and Rashied Ali. And by "vein" I mean exactly that, for what he does (or so it seemed to me that night) is insists upon a hemorrhaging, a dilation of one's way of looking at time. What struck me most was his playing's apparently absent yet all the more convincing regard for linearity, his having collapse and consolidation, qualm and quanta, find their way to one another.[31]

N. describes SunStick's manipulation of time within a tradition of free jazz drumming outlined by Graves, Murray, and Ali, citing their ability to refashion sound through a withdrawal of finitude, recasting the beat outside its timekeeping role through what he calls "dilation," a practice of expansive rupture that refuses to maintain patterns of musical sound strictly within linear frameworks. Dumas's depiction of the afro-horn's sound exemplifies Mackey's idea of sonic dilation. These temporal and phenomenological disruptions are featured through Dumas's use of free indirect discourse to fluidly shift the narrative perspective between the thoughts of Probe, an omniscient voice, and the perspective of the sound itself.

Probe, hearing "the whistle of the wind," notices Jan, Ron, and Tasha entering the club as "three ghosts, like chaff blown in from a wasteland." The circle contracts, and "movement began from within it, shaking without breaking balance." The circle becomes a reverberating womb that Probe has to prepare "for the afro horn," and the instrument is described as beyond Probe's control: "Its vibrations were beyond his mental frequencies unless he got deeper into motives."[32] The vibrations move beyond conscious patterns of thought, but the "motives" that Dumas alludes to serve as short, rhythmic, improvisational statements that begin to make the vibrations of the afro-horn more present within the performance. The vibrations resonate within the regenerative circle creating a synergy between the experimental aurality of the moment and the collectivity fashioned by the musicians and listeners.

The entrance of Ron, Jan, and Tasha is signaled by the interactive, synesthetic projection of the sound as "the blanket of the bass rippled and the fierce wind in all their minds blew the blanket back, and there sat the city of Samson. The white pillars imposing . . . but how easy it is to tear down the building with motives." Rather than simply describing the music through recognizable musicological terminology, Dumas depicts its synesthetic expansiveness through ideas of rupture and regeneration. Dumas's narration fuses fragments of the music within and against its more attenuated, extended, deliberative narrative qualities that both complicate and sustain its sound: "Inside the center of the gyrations is an atom stripped of time, black. The gathering of the hunters, deeper. Coming, laced in the energy of the sun. He is blowing. Magwa's hands. Reverence of skin. Under the single voices is the child of a woman, black. They are building back the wall, crumbling under the disturbance."[33] The audiovisual framing of rebirth and regeneration underscores a cyclical, circular basis to the sense of unified, pluralistic collectivity that is symbolized by the breadth and multi-directionality of the sound. The final line of description is perhaps most intriguing in suggesting a suspended or elongated temporality of reconstruction amid destruction. Within this temporal–sonic continuum Ron, Jan, and Tasha begin to experience an alteration in their consciousness; a renewal not so dissimilar from the creative destruction the sound enacts in its invocation of Samson's destruction of the pillars.

Dumas describes the sound of the music as a "volt," one that Jan "did not hear" but that through its formal, interactive dissonance connects the "shock waves" of the afro-horn and the memories and thoughts of Jan, Ron, and Tasha. The fact that Jan's "mind went black" as he "recalled the feeling when his father had beat him for 'playing with a nigger!' and later allowed the feeling to merge with his dislike of white people," reflects the sonic complexity of Probe's motives and extensions that refuses the deterministic elimination of whiteness through radical black sound. Instead, the idea that Jan's mind "went black" as his saxophone case opens, "revealing a shiny tenor saxophone that gleamed and vibrated in the freedom of freedom," while Ron "fell face forward across a table, his heart in silent respect for truer vibrations," positions the blackness of the sound as an opening or possibility for an evaporation of whiteness. In this formulation whiteness can be understood as an objectified deformation that is much less a reflection of one's phenotypic properties than it is indicative of a perspective of power and privilege that amounts to a masking of the humanity beneath its artifice. Dumas extends the sense of ritualistic regenerative power circulating from the waves of the afro-horn's sound as the story concludes: "The horn and Probe drew up the shadows now from the audience. A child climbed upon the chords of sound, growing out of the circle of the womb, searching with fingers and then with motive, and as the volume of the music increased—penetrating the thick callousness of the Irishman twirling his stick outside of black flesh—the musicians walked off one by one, linked to Probe's respectful nod at each and his quiet pronouncement of their names."[34] The womb-like circularity of the body of the audience fashions "chords of sound," which create the conditions for new life through an organic, expansive vision of collective improvisation.

As Larry Neal's quotation at the beginning of this chapter suggests, "Will the Circle Be Unbroken?" can be read as a liberatory tale of black aesthetic and creative power to create a ritual space for black collectivity and authority. The divide between the white characters and black creativity, indeed the seeming violence enacted on the white characters, is complex and contains more than just visceral reaction. Considered in this light, perhaps the weight of the conclusion lies in growth and expansion rather than in death. While the voices of authority close the story with exclamations that focus on the supposed deaths of the three white friends, these words can almost be heard as an afterthought to the suggestion of rebirth through the chords of sound, personified as a child who searches and finds "motive" amid an escalating volume of music. Listening to the sound of the music as a counterweight to the harnessing of tonality allows for a reading of their minds "going black" as an opening, and one not unlike Mackey's sense of Sunstick's sonic dilation, which fuses foreclosure and possibility through an improvisatory rethinking of death and rebirth. Dumas's contemplation of sonic temporality, as it relates to life and death, becomes indispensable in his rethinking of black radical politics as a disruptive and dissonant force. As a signal, flagship story of the Black Arts Movement, "Will the Circle Be Unbroken?" ultimately projects Dumas's innovations in literary sound as the grounds for critical reflections on the ideological possibilities rather than more foreclosed visions of black consciousness.

Reverberation

Jay Wright highlights this convergence between the literary, critical, and sonic in his introduction to Henry Dumas's first posthumously published volume of poetry, *Play Ebony Play Ivory*, noting that Dumas's writing generates a "rhythm of perception" through a linguistic and imagistic musicality that posits tone not simply as aural, but as a broader aesthetic orientation Wright understands as Dumas's belief that "there are racial and social determinants of perception." Wright sees Dumas's projection of tone as a reflection of his "sense of history," his comprehensive vision of overlapping spheres of phenomenological, environmental, social, and political experience. Making an analogy between Dumas's valuing of literary tonality and his love of gospel music, Wright explains, "Dumas haunted gospel concerts, photographing, when he could, the singers and the action. For him, the songs and the style of the singers linked him to the land, pinpointed that sense of dispossession that he felt, living in the alien, crass and prejudiced cities." This attentiveness to the totality of sound, for Wright, underlines Dumas's rendering of black life in all its expressive and political fullness. As Wright suggests, Dumas's attention to sound reflects a synthesis of the cultural, ideological, and environmental texture of black consciousness understood as "mythic gesture" that is "able to carry the burden of direct participation in the act of living."[35] Wright's focus on the vitality of Dumas's work, the way its sound organically emerges from and reflects substantive material and ethereal dimensions of black life, and specifically how this literary sound often "linked him to the land," provides a starting point for my inquiry onto Dumas's exploration of black consciousness through the natural soundscape within his story "Echo Tree."

The idea of an echo tree at the center of the story embodies the acoustics of the natural world, connecting the sensory dimensions of the land and the consciousness of a young African American man who is being pulled between forces of modernization and the spiritual power embedded within the natural world. Dumas's narrative offers a vision of transformation fashioned out of the soundscape of the surrounding environment. In doing so he frames the longevity of the negative material and spiritual impact that capitalist development in the United States continues to exert on the horizon of black historical experience and consciousness from the forced labor of chattel slavery through Dumas's present context of writing within the indeterminacy of the Civil Rights–era. Centering the echo as the conceptual and critical grounding of the story, Dumas considers its acoustics as theoretically distinctive in its conflation of return, repetition, delay, and fragmentation. Brandon Labelle describes the formal properties of an echo by focusing on its ephemerality as a path toward resistance: "The echo, as an underground sonic figure, gives way to enlarging the possibility of imaginative transformation; shifting our cognitive focus away from the text and toward an acoustical dynamic ultimately makes unsteady, through a mesmerizing shift in clarity, the movements of meaning. In doing so, the echo is a strategy for resistance and rebellion—a sonic mirroring to the point of defusing the reign of established culture. The echo performs as an acoustic bomb, exploding the vector of time, of relations, of origins, for other perspectives."[36]

Reverberation, as a kind of ontological horizon of the echo, points to a provocative framework of accumulation and recession as the grounds through which memory and temporality are both sustained and dislocated. For Dumas, the echo presents a form of asymmetrical resistance that, similar to the visions of Jamaican dub musical innovators working during the late 1960s, offers the possibility for fashioning resounding improvisational remixes through technological manipulation that, to quote Michael Veal, might "evoke a cultural memory of ancestral African roots through heavy use of the reverb and echo effects and various musical strategies of African origin."[37] As a soundscape of black resistance, "Echo Tree" provides a means for Dumas to imagine the aurality of black historical consciousness as a resounding challenge to forms of social alienation.

The story unfolds as two African American young men arrive at the location of the echo tree amid the intensifying phenomenological forces animating the natural setting. As they approach what we come to learn is a sacred location, Dumas depicts the movement, force, color, and sound of the land: "The wind fans up a shape in the dust: around and around and over the hill. Out of the cavity of an uprooted tree, it blows up fingers that ride the wind off the hill down the valley and up toward the sun, a red tongue rolling down a blue–black throat. And the ear of the mountains listens..."[38] Dumas's initial invocation of the natural soundscape positions its synesthetic emanations as both a sensory and an ideological context for the story. He articulates this natural soundscape as a dissonant presence—both in its sound and in the links between the environmental sound and a broader critique of alienation.

This aural, philosophical framework of the story becomes more evident through the interactions of the two young men. Dumas draws their connection through the haunting absence of Leo, the recently deceased brother of the young man being led to the echo tree by Leo's friend who informs him, "He my friend more'n your brother," a point that the young man emphasizes to Leo's brother by pointing to the wariness he and Leo shared of the "way up yonder," his term for the urban North that Leo's brother ventured into. Dumas conveys this crucial epistemological discrepancy emerging between the two young men through the following exchange initiated by Leo's brother:

"Did Leo used to want to come up to New York?"
"He ain't thinkin bout you whilst you way up yonder."
"How come you say that? What's wrong with up there?"
"Leo's grandpa, *your'n too*, well he say up in the city messes you up."[39]

Throughout the story, Dumas remixes the ongoing conversation between the acquaintances against the frequent, vibrant eruptions of sound across the landscape, and through these intersecting narrative lines gestures toward otherworldly conceptions of black life amid a radical (re)imagining of the present. This fusion of commentary from the young men is set against Dumas's depiction of environmental sound and creates a synthesis of the political and spiritual contestations of black consciousness running through the soundscape of the story.[40] Dumas's focalized narration shifts between overhearing the dialogue between the young men and projecting an omniscient, almost deific tonality that frames the interaction between the sounds of the natural surroundings and the existential questions facing the characters.

Dumas's articulation of sound as both a narrative presence and a diffuse epistemological force suggests an alternate construction of African American struggle outside the familiar representation of organized social movements and interracial conflict. "Echo Tree" asks us to consider, through the sonority of the land, the dissonant relationship between a linear idea of transformation through teleological progress and the more cacophonous, unbridled potential for change emerging from the haunting resonance of spiritual possession. Dumas's story proposes the following query: how might the supernatural and transcendent potential of black historical memory become embedded within our surroundings, and how might we unearth this potential from the environment?

As the story builds, the political and the sonic more obviously converge through the ideas of supernatural sound invoked by the echo tree. As the two young men survey the area from the hill, Leo's friend explains to Leo's brother that there are echo trees throughout the area, and that "if you don't believe in the echo tree and believe what it hears from the spirits and tells you in your ear, then you're in trouble."[41] Exactly what an echo tree is remains a mystery. Dumas never provides a physical description, although the narration makes it clear that both characters in the story are looking at echo trees at different times. Leo's friend's statement to Leo's brother about the danger of not taking the echo trees seriously is the most direct statement about them, and his perspective depicts the function of the echo tree as quite similar to that of the African diasporic presence of bottle trees. Robert Farris Thompson describes bottle trees as branches or entire trees adorned with an array of colored bottles or glass placed on or hung from limbs. As "Kongo-derived" fixtures "blocking the disappearance of the talents of the important dead," bottle trees sustain and carry forth the Kongo perspective of honoring the grave sites of the deceased with the understanding that these spaces are not only sacred, but possess the power to project the otherworldly back into the present.[42] As Thompson imagines the message and meaning of bottle trees, the synergy of his descriptive reflection resonates strongly with Dumas's characterization of the echo tree through the perspective of Leo's friend. Thompson offers a particularly vivid rendering of the epistemology of bottle trees, imagining the message they carry as follows: "The cemetery and the yard are one. The dead watch over us. If you come to do us harm, here are dead trees and dead branches from their woods and glass from their scintillation. Join them! But if you come in good faith may your soul be strengthened in the strength of your flash."[43]

The pivot Thompson suggests between the dreadful punishment and spiritual sustenance bottle trees may enact outlines Dumas's imagining of the echo as it orchestrates the natural soundscape and responds to oral invocations. The echo resonates through the presence of the trees as spiritual manifestations of ancestral protection and judgment.

Dumas renders the perspective of Leo's brother as poised on the line between these alternate possibilities marked by the power of the echo tree. His apparent disbelief in the echo tree becomes problematic, as Leo's friend contends, "If you curse the echo tree, you turns into a bino." He elaborates, explaining that "nothin's worse than a bino, nothing. A bino is anything or anybody that curse the echo tree and whichever spirit is restin there." Essentially, in a zombielike state of spiritual and metaphysical emptiness, one becomes a bino "cause the spirit leave out your body, you pukes, you rolls around on the ground, you turns white all over, your eyes, your hair. Even your blood, 'n it come out your skin, white like water." Clearly, the condition runs much deeper than the pigmentation it seems to denote, as Dumas uses this portrayal of possession as a reflection of existence in a spiritual vacuum. When Leo's brother asks if a bino and an albino are the same thing, Leo's friend responds, "Naw. That's different. If you let yourself to taint all the way till you's a bino, then you don't eat, you don't sleep, you can't feel nothing, you can't talk or nothing. You be like a dead dog with a belly full 'o maggots, and you thinks you livin."[44] The unfeeling, numb, lifelessness of a bino is chromatically marked through the "taint" of a desensitizing, automatizing paralysis taking hold of one's body, soul, and mind. This possessed state of zombification is, in political terms, akin to the alienation of late capitalist "one-dimensionality," described by Herbert Marcuse as "a comfortable, smooth, reasonable, democratic unfreedom . . . in advanced industrial civilization, a token of technical progress."[45] Marcuse elaborates on the concept of one-dimensionality as a corrosive force that upholds alienation through the sweeping away of what Michael Hardt and Antonio Negri (and Machiavelli, Hobbes, and Spinoza before them) refer to as the "multitude," that is, the possibility of multifaceted, pluralistic, revolutionary movement. The sweeping away and supplanting of this possibility through the crafting of a one-dimensional society is subtle, however, and is upheld through self-coercion and the "absorption of ideology into reality" facilitated by the mass production, distribution, and consumption of technological advancements that seem to reflect progress, but as Marcuse points out, actually work toward the whittling down of possibility through advanced industrial society's "suffocation of those needs which demand liberation . . . while it sustains and absolves the destructive power and repressive function of the affluent society."[46] "Echo Tree" represents a sensory, aural, and synesthetic challenge to this "implanting of material and intellectual needs that perpetuate obsolete forms of the struggle for existence."[47] For Dumas, it is the idea of the echo, its resonance, delay, and reverberation across dimensions of time and memory, that offers the possibility of an intervention within the fabric of the establishment's manufacturing of coerced consciousness. The echo tree is a hinge between the spiritual strength of the African diaspora and the possibility of a renewed futurity expanding outward from the fading and resounding sonic trajectory of the echo.

The dynamic between the two young men increasingly revolves around the sonic contours and epistemological elements of the echo as Leo's friend reveals himself to be a conjurer, explaining that Leo "taught me how to call . . . how to use callin words for spirit-talk," a statement punctuated by his calling out, "*Swish-ka abas wish-ka. Saa saa aba saa saa.*" His call is echoed by Dumas's italicized rendering of the response of the surrounding natural world: "*The wind comes. Goes. Comes again. Across the sky, clouds gather in a ritual of color, where the blue–black, like muscles, seem to minister to the sides of the sun.*"[48] Dumas's crafting of a literary soundscape through the acoustics of the echo reflects this consistent exchange between the prophetic calls of Leo's friend and the synesthetic responses of the natural world. The aurality of the natural world's keynotes, what R. Murray Schafer terms sounds that "do not have to be listened to consciously" for "they are overheard but cannot be overlooked," are crucial to the aesthetic and ideological configuration of Dumas's narrative. The "archetypal significance" of keynotes sound in the natural world, "imprint[ing] themselves so deeply on the people hearing them that life without them would be sensed as a distinct impoverishment," is elevated through the distinctiveness of the "hi-fi soundscape" of the rural setting, as Schafer explains, "one in which discrete sounds can be heard clearly because of the low ambient noise level," in contrast to the "overdense population of sounds" dominating urban contexts in which the increased manipulation and amplification of sound erodes a purer, more unfiltered relationship to the aural dimensions of one's contextual space.[49]

Dumas focuses on the purity of sound through his depiction of Leo's friend who occupies and orchestrates the spiritual center of the narrative. As he explains to Leo's brother the acoustic basis of his ability to commune with the spirit world through the landscape of echo trees, the sun is setting in the distance; he points to it and says, "Well, he's gatherin in all the words talked in the daylight. Next, them catcher-clouds churn 'em up into echoes. When the time is right, the echo tree will talk."[50] The long italicized description immediately following the young man's comments conveys the land's demonstration of his prediction in Dumas's synesthetic fusion of the visual and aural:

> *Shadows begin to fade into a tinted haze.*
> *Red Oklahoma clay darkens.*
> *Green stretches of Arkansas pine finger their way into the land.*
> *White blotches of clouds edge into open sky, fading into oblivion.*
> *Orange filaments stream from the sun.*
> *And blue–red–blue, green–blue, white–blue—all ink the sky.*
> *Shadows become fingers of wind in the night.*
> *Shadows take on shapes. They come to breathe.*
> *And the blue–blue prevails across the heavens, and the weight of the*
> *   mood is as black as night.*[51]

The sensory elements of the passage escalate through the various movements of color that culminate in the respiration of shadows, a movement from the visual to the aural that erupts to define the concluding movements of the story. The depth of epistemological movement is thus expressed through the ability to conceive the radical connections between the natural states of the land, the sensory, and the possibility for existence that challenges the systematized yet subtle cultural repression "one-dimensional society" is built upon. Leo's friend emphasizes this fact as he "stands behind the other boy and dances a strange dance . . . with his arms, and jerks his body toward the valley and the sky." His movements, seemingly in praise of, or in communication with unseen yet felt forces, culminate in his calling of "Laeeeeeeeooooooo!": "The sound pierces the wind. It rides down into the valley, rolls up Laelaelaeooo! Toward the sun. It resounds like notes of thunder made by children instead of gods. It comes back LaeLae-eee-ooo! . . . There is silence . . . the silence of an empty lung about to breathe in. Again the sounds vibrate and answer from the boy's throat. Again they travel and return as though wet, as though spoken."[52] The echo resonates, gradually fading away while leaving the clear impression that the calling of Leo represents a point of transformation, as Leo's brother witnesses the transcendent movement of sound that Dumas portrays as a kinetic as well as sonic force. An invocation of his brother's spirit vibrates through the call and response form of the echo, resituating the antiphonal dynamic in order to worry the line between Leo's loss and the ancestral spirits manifested in the aural dimensions of the landscape, simultaneously redefining loss through a temporal past and an active communal present.[53]

Dumas's literary extension of this sonic landscape opens the possibility for Leo's brother to comprehend experience outside a controlling rationality, within the sound's "ontology of vibrational force." Steve Goodman defines the concept as one that "exceeds the philosophy of sound," as it "delves below a philosophy of sound and the physics of acoustics toward the basic processes of entities affecting other entities." Goodman terms this ontological status "the vibration of vibration," as the immeasurable autonomy of sound manifested through its phenomenological effects and creations of affective states creates a "politics of frequency" pushing beyond the categories of "sonic physicality and the semiotic significance of its symbolic composition or content."[54] Dumas continues to explore this visionary and theoretical capacity of sound, as Goodman suggests, on its own terms of deployment. Returning to the earlier framing of "bino"-ism, Dumas places this tension into sharper relief when Leo's friend who calls on the spirits, warns Leo's brother of the cost of not acknowledging the power of the spirit world and its relevance to the present: "I been splainin it all to you, but you got so much city taint in your blood, you be a bino fore you go back." After Leo's brother dismisses this warning, "whispers echo from the valley throat, and all motion becomes sound, words, forces," leading to "a moanful resonance, a bluish sound, a wail off the lips of a wet night." The interaction between Leo's brother's doubt and the environmental sounds disclose a point of transition in the arc of the narrative, as the moans can be heard as protests against Leo's brother's alienation, while they also open up into a symphony of sound orchestrating the harmonic reverberating landscape within the intensifying dynamic between the young men. Dumas establishes the wind as the primary signifier of spiritual awareness eroding Leo's brother's resistance to the ancestral presence of the echo tree: "The wind, the wind. All of a sudden it sweeps across the top of the hill like an invisible hand swirling off into the darkening sky. Whispers echo from the valley throat, and all motion becomes sound, words, forces." The sound of the wind is manifested as a thematic element marking the sensory perceptions of the young men and the environmental expanse of the setting, yet Dumas further articulates it as a narrative device increasingly dominating the textual spatiality of the conclusion and creating another temporal dimension for the story to operate through. The strange quality of Dumas's synesthetic description and the "bluish sound" that "sweeps over them" open a new sensibility through which the transformation of Leo's brother can be more fully imagined. Dumas does not offer a smooth linear progression in which Leo's brother suddenly awakens to a new awareness; rather, the narrative dilation through Dumas's description of the sound poses an open, unending sense of possibility through its alterity, one that Leo's brother ultimately cannot ignore: "Shhhwsssss! The small valley seems to heave and the sounds come from the earth and the red tip of its tongue. And then a harmonic churning swells up and up! And as the ink-clouds press in on the sun, a motion in the sky, a flash of lightning, a sudden shift of the cloud, churns up, and a speck of sunlight spits out to the Shhwssss! Of the spirited air, and the ears of the boys hear and the sounds are voices—remade, impregnated—screaming out to the world." As Dumas relates the heaving of the valley at the end of the story, it initiates a progression of sounds—first a "harmonic churning" and then the "Shhwssss!" of the air that transform into voices "screaming out to the world." Dumas depicts the transformation as one where the voices are "remade" and "impregnated" with the forcefulness of screams that fuse the sensoria of the young men with the environmental soundscape. The conflation of voice and the natural world intensifies through Leo's friends chanting, as he configures the sound of the wind within his calls against the negative possession of tainting:

> Swish-ka aba, take the tainter,
> Swish-ka aba, count to three,
> Swish-ka aba, take the hainter,
> Saash-ka Lae, don't take me.

Leo's friend's chanting through and within the wind helps Leo's brother ultimately find his voice, as he forcefully states to Leo's friend, "Stop! Don't say it! I'm not cursing anymore!" followed by his desire to "hear it too." In order to do this, he must, as Leo's friend instructs him, "seal 'em out!" which he finds the ability to do as the concluding lines of the story demonstrate his realization of the ancestral power of the echo tree to conjure an alternate state of being:

Saaaa . . .
Saa saa aba saa saa.
Saa saa aba saa saa.
Two shapes on a hill. The sun has fallen down.
Two forms running the slope. And in the wind it is whispered to the ear
    of the hearer . . . The sun will rise tomorrow.[55]

The final lines of the story are hardly a conclusion, offering more possibility than finality. Dumas reinforces this sensibility by enacting a measured narrative break that highlights Leo's brother's ability to conjure, as the sound of his calling coincides with a sudden shift in time and perspective whereby the young men become part of the fluidity of the landscape. Dumas's concluding movements in the story generate a confluence of sonic and temporal distortion, a bending of time through the sensory dimensions of literary perception that creates a synesthetic reverberation of the *"forms running down the slope"* within the whispering wind and toward the futurity signaled by the fact that *"the sun will rise tomorrow."* The story itself becomes an echo of hope and resistance resonating against and within the longevity of black memory, its ancestral force of dispossession and struggle that cannot be contained through an archive, but must emerge through the inchoate energy of sound embedded within and erupting from environments that have been imprinted with asymmetrical histories of abjection and communion.

Sonic Warfare

While both "Echo Tree" and "Will the Circle Be Unbroken?" present moments of struggle and transcendence outside of more obvious scenes of political conflict, Dumas's story "Strike and Fade" situates the reemergence and evolution of black consciousness during the tumultuous years of the mid-to-late 1960s within the recognizable setting of a black rebellion in a large northern city. In "Strike and Fade," Dumas creates an aural portrait of black urban space under siege. His investment in the sounds of the cityscape and of the voices of those inhabiting it reflect his understanding of aurality as a pivotal contextual marker of the immediacy of struggle. Dumas works with sound, both in representing its acoustic dimensions that mark the setting, and through a tonally and rhythmically structured narrative approach that captures the sudden, unpredictable shifts, movements, and interactions emerging in the politically charged situation of urban guerilla warfare and state counterinsurgency.

The compressed text of "Strike and Fade" offers a layered snapshot of the historical moment of the mid-to-late 1960s that was gripping the nation, as the early, unifying Civil Rights optimism was beginning to lose sway, particularly in larger urban environments where significant concentrations of black dispossession, disfranchisement, and disenchantment had complicated a linear narrative of Civil Rights progress. Given the frequency of civil unrest between 1964 and 1968, a counter-narrative emerged in which black urban rebellion arose as not simply rage but as an expression of the need for socioeconomic redress to be elaborated rather than attenuated as the signing of the 1964 Civil Rights Act receded further into the past.[56] Countering this narrative, perspectives emerged within what might be considered a mainstream American popular consciousness, which expressed a mounting fear of the energy and meaning of black rebellion, and through this fear justified the intensification of militarized policing, occupation, and incarceration as a means of exercising control over black urban space. For example, this fear of urban black self-determination was rhetorically deployed quite forcefully in 1964 by Barry Goldwater, who claimed during the presidential election campaign, "If it is entirely proper for the government to take away from some to give to others, then won't some be led to believe that they can rightfully take from anyone who has more than they."[57] Goldwater critiques what he views as excesses of the social welfare state providing the impetus for those on the margins to increasingly demand more from the center. His belief fuses white racist fearmongering with a claim to the defense of property and rights, which he would argue are earned through merit and responsibility rather than structural privilege. This becomes a key ideological context for the contestation over black space that Dumas captures in the story "Strike and Fade."

Dumas narrates "Strike and Fade" through the observations of an unnamed main character and a first-person voice that link the sensory and structural details of the cityscape through a vernacular, fragmented, and ideologically weighted sound: "The word was out. Cool it. We on the street, see. Me and Big Skin. We watch the cops. They watch us. People goin and comin. That fire truck still wrecked up side the building. People say we riot, but we didn't riot. We like the VC, the Viet Cong. We strike and fade."[58] Rhythm is central to Dumas's narration, as a staccato vocal sound is measured to reflect the contingencies of the specific environmental context of the occupied urban space in which the main character moves. The narrative lens of the story reflects the audiovisual immediacy as well as the historically contextual and structural underpinnings of the intense regulation of black life. The sound of the narrative voice reflects the conditions of its emergence; its vernacular tonality has a political causation, its style an iteration of resistance to the necropolitical framing of black ghetto life under siege.

In his depiction of mid-1960s black urban rebellion, Dumas also references the interplay between internal colonization and foreign military aggression, linking U.S. imperialism and the idea of domestic colonialism that was becoming a central contention within Black Power ideology. He weaves this thread of dispossession into the story through the main character's vocalization of the term "Mowhite," a designation of economic super-exploitation that the narrator explains represents ownership of "the cleaners, the supermarket, the laundry, the tavern, the drugstore, and all the rest."[59] The critical sound of "Mowhite" depicts structures of white power that expand beyond the visual presence of whiteness and more capaciously represent the maintenance and permanence of racialized economic domination of black space. As Walter Rodney points out, "The essence of white power is that it is exercised over black peoples—whether or not they are minority or majority, whether it was a country belonging originally to whites or to blacks. It is exercised in such a way that black people have no share in that power and are, therefore, denied any say in their own destinies."[60] The sounds of extraction and brutality engendered through this category of "Mowhite" also converge with the words of Stokely Carmichael in 1967:

> There are over thirty million of us in the United States. For the most part we live in sharply defined areas in the rural black belt areas and shantytowns of the South, and more and more in the slums of the northern and western industrial cities . . . In these cities we do not control our resources. We do not control the land, the houses or the stores. These are owned by whites who live outside the cities. White power makes the laws and enforces those laws with guns and nightsticks in the hands of white racist policemen and black mercenaries.[61]

Carmichael's description lingers within the economic reality of Dumas's story as state-sanctioned violence is used as an instrument of white power—

both in its protection of white capital interpenetrating the ghetto landscape, and through the physicality of what another character in the story, Mace, refers to simply and repeatedly as "raw oppression." The substance of Carmichael's critique reverberates through Dumas's attention to the immediacy of the situation, as the cadenced observations and thoughts of the narrator resonate through the following lines: "Me and Big Skin, we scoutin the street the next day to see how much we put down on them. Big Skin, he walkin ahead of me. He walkin light, easy, pawin. It daylight but you still got to walk easy on the street. Anytime the Mowhites might hit the block on rubber, then what we do? We be up tight for space, so we all eyes, all feet an easy. You got to do it."[62] Dumas's first-person narration does not simply rely on the sound of the vernacular, but more deeply reinhabits those sonic spaces with added political depth in conveying the complexities of repression and resistance through the constellation of meanings ingrained within the shifting relationships among language, sound, and meaning. "Pawin," for instance, in referencing a catlike stealth, more precisely invokes the ease of movement needed to guard against the omnipresent threat of repression. This cool quality, as Dumas's story seems to suggest, is deeper than an abstract sense of smoothness, reflecting instead a tactical anticipation of antagonism through soft, dampened movement.

Dumas's rendering of the main character's calculating and vigilant voice is set within a broader radical chorus of compressed verbal analyses of the situation. As the narrator congregates with a group of like-minded neighborhood men at Bone's place ("Bone, he the only blood on the block got a business"), he relays the critical observations of another rebel, Mace, and provides a window into his understanding of this sociopolitical context: "A cat name Mace, he talkin. Mace just got out the Army. 'Don't worry, man. It's comin.' He point out the window. 'This is raw oppression, baby. Look at them mf's. Raw oppression.' Mace, he like to use them two words so he sayin them over and over again. He say them words all the time. It ain't funny cause they true. We all look out the window at the cops." The narrator's rendering of Mace's repetitive call of "raw oppression," through its phonic consistency, exemplifies a level of sonic, syntactic compression that bridges its critical sound with the increasingly tense action of the story. Dumas, as literary aesthetician, approximates through his prose not only the sound of Mace's words, but also the sense that the phrasing resonates as "true." Through this bridging of literary acoustics and thematic focus, the plot builds toward a brief yet brutal encounter with the police as he, Duke, and Big Skin attempt to move from Bone's place to the apartment of the legendary black Green Beret, Tyro, who has recently returned from Vietnam. Simply traveling the short space between Duke's and Tyro's involves carefully negotiating a cityscape in which any movement is a potential trigger for "raw oppression":

> Duke say he makin it to Tyro's now. We walk on. I kick some glass. We see a store that is burnt out. A cop is watchin us. We stakin easy, all eyes, all feet. A patrol car stop along side us. The gestapos leap out. I see a shotgun. We all freeze.
>
> The man is talkin.
>
> "You niggers got one hour to get off the street." Then he change his mind. "Against the wall!" There is three of them. Down the street is more. They frisk us. We all clean. One jab the butt of a gun hard on my leg. It give me a cramp in the ball.
>
> They cuss us and tell us to get off the street. We move on. Around the block. Down the street.
>
> I'm limpin. I don't say nothin. I don't curse or nothing. Duke and Big Skin, they mad, cursin and sayin what they gonna do. Me, I'm hurtin too much. I'm letting my heat go down into my soul. When it comes up again, I won't be limpin.[63]

Dumas highlights the quickly shifting context through synesthetic narration moving between vocalized sound and terse visuals of the city. The immediacy of state violence is present through the martial control the police exercise over the neighborhood, and is underlined by the short temporal spacing Dumas opens and closes between observations and events. The police watch, stop, and "leap out" to confront the young men, frisking them, and jabbing the narrator in the leg with the butt of a gun. The narrator's meditative reflection on the quick series of events interrupts the quickly moving temporality of the narrative, mediating his rage with the recognition that forging any meaningful resistance to these conditions will only come about through a more lasting critical patience reflected in an inversion of the terms comprising the title of the story. He fades in response to the police-state violence in order to let "the heat go down into my soul," in preparation for a retaliatory strike when the time is right.

Dumas's black resistance sharpens as the narrator, Duke, and Big Skin venture to the home of Tyro. As they "paw" through the streets, armed and angry young men from the neighborhood prepare for a direct confrontation with the police and National Guard: "We see some more cats pawin along the block. About fifty. We join. They headed to 33rd. Some cats got heats, some got molotovs. One cat got a sword." They break off from the group upon arriving at Tyro's building. As they ascend the stairs, the narrator hears the circularity of sound cascading from a siren, signaling the inevitability and recursive nature of black urban struggle against the specter of authoritarian policing as he explains, "The shit done already started," perhaps anticipating the temporal space between the narrative utterance and readers decades later responding, "and it never stops," in accordance with the cyclical oscillating sound of the siren. The resonance of the siren, its sound and the exteriority of that sound traveling through space and time, set the context for the meeting with Tyro and his understanding of resistance to formations of American imperialist aggression gained at the expense of his limbs lost during the Vietnam War. Tyro is revered by the young men in the ghetto as a prophet who offers ideas about how to move forward in the intensely racialized environment by imparting lessons learned from his near-death experience in an ambush during the war:

> The Cong are masters of the ambush. Learn this about them.
> When we fell back under fire, we fell into a pincher. They cross-
> fired us so fast that we didn't know what hit us. Out of sixty men,
> I was left. I believe they spared me so that I could come back and
> tell you. The cat that found me was hit himself, but he didn't seem
> to care. He looked me in the eye . . . for a long time. My legs were
> busted up from a grenade. This VC stood over my blood . . . he
> raised the rifle . . . It was one of the few times my prayers have been
> answered. The cat suddenly turned and ran off. He had shot
> several of my buddies already, but he let me go.[64]

The swirl of images and sounds, from Castro in fatigues, to the attempts at U.S. imperial expansion in the Vietnam War, to the transnational communion discovered through Tyro's spared life, grows into a black international consciousness[65] that Tyro has brought back to the rebellious streets on his home front:

> All I can figure is that one day the chips are all comin down.
> America is gonna have to face the yellow race. Black and yellow

might have to put their hands together and bring this thang off. You cats out in the street, learn to fade fast. Learn to strike hard, but don't be around in the explosion. If you don't organize you ain't nothing but a rioter, a looter. These jigs won't hesitate to shoot you. . . . Naw. I ain't tellin you to get off the streets. I know like you know. Uncle means no ultimate good, brothers. Take it for what it is worth. I'm layin it down like it is. I got it from the eagle's beak. That's the way he speak. Play thangs careful. Strike and fade, then strike again, quick. Get whitey outta our neighborhood. Keep women and children off the streets. Don't riot. Rebel. You cats got this message. Do what you got to do. Stick together and listen for the word to come down. Obey it.[66]

There is an interesting echo in the cadence of Tyro's message, as it recalls Gwendolyn Brooks's poetic provocation to "first fight. then fiddle," through his staccato imperatives to strike and fade, that correspond to Brooks's lyrical call for a mediation between engagement and evasion. Brooks frames a tension between an effort to "Be remote / A while from malice and from murdering," and the imperative to "Win war. Rise bloody, maybe not too late."[67] The echoes between Dumas's story and Brooks's poem are notable through their shared focus on the possibilities and costs of potentially violent engagement. For Brooks, however, the perspective of the poem offers a less overtly masculine idea of self-defense. Her address never designates black revolutionary empowerment as a goal to be achieved by men on behalf of women, as Tyro's words suggest. While Dumas may simply have been replaying dominant ideas of the gendered dynamics surrounding black urban rebellion, the relationship between his portrayal and Brooks's speaks to an opportunity Dumas seems to have missed to expansively reimagine black radical consciousness outside a reductive reading of gender. By not complicating Tyro's statements, Dumas creates a degree of verisimilitude that downplays the space between an almost stock representation of black urban rebellion and the very real and imaginable possibility that this resistance could be articulated through a more complex vision of gender. As Brooks reminds us, resistance might be strategically guided by a need to civilize living space and expression in a way that complicates notions of vulgar retributory violence. Rather than castigate Dumas for his oversight, we might think about this critical impasse as one that reflects a potential limitation of the sonic when it is used primarily as a documentary reflection of the real—even as that reality is being fictionally constructed. While it is crucial to replay these contexts, reproducing them in and of themselves can create constraints on how we might reimagine the specificities of certain conditions.

After Tyro's words, "Strike and Fade" concludes with a final set of sounds and images as the narrator ventures into the battlefield of the streets. Through his synesthetic relaying of the scene, it is clear that the sound of the "word" has come down, and the situation has intensified: "The word is out. Burn, baby, burn. We on the scene. The brothers. Together. Cops and people goin and comin. Some people got good loot, some just hoofin it. A police cordon comin. We shadows on the wall. Lights comin towards us. We fade. Some-body struck them. The lights go out. I hear shots. I fall. Glass get my hands. The street on fire now. We yell. 33rd Street here we come! Got to get to-gether!"[68] The economy of prose reflects Dumas's sense that there is no time to offer extended, elaborate descriptions of the events; the exigency can only be conveyed through abrupt observations and succinct sounds of the landscape: the staccato of shots being fired, feet hitting the ground run-ning, police sirens, and the portentous breaking of glass. The backdrop of breaking glass set within the evaporation of temporality in the story signals a level of disruption that accentuates the overarching framework of experi-mental sound motivating Dumas's writing. The specifics of breaking glass as a sonorous representation of epistemological rupture become equated, in the view of Robert Levin (writing the sonic interventions of visionary drummer Sunny Murray, with an attack on the American commitment), "to the suppression, the dispersal, enervation, and neutralization of passion." Levin contends that "the particular anxiety which a Sunny Murray, a Cecil Taylor, an Archie Shepp, or an Albert Ayler provokes in many people is only by degrees different from that which a riot will stir in them—the same circuits are disrupted." For Levin, the destruction of property marked by the "continuous cracking of glass" represents a challenge to "the upright emo-tional order which that property represents." Levin leans heavily on the words of Murray regarding his relationship to sound, suggesting how sound might radically operate across musical and political contexts, highlighting the continuum of freedom and the sensory. As Murray notes, "It is also about getting back to the natural, everyday sounds . . . I try to condition myself to be able to hear all of them. Society tries not to hear natural sounds—they disrupt the hearing of the people, they aren't 'listenable.' But to disturb people—at least what *they* mean by disturb—that's the whole point. That's why we have to bring natural sounds up front again."[69]

The presence of what Murray refers to as "natural sounds" provides openings within Dumas's narration for a grappling with the ideological dissonance between systems of black oppression and the struggle to imagine and create forms of resistance that exceed the teleology and empiricism that so often return to quietly underline articulations of struggle. Pushing beyond the registers of the anarchic and the utopian, Dumas's invocation of striking and fading, advancing and retreating through a constant state of guerilla insurgency, as lived practice, is exemplified but outlives the context of urban rebellion. The fragmentary quality of shards of glass erupting in the chaotic sound of shattering begins to conceptualize the sonority of such a political vision.

· CHAPTER 3 ·

Peering into the Maw

Larry Neal's Aesthetic Universe

Everybody wants to cop the black voice, that eternal vibratory force trying to assert itself in Babylon. The black voice, needing its own space, its own place, but consistently contained by the jive shapers of public taste.

—Larry Neal

Muntu/Marcuse

As a central theorist and creative writer within the Black Arts Movement, Larry Neal produced a significant body of writings from the mid-1960s until his unexpected death from a heart attack in 1981, at the age of forty-three. Perhaps the most prolific, influential, and understudied major figure in the movement, Neal creatively and theoretically conceptualized the sensory, phenomenological, and particularly sonic dimensions of black experience. He created a diverse body of work that includes his coauthored Black Arts Movement anthology with Amiri Baraka (LeRoi Jones), *Black Fire* (1968); numerous critical essays and creative work published in influential publications of the 1960s and 1970s including *Liberator, Journal of Black Poetry, The Cricket, Black Theatre,* and *Negro Digest* (later *Black World*); two volumes of poetry, *Black Boogaloo: Notes on Black Liberation* (1969) and *Hoodoo Hollerin' Bebop Ghosts* (1974); as well as two plays, *The Glorious Monster in the Bell of the Horn* (1976, 1979), and *In an Upstate Motel* (1980, 1981). Neal's exploration of sound is central to his understanding of and his commitment to the vitality of black aesthetics, which represents a pathway toward the "new space" he frequently writes about as the inchoate possibility of black expressive and political freedom. In critically framing the pivotal role of sound within the formation of black aesthetics, Neal envisions African American culture during and in the wake of the Black Arts Movement, not as a monolithic foundation, but as a dynamic field of aesthetic and political interaction.

Neal may be best known for his aforementioned coeditorship of *Black Fire* with Amiri Baraka. The volume was (and still is) seen as a signal contribution to the Black Arts Movement literary oeuvre, yet its publication in 1968, and Neal's relationship with Baraka—as fellow critics, artists, and activists—follows an already rich trajectory of intellectual and artistic development, which shaped Neal's perspective on aesthetics and political thought. Baraka's ideas on sound and black expression, as I demonstrated at the end of chapter 1, are largely borne out through a tensely articulated relationship between the acoustic and political expressions of black cultural nationalism. Neal is in conversation with Baraka regarding these convergences; they both understand the centrality of black innovation as a conceptual foundation for imagining sound. As I will show in this chapter, however, Neal's conceptualization of sound furthers an expansive phenomenological perspective, increasing the possibilities for liberation through multidimensional resistance and transformation.

In charting this critical approach, my chapter engages with the rich history of conversations and debates over black aesthetics during and in the wake of the Black Arts Movement. Evie Shockley, in her study of innovation in African American poetry, *Renegade Poetics* (2011), rightly points out the flaws in relying on an overdetermined version of a militant, separatist idea of black aesthetics to mark the period definitively, yet she also cautions us to not forget the "constricting, racially essentialist limitations some BAM theories placed on what a black aesthetic could encompass." Shockley's call to redefine and nuance our approach to the theory and practice of black aesthetics provides a contemporary critical view that reprises and fruitfully expands the wide angle through which Larry Neal ultimately wished artists and critics to imagine their work: "I propose that we think of not 'a black aesthetic' or the Black Aesthetic, but of 'black aesthetics,' plural: a multifarious, contingent, non-delimited complex of strategies that African American writers may use to negotiate gaps or conflicts between their artistic goals and the operation of race in the production, dissemination, and reception of their writing."[1] The qualities of flexibility and multiplicity that Shockley points to as crucial for the expansion of black aesthetic theory and practice are fundamental aspects of Neal's sonic reconfiguration of black artistic and political consciousness. Moving between essays and poetry, Neal turns to music, phenomenology, and ideas of the supernatural to help reframe black aesthetics outside the constraints that often emerge within the discursive realms of black cultural nationalism and literary theory. Certainly, he did not ever forfeit his commitment to either of these pursuits, but through his understanding of the shifting ephemerality and profundity of black sound Neal was able to stretch the capacities of both. His contributions as a Black Arts Movement creative artist and theorist might be most accurately noted through his ability to recursively refashion black aesthetics as malleable fields of creative expression and critical resistance.

James Spady, a close friend, associate, and chronicler of Larry Neal (particularly in terms of Neal's North Philadelphia roots), brings into focus many of the important early contextual elements that contributed to Neal's evolving ideas regarding black art and cultural politics. He contends that "in assessing Larry's life, one is able to see many of his earlier interests (from at least teenage days) sustained throughout his career. Contrary to popular belief, his activist/artistic life began at least 4 or 5 years before moving to New York."[2] Spady considers Neal's intellectual growth in Philadelphia, and his conceptualization of black expressive culture more broadly, in connection with a group of African American artists and activists known as the "Muntu Circle."[3] Initially comprising Neal, the playwright Charles Fuller, the educator Marybelle Moore, as well as the musician and critic Jimmy Stewart, this collective provided Neal with a black intellectual space through which he could begin contemplating new models, theories, and approaches to black aesthetics. Partially shaped by the cultural Pan-Africanism of Jan-heinz Jahn's *Muntu: African Culture and the Western World* (1961), but also heavily influenced by Marxist theory and notions of a popular avant-garde, the Muntu group's innovative black cultural nationalism, as Spady recounts, also emerged in relationship to Jimmy Stewart's critical explorations of black music.

In chapter 1 of this book I discuss the importance of Stewart's essay "Introduction to Black Aesthetics in Music" as an analysis of the revolutionary potential within the sonic formations of experimental black music. Spady notes that Stewart also understood his critical writings in the late 1960s journal of black music, *The Cricket*, as closely related to the distinctive orientation toward musical aesthetic innovation termed "Kuntu," which had emerged from the intellectual context of the Muntu group.[4] Stewart explains this orientation in his essay "Just Intonation and the New Black Revolutionary Music," through his analysis of the gaps between the "distinctive harmonic structure" of "Western European music" and the "vast field of musical possibilities" found in "the distinctive timbre, the treatment of pitch" in black music.[5] Stewart critiques "Western musical hegemony" as an epistemological force based on a regulation of sound that is confronted by the texture of free jazz sonic experimentation and its engagement with structures of tonality, harmony, and time, which are based on a "just" rather than "tempered" sense of tonal possibility. Stewart understood this tension as indicative of new dimensions of black nationalist struggle, as the more relational and shifting quality of a justly intoned sound begins to define part of the conceptual break that free jazz articulates against the constraints of hierarchically ordered Western musical scales. Spady, in relating an exchange between Neal and Charles Fuller, which Fuller recounts to him, explains how Neal was building on these ideas to concertedly chart a connective line between sound and revolutionary action:

> One afternoon Larry came running down 2nd street. He said, "Charlie, we are going to bring this motherfucker down." I said, what? He said we are going to bring this country down. Before he went to New York. He said we are going to change this country. We got the power, don't you know that. I said, how are we going to do it? He said "I just found Muntu. This explains all the rhythm. Force and rhythm." He and Stewart had talked about it. Stewart was involved in all of this. We created a new poetry. We created a poetry that involved the real force of rhythm . . . How do you get rhythm, how do you get music into what you are doing? How do you combine the rhythm of our people with the force to move our people toward revolution[?] Larry was the person who did that. Larry was the person who brought that to us, man.[6]

This exchange situates Neal's creative and theoretical work during the Black Arts Movement within a North Philly cultural and political matrix that is heavily invested in the politics of sound as an expressive force of black revolution. This context becomes a foundation for the distinctiveness of Neal's artistic ideology in the Black Arts Movement, a position marked by his conceptualization of black aesthetics across a field of artistic and political interaction, largely mapped in relationship to black sound. The early years of Neal's aesthetics, developed through the Muntu–Kuntu framework, represent a foundation of thought and practice that Neal consistently builds on as he maintains a view of black expression that is fluid in its refusal of rigid formal definitions while maintaining a political commitment through the dynamism of this innovative impulse. For Neal, maintaining a focus on the expansive, ineffable qualities of black art necessitated modalities such as the sonic that might accommodate the contingencies of mood, atmosphere, style, memory, and political experience. Beginning with a sense of this early point in Neal's career, the remaining pages of this chapter examine Neal's recursive attention to constantly expanding the role and possibilities of black aesthetics through their relationship to modes of sonority. Not simply focusing on music (although this manifestation of sound is still quite important), as is often the case when matters of sound are considered within black expressive culture, this chapter frames the role of sound in Neal's work more broadly as a critical inclination or orientation that moves between representation and method, object and practice, positioning the sonic as a black modernist framework through which Neal reconsiders the limits and possibilities of black artistic and political consciousness.

In an undated letter included in his archived papers, composed at least fifteen years after the initial formation of the Muntu group, Neal writes to Amiri Baraka, "Hey LeRoi Amiri Chairman Baraka Amiri Baraka! I understand you're working hard on that Coltrane book. Would you please take a look at the Herbert Marcuse book, *The Aesthetic Dimension: Toward a Critique of Marxist Aesthetics*[?] You will get this book I know." Neal continues by providing a block quote from Marcuse's text that establishes one of the primary contentions of Marcuse's rejection of orthodox Marxist social and artistic theory: that the revolutionary potential and truth of art can no longer be measured simply by its ability to reflect proletarian consciousness. Neal then puts interpretive pressure on this point by laying out his reading of Marcuse to Baraka: "In general Marcuse puts forth the position that Marxism cannot contain and define the conditions of art, since these conditions are not always grounded in objective social and economic reality on a one-to-one basis."[7] Neal contemplates Marcuse's critique of the standpoint within much Marxist theory of a rigid correspondence between proletariat identity and the "truth" value of artistic production. He dissects this rigidity as a disavowal of the formal political complexity within dialectical thought, as this orthodox atomization of subjectivity reduces it to an objective reflection of collectivity, and strips it of the preconditions of revolutionary ideology that may exist within individual formations of consciousness and experience. This stripping occurs in the realm of art, through the reductive qualification of what Marcuse, building on the late aesthetic theory of Theodor Adorno, calls the "uncompromising estrangement," which defines the autonomy of art as decadent and elitist rather than "authentic forms of contradiction."[8] Neal underlines his view of Marcuse's ideas to Baraka by stating, "My note concerns the relationship between economic and social liberation in reality, and their relationship to the question of complexity in art."[9]

Neal's citation of Marcuse to Baraka is perhaps intended as a provocation, in that he knows Baraka believes that revolutionary black cultural nationalism involves a cyclical circuitry whereby art is a functional weapon in the struggle, serving as an organizing principle to the extent that it is reflective of a determinate, objective sense of political reality. Neal takes up this question in his letter by raising a point posed to him by the jazz drummer Max Roach, whose biography Neal was in the midst of writing. Roach explains to Neal the experience of playing at a club in Chicago that was divided into a downstairs jazz club and an upstairs disco. Neal recounts Roach's dismay regarding the racial dividing line in which a predominately white, middle-class, college-educated audience consumed his music, while "our Afro-American comrades were on the disco floor upstairs." For Neal and Roach, this scenario puts into relief the larger question regarding the access one may have to different levels of transformative artistic experience, and how the lived realities of race and class affect that access. Neal contends that "the oppression of the people is such that they are rarely even given a chance to really decide whether Coltrane or Smokey is what's happening." Neal understands the relationship between aesthetic and political struggle to revolve, in part, around the ways in which structures of economic oppression and restricted access to education may foreclose the ability one has to develop insight into and appreciation of more complex processes of artistic abstraction. Neal's point is not that Smokey Robinson's falsetto is necessarily any less revolutionary than Coltrane's scream in its sound and affect, rather he is pointing to the fact that a limited range of sounds are made available to the imaginations of many African Americans. The challenge that emerges for both Neal and Marcuse, then, is to realize art as a tool of revolutionary transformation, what Marcuse refers to as "the political potential of art in art itself," or the qualities of contradiction and estrangement that both mark art's subversive orientation and make it challenging to grasp as a collectively felt experience of revolutionary transformation.[10] In referring back to the work of Coltrane in this context, Neal underlines the value of his music (and here he seems to have Coltrane's later career efforts in mind) as a "challenge [to] the minds and possibility of himself

and his audience." Valuing artistic rigor, complexity, and abstraction as definitive markers in the relationship between black aesthetics and political transformation, Neal points to Baraka's 1970s dramatic work as examples of
revolutionary art that require a high level of education and critical thought
to fully grasp. Rather than qualify this approach to artistic production and
reception as elitist, Neal contends that "the point is we should encourage
the mental discipline posed by the complex . . . That is the only way we
gonna build an audience with the consciousness and mental discipline
required to restructure society to something more human than it is now."[11]
Neal's epistolary meditation reflects back on the initial Muntu principles
of black aesthetics that were a foundation in his efforts to help guide the
creation and manipulation of politicized art throughout the Black Arts
Movement, as he attempts to envision the path toward a liberated future.

Ellison's Sonic Rites

Writing in a 1970 reconsideration of the work of Ralph Ellison, Larry Neal
outlines the strong connection between approaches to black aesthetic innovation, art as a form of critical resistance, and the ritualistic convergence
between writing and sound. In recognizing that sonic forms offer means of
accessing the inchoate political possibility within black expression, Neal
reaches back against the grain of his earlier dismissal of Ralph Ellison as an
apolitical artist, to recover the importance of the mythic politics at work in
Ellison's aesthetic universe. He quotes Ellison's evocative description of the
blues as a form containing and expressing "an impulse to keep the painful
details and episodes of a brutal experience alive in one's aching consciousness, to finger its jagged grain, and to transcend it, not by the consolation of
philosophy but by squeezing from it a near-tragic, near-comic lyricism."[12] As
a method of critical inquiry the blues can potentially chart political possibility through a formal reflection of the conscious and unconscious elements of
black life that have emerged and evolved in respect to musical creation. This
point must be understood with attention to form as an aspect of—rather
than a supplement to—content. For Ellison, it does not particularly matter
whether an artist has grown up with bits of knowledge imparted through
blues songs inasmuch as the form represents a way of comprehending
the power of cultural redefinition outside prescribed roles; as a movement
through space—the space of memory, the space between defined identities—
naturally occurring during struggles for the recognition of a group identity.

Neal's reading of Ellison expands the space of black cultural politics, as it is shaped by the sonic and ideological intersections within the notion of a black aesthetic. The first words of Neal's essay draw attention to his analytical and vernacular registers:

> Well, there is one thing that you have to admit. And that is dealing with Ralph Ellison is no easy matter. It is no easy task to fully characterize the nature of Ellison's life and work. He cannot be put into any one bag and completely dispensed with. Any attempt to do so merely leads to aesthetic and ideological oversimplifications. On the surface, oversimplifications may appear pragmatic and visible but, in the long run, they weaken us. To overlook the complex dimensions of a man's ideas, character, and personality is to do a great disservice to the righteous dissemination of knowledge.[13]

Neal begins by framing the complexities of reading Ellison as a way of suggesting the dangers of a critical myopia within attempts to interpret black expression. His articulation of the statement is crucial in that the opening—"Well, there is one thing you have to admit"—is embedded with a deep and shifting degree of critical self-reflexivity. As the essay develops, it becomes clear that "you" is really Neal both considering himself and the way his place in the movement might stand for a broader critical perspective. Considering his artistic relationship to Ellison amid the ideological struggles over black art and politics circulating around the Black Arts Movement, Neal contends that the critical exchanges between these artistic genealogies need to be treated in a sustained, analytical form. Notions of creativity and ideology are central to Neal's argument as he quickly breaks down the fact that "much of the criticism directed against Ellison is personal, oversimplified, and often not based on an analysis of the man's work and ideas." The real crux of Neal's problem with this criticism is that it also "springs from a specific body of Marxian and black neo-Marxian thought . . . called 'social realism.'"[14] These opening thoughts provide a foundation for Neal to develop a layered theorization of, and resistance to, efforts to contain black radical expression by elements of both the white left and conservative black nationalists.

The first sections of Neal's essay elucidate these ideas by refuting the totalizing nature of the dichotomy between the "protest" writing of Richard

Wright and Ellison's perceived aesthetic and personal detachment from black radical ideas, which has been enforced by notable white leftists within literary circles. After recounting the well-documented exchange between Ellison and Irving Howe regarding the urge to define black art and creativity through primarily sociological lenses, Neal points out the fact that even as critics try to insert this ideological wedge within black intellectual production, Wright himself speaks to the imprecision of white Marxist formations of black resistance, as Neal quotes him from the introduction to George Padmore's *Pan-Africanism or Communism?*

> The Negro's fundamental loyalty is, therefore, to *himself*. His situation makes this inevitable. (Am I letting awful secrets out of the bag? I'm sorry. The time has come for this problem to be stated clearly so that there is no possibility of further misunderstanding or confusion. The Negro, even when embracing Communism or Western Democracy, is not supporting ideologies; he is seeking to use instruments [instruments owned and controlled by men of other races!] for his own ends. He stands outside of those instruments and ideologies; he has to do so, for he is not allowed to blend with them in a natural, organic, and healthy manner.)[15]

Interestingly, the Wright whom Neal invokes here is being captured at a moment (the last years of his life, in the late 1950s) when he, too, is under severe questioning regarding his commitment to the struggle for black equality in the United States. His expatriation to France made him, in the eyes of many black American writers and intellectuals, disconnected from the realities of racial politics in the Unites States—a claim that his politically layered novelistic depiction of the economic and social complexities of southern U.S. race relations, *The Long Dream*, would nonetheless seemingly challenge. At any rate, Neal assesses black experimental practice in the face of traditional or orthodox notions of black cultural expression in his appraisal of the situations facing both Ellison and Wright; and here "black experimental practice" is meant to encompass both artistically and politically radical constructions of black cultural identity and resistance.

The other intertwined theme of Neal's essay emerges as an implied question: what might Ellison's work tell us about the centrality of myth in constructing a radical black political vision? For Neal, this query represents another level through which notions of sound, the aesthetic, and the political converge as he frames his ideas on black aesthetics, moving away from a strict notion of a newly defined black cultural nationalism being mobilized around various manifestations of Black Power and the Black Arts Movement, to a broader idea of black cultural production that materializes out of the wide-ranging, "even noumenal set of values that exist beneath the surface of black American culture." Neal's analysis of Ellison revolves around the idea that political engagement might best be imagined through manipulating aesthetic form. Flowing between an unsigned 1943 editorial believed to have been penned by Ellison, and scenes from *Invisible Man*, Neal considers deeper exchanges between the political and aesthetic levels of black art, where Ellison's "counter-Marxian thrust" gives rise to "a unique cultural theory, one that is shaped on the basis of cultural imperatives integral to the black man's experience in America."[16] Neal's reading of Ellison reflects another tension between his desire for black aesthetic liberation and the gendered dimensions of his black aesthetic thought, and serves as a necessary reminder of the general masculine hegemony within the movement.[17] Yet it is equally important to understand Neal's contributions as part of a theoretical line within black aesthetic discourse that questions the hegemonic reproduction of hierarchical orders (including patriarchy) within black political culture through formal innovation. A likeminded black aesthetician of the Black Arts Movement, Sarah Webster Fabio, addresses this complex relationship between aesthetic form and ideology in her essay "Tripping with Black Writing," included in Addison Gayle's signal edited volume, *The Black Aesthetic*. Fabio, not unlike Neal, points to the limitations placed on black subjectivity through manifestations of white supremacy that delimit the free expression of black thought by linguistically and expressively binding black artists to "a tree with 'the man's' rhetoric and aesthetic, which hangs them up, lynching their black visions." Fabio frames black aesthetics as a severance from the tethers of expressive and epistemological violence that confine and silence black artists. This severance amounts to what Fabio refers to as a "flying home" in which revolutionary black expression incorporates "black perspective, black aesthetic, black rhetoric, black language to add authenticity to the felt reality." Rather than offering an essentialist or reductive sense of identity by making claims to a correspondence between black aesthetics and reality, Fabio, in concert with Neal and other theorists of the complexity of black cultural politics, poses this correspondence as capacious and rhizomatic rather than sedimented and hierarchical. Most important, the correspondence is distinguished by a resistance to the imposition of a reductive and false construction of American universality. As Fabio explains, this black aesthetic resistance is based on a deeply felt critical awareness of the strategic importance of what we might now refer to as black essentialism, and a willingness to express oneself in accordance with the unflinching quality of this intuition in order to more substantively achieve a pluralist society:

> Knowing America has no rhetoric matching its racist reality; no reality matching its "Universal" and "democratic" idealistic state of existence. Knowing the simple-minded, fascist, pseudo-Europeanized mandate of universality to be a funky issue in any aesthetic consideration. A hustle to make walleyed, white-eyed America to be the all-seeing Cyclops of our age.
>
> Giving the finger to blind justice. Peeping the loosened blindfold. Peeping her peeping; favoring the apples of eye-rotten though they may be. Playing the game of dozens with her. Combatting her status-quo games. Knowing the truth about this society. One that devaluates the lives of a people for the duration of its existence. One that dehumanizes them for fun and profit. A mere matter of pragmatism and utilitarianism. Knowing that society to be guilty of: emasculating manhood; deflowering womanhood; exploiting spirit and soul; blinding vision; binding motion; dulling sensitivity; gagging speech.[18]

I quote Fabio at length to render her voice within the fullness of its critical texture and vernacular grain. Fabio's sound emerges at the intersection of aesthetics and politics (not unlike the political sonority of W. E. B. Du Bois that I analyzed in the introduction), as she emphasizes the gravity of her points through a tightly measured poetic rhythm that puts consistent pressure on the circulation of injustice that defines the tension between the veneer of American democracy and the reality of racial marginalization. Fabio points out that formations of white supremacy are effectively "gagging speech" by maintaining false lines of division that facilitate the accumulation of profit, pleasure, and comfort for those at the top of the hierarchy. She understands the devaluing of sensorial, phenomenological, and political possibilities contained in the speech of black creative artists and political activists as an attack on the transgressive potential of black thought. Fabio is less concerned with determining the particular relationships between race and gender than with breaking all forms of hierarchical regimentation and subjection, and in this way addresses the issues of inter- and intra-racial gender inequity through her broader irruption of radical critique.

Fabio's essay, in style and substance, reflects the totality rather than narrowly separatist line of black aesthetic thought that Larry Neal was so instrumental in pushing forward. Within the breadth of these literary, sensory, and political possibilities Neal envisions Ellison's ideas of the mythic and ritualistic modalities of black culture as an approach through which Ellison "turns Marxism on its head and makes the manipulation of cultural mechanisms the basis for black liberation," bringing "the hidden cultural compulsions of black American life" to light, serving as an example for Neal of the distinct, yet broad political usefulness he envisions within black aesthetic practice: "We are going to have to be careful not to let our rhetoric obscure the fact that a genuine nationalist revolution in the arts will fail if the artistic products of that revolution do not encounter our audiences in a manner that demands their most profound attention. I'm talking about a black art that sticks to the ribs, an art that through the strength of all its ingredients—form, content, craft, and technique—illuminates something specific about the living culture of the nation, and by extension, reveals something fundamental about man on this planet."[19] For Neal, the ongoing search for truth that is present throughout Ellison's writing becomes the correct way of formulating a theoretical basis for black aesthetics. Through an idea of flexible truth, Neal imagines the potential for individuals to step outside the imposed drama of racially determined existence and refashion political and social interaction on their own terms. Remaining cognizant of the fact of Neal's skepticism of Marxism's doctrinaire aspects, it becomes clear that, more than a criticism of the theoretical content of Marxist thought, Neal is focused on the overdetermined systematization of knowledge and historical truth as a constraint on the productive theorization of black historical memory and political experience.

Neal's grappling with Ellison's ideas frames the mythic and ritualistic elements of black life as expressive impulses that force a convergence of the political and the sensory. His understanding of Ellison expands the possibilities for constructing, in Hortense Spillers's phrasing, "a coherent system of signs that brings into play the entire repertory of American cultural traits"—one which resists "the modernist inclination to isolate issues of craft from ethical considerations," and in this way, Ellison's creative vision becomes a crucial juncture for Neal in theorizing black aesthetics.[20]

Neal's analysis of Ellison's aesthetic innovation as a model of aesthetic and political indirection relates to the promise Neal finds in the multidimensionality of black sound. Although he is not as renowned for his writings on music as fellow Black Arts Movement–era writers Amiri Baraka or A. B. Spellman, Neal frequently turns to the phenomenological levels of sonic expression and reception as openings that may disrupt linear understandings of time. The idea of rupture that Neal reads through the manipulation of sonic expression is instructive in its marking of and movement between expressive and political realms. In turning to music, Neal is often interested in taking its specificity seriously, but also in moving beyond that specificity in order to expand the possibilities of fusing the artistic, experiential, and political dimensions of black aesthetics. In the opening to his unpublished book-length manuscript, "Black American Music," Neal explains, "We should attempt to avoid labels like 'old' and 'new' music. Mainly because Afro-American music is not historically linear, but rather it is multi-directional. It goes back & forth in time . . . The music is informed by the past & present. It is time itself rather than any particular time. It is non-matrixed always in motion & free." Neal describes the sound of black music as a challenge to linear ideas of history and temporality, as the "intrinsic qualities of the music . . . what makes it go," represent the sonic formulation of a "new vocabulary" that deploys resistance through a transcendent "longing for a new world to come into being." The asymmetry of experimental black sound, for Neal, reflects what he refers to in his manuscript and in other writings as the "ethos of Black America," an inclination toward understanding the relational tension comprising Ellison's vision of black American identity, in which black music and culture have "greatly influenced the music of the dominant white culture," as well as a concurrent "symbolic separation of the black man from white America."[21]

Exploring this tonal and epistemological orientation in a later section of the manuscript that engages specifically with free jazz, or what he terms "New Music," Neal analyzes more abstract, expressionistic sound, through its own terms of improvisational energy and time, rather than through Western conceptualizations of musical sound structure. Neal's turn toward experimental black music highlights the need for listeners to reorient themselves in relationship to distortions of time and space. He goes into detail regarding this point, and I'll quote his words at some length in order to best convey his perspective on this productive convergence of the aural and the epistemological within the "New Music":

The listener experiences a greater sense of release. This music is
particularly demanding because most of us are unaccustomed to
so much energy coming at us in such force. Or where there is an
abundant use of space some people can't relate to the tension.
Many of our problems with the New Music are linked to the inability of great many listeners to overcome our Western biases. These
culturally determined biases prevent us from listening to the music
on its *own terms*. Instead of hearing the thing itself, many people
keep listening for elements, melodic and rhythmic, that are
familiar. Essentially, we are lazy looking for clichés or convenient
props on which to hang things. The beauty of the New Music lies
primarily in its "purity." It presents an entirely new way of looking
at the world. Not merely interested in *swinging* in the old sense of
the word. The New Music proposes a music whose dynamic is
based on the creation of energy and time. Notes and rhythmic
figures are subservient to the *act* of improvising. It is the act that
counts above all things. The music radically commits itself to some
kind of point-of-view, to a specific stance. It challenges the regular
systems of Western music, distorting and transmuting ordinary
ideas of harmony, tone, pitch, and rhythm.[22]

The sound of the music represents something beyond music for Neal. It has
both a formal and theoretical presence in that its sonority of distortion, displacement, and abstraction audibly oppose the regulation of Western measures of artistic order. In establishing these sensory breaks with standard
listening practices, this experimental music challenges listeners to hear the
music outside the familiarity and expectation created through what Neal
refers to as "Western biases." Neal's formulation, however, grants that his
audience may be subject to and reliant on many of the assumptions that these
forms of expression seek to break away from. In suggesting this configuration
between audience and phonic matter, he anticipates an epistemological
expansion in the formal horizons of listeners, rather than simply relying on a
dichotomy between black culture and Western culture in which the oppressive forces of Western culture are directly and linearly overturned through
the force and energy of the music. Distortion and transmutation embody the
radical edge of sound for Neal, operating both within the music and more
broadly as a critical orientation posed in opposition to the production of
"culturally determined" patterns of value. In conceptualizing the sound of the

music, Neal suggests a cultural distinctiveness to black music, and claims that this approach to sonic innovation represents a revolutionary idea of expressive abstraction that blends modernist and cultural nationalist perspectives. Neal's theorizations and representations of sound are entangled and in tension with ideas of modernism and the avant-garde. As Kimberly Benston states, regarding the creative impulse behind much Black Arts Movement theater, "African American modernist performance works to align disruptive play with cultural reconstruction, resituating rather than deconstructing the subject as an agent of historical ferment."[23] Benston's notion of resituation parallels Neal's sense of bending sound, as both expressive configurations depend on a fusion of innovation and ritualistic tradition.

Neal's perspectives on the experimental sonority of black music and the contours of black expressive culture as political in and of themselves complicate his presence within the Black Arts Movement, locating it well beyond a flattened convergence of aesthetics and politics. While it has become common for critics to cite Larry Neal's frequently anthologized 1968 essay "The Black Arts Movement" as a central statement of his artistic and political philosophy, revisiting his statement of black cultural nationalism through his attention to the flexibility of sound illustrates Neal's layered and dynamic vision of black cultural autonomy and his understanding of the centrality of the sensory and phenomenological registers of experience and expression to his critical perspective. Published at the height of the movement in 1968, a year marked by perhaps the most visible social unrest in the late twentieth-century United States, Neal's essay argues for black art as "the aesthetic and spiritual sister of the Black Power concept." Framed through a fusion of ethics and aesthetics, Neal envisions the role of black artists as impelling "black people to define the world in their own terms," through an aesthetic commitment to "the destruction of the white thing, the destruction of white ideas, and white ways of looking at the world."[24] As a paean to the urgency and confrontational nature embodied within the foundational works of the movement, Neal's essay still serves as the primary statement used to encapsulate the period within many literary historical accounts. The overtly ideological overtones of Neal's perspective reveal themselves through examples of these cultural nationalist motives and the techniques used to achieve them in the poetry, drama, and at times prescriptive statements of writers such as Amiri Baraka, Don L. Lee (Haki Madhubuti), and Maulana Karenga.

What is perhaps most notable about Neal's critical perspective, however, is his focus on the felt, experienced, and sensory manifestations of artistic production, as he considers, for example, how the Amiri Baraka play *Slave Ship* projects an idea of historical consciousness through an "expressionistic tableaux" of the sensory, in which "there is no definite plot (LeRoi calls it a pageant), just a continuous rush of sound, groans, screams, and souls wailing for freedom and relief from suffering." He goes on to explain that "this work has special affinities with the New Music of Sun Ra, John Coltrane, Albert Ayler, and Ornette Coleman. Events are blurred, rising and falling in a stream of sound . . . It is a play which almost totally eliminates the need for a text. It functions on the basis of movement and energy—the dramatic equivalent of the New Music." Neal understands the presence of sound in Baraka's work to enact a formal break with what he terms the "alien sensibility" of Western culture. This break, however, is not reducible to ideas of ontological, essential racial difference seemingly signaled by Neal's framing of it as "the destruction of the white thing, of white ideas, and white ways of looking at the world." When Neal diagnoses whiteness as oppositional to the intentions of the Black Arts Movement, he admittedly leaves open the door for those who might use his pronouncements as fuel for an essentialist vision of black separatism, yet a more deliberate engagement with the implications of Neal's perspective reveals that his dividing line hinges less on one's racial identity than the degree to which one recognizes the indivisibility of aesthetics and politics. His framing of the problem revolves around the fact that "much of the oppression confronting the Third World and Black America is directly traceable to the Euro-American cultural sensibility," an orientation he calls "anti-human in nature" and, because of its manifestation across racial lines, Neal notes that this sensibility "must be destroyed before the black creative artist can have a meaningful role in the transformation of society."[25] Neal's idea of black cultural nationalism offers an intriguing dialectic as he defines black aesthetics in both a focused sense of speaking to the distinct needs of black people in struggle against forces of racist dehumanization and subjection, but simultaneously understands the racial and cultural precision and basis of this push to ultimately affect a far more capacious formation of the social than simply black culture.

Tonal Memories

In Neal's vision, black aesthetic critical thought reflects the global and local conditions of resistance to historical and political subjection, while also operating within a broader field of critical resistance to elements of Western culture that includes views often fashioned from within the culture itself.[26] These overlapping aims of artistic resistance are signaled through Neal's definition of black aesthetic creativity as a "radical reordering" through the "concrete" nature of expression that "comes to stand for the collective conscious and unconscious of Black America." The idea of reordering that Neal argues for is perhaps less direct than he at first alludes to in his commentary on Amiri Baraka's "Black Art," insofar as in the middle of a reading of Baraka's poem that he uses to begin mapping his argument in "The Black Arts Movement," Neal states, "Poetry is a concrete function, an action. No more abstractions. Poems are physical entities: fists, daggers, airplane poems, and poems that shoot guns. Poems are transformed from physical objects into personal forces."[27] Neal's refusal of abstraction in favor of concrete, active physicality is complicated only a year later in the statement he includes as the final page of his 1969 volume of poetry, *Black Boogaloo*, as he outlines the potential for poetics to achieve political ends through less determinate relationships between aesthetic creativity and political action: "Poems are ways into things, the opening of the natural spirit in us. Poems do not shoot guns; they are spiritual cohesives, tightening us up for the future war, if there be one, and giving us the strength to build a nation. These are dimensions of our consciousness; ourselves extended as far as current possibilities allow." Neal's statement concluding *Black Boogaloo* is notable in its move away from a vision of art operating within a field of recognizable objects, suggesting instead that art may reflect an idea of metaphysical expansion through less tangible expansions in the "dimensions of our consciousness."[28]

Amiri Baraka in "Sound for Sounding," his introduction to Neal's poetry collection, describes expressive expansion through what he refers to as a "Post 'literary'" tonality. He defines Neal's poetics as projecting "literary sound like somethin' else . . . sound like it ain't sound. And sound is what we deal in . . . in the real world . . . sound for sounding."[29] Baraka's prefatory remarks focus on Neal's poetic mediation of sound, movement, and energy. The fluidity of sound represents "somethin' else" for Baraka, and through this shifting quality of sound, Neal's verse offers a window into formations of black historical consciousness. In a signal poem in Neal's collection, "Don't Say Goodbye to the Porkpie Hat," this fluidity is narrated as a sonic presence that marks a historical trajectory of black musical expression. Neal's poem suggests and refuses the elegiac mode as a limited horizon in its titular representation, and this inclination is extended throughout the work's fashioning of sound as synesthetic "tonal memories" and "blue streaks of mellow wisdom" that take the reader through historical moments in the formation of black musical and sonic traditions, connecting these expressive constructs to evocative distillations of memory and experience that begin to impressionistically suggest black consciousness as a multidirectional force. The compositional sound of Charles Mingus's 1959 brief, yet sonically elongated bluesy ode to the recently departed Lester Young, is not necessarily used as a direct sonic corollary for Neal; he is more interested in translating Mingus's sonic projection of black memory, loss, longing, and hope into the spiraling sonic dimensions of his verse. The poem situates Mingus's composition as both point of reference and departure in order to create a new possibility for the sound's existence on the page; an existence that might extend temporally outside the music, always keeping it in the forefront of its sensibility, but using it to demarcate the sound of black memory and consciousness. Neal opens with a brief epigraph, dedicating the poem to *"Mingus, Bird, Prez, Langston, and them."* The first sections of the poem follow the epigraph with lines that establish the fluidity, multidimensional movement, and temporal displacement embedded in the figure of the Porkpie Hat:

> Don't say goodbye to the Porkpie Hat that rolled
> along on nodded shoulders
>   that swang bebop phrases
>   in Minton's jelly roll dreams
> Don't say goodbye to hip hats tilted in the style of a soulful era;
> the Porkpie Hat that Lester dug
> swirling in the sound of sax blown suns
>   phrase on phrase, repeating bluely
>   tripping in and under crashing
>   hi-hat cymbals, a fickle girl
>   getting sassy on the rhythms.
> Musicians heavy with memories
> move in and out of this gloom;
> the Porkpie Hat reigns supreme
> smell of collard greens
> and cotton madness
>   commingled in the nigger elegance of the style.

The Porkpie Hat sees tonal memories
of salt peanuts and hot house birds
the Porkpie Hat sees . . .[30]

Much like the sound of jazz music that often expands through its compositional and tonal breadth, Neal's poem dilates its scope through the movement of the Porkpie Hat in time and space, and through the shifting rhythmic
temporality created as Neal both elongates and syncopates the phrasing,
fracturing it by alternating enjambment against more measured demarcations of line structure. Across the expanse of the poem, Neal blends direct
references to actual musical sound alongside the tonal depth and complexity
of his verse. Perhaps the most intriguing sonic element of the poem, however, exists in the levels of imagined sound that extend the poetic expanse
of the work beyond the sonic points of reference evoked by the artists and
compositions through which Neal propels the poem. Neal creates a sounding of temporal memory signaled initially by the many reference points in
jazz history populating the poem, but that ultimately becomes, through the
formal operation of the verse, a haunting echo, a sonic embodiment of the
refusal of loss. Through the poem, Neal frames loss as a nonlinear phenomenon, and in his exploration of this condition seeks to refashion its
meaning and possibility through the ephemeral qualities of its resonance:

Stop-time Buddy and Creole Sydney
wailed in here. Stop time.
chorus repeats, stop and shuffle.
stop and stomp.
listen to the horns, ain't they mean?
now ain't they mean
in blue
in blue
in blue streaks of mellow wisdom
blue notes
coiling around
the Porkpie Hat
and ghosts of dead musicians drifting through
here on riffs that smack
of one leg trumpet players
and daddy glory piano ticklers

who
twisted arpeggios
with diamond-flashed fingers.[31]

The "stop-time" that Neal invokes immediately following the stanza break reflects the highly syncopated New Orleans jazz sonority of Buddy Bolden and Sidney Bechet, suggesting a modality of expression and critical orientation based on the simultaneity of freezing and expanding time through interrupting the steadiness of a rhythm and filling the gaps with improvisational sound. While the lyricism and poetic structure around Neal's direct reference to "stop-time" certainly suggest a formal correlation to the musical practice, Neal is also asking us to understand this temporal disruption as an opening of the poem that might facilitate and be defined by the haunting drift of sonic memory. Hearing stop-time outside of simply a musical context, through "blue streaks of mellow wisdom" and "blue notes / coiling around / the Porkpie Hat," Neal expands the domain of the poem beyond solely the musical into a philosophical and critical sphere that complicates the relationship between sound, temporality, and the aesthetic imagination. The wailing of "Buddy and Creole Sydney," the coiling of "blue notes," and the drifting "ghosts of dead musicians," all reflect a desire to understand the interminable sonic force of black music and cultural memory as a productively haunting blurring of time. Neal's configuration of sound as a critical force is perhaps best approximated by Ralph Ellison through the narrative voice in the prologue to *Invisible Man* as he interrogates the meaning of racial invisibility through a meditation on Louis Armstrong's "(What Did I Do to Be So) Black and Blue?": "Invisibility, let me explain, gives one a slightly different sense of time, you're never quite on the beat. Sometimes you're ahead and sometimes behind. Instead of the swift and imperceptible flowing of time, you are aware of its nodes, those points where time stands still or from which it leaps ahead. And you slip into the breaks and look around. That's what you hear vaguely in Louis' music."[32]

Much of Neal's poetry enfolds such temporal disruptions within its aesthetic dimensions, calibrating a formal exploration of and through sound with an ability to accumulate images, and to manipulate that accumulation in a way that generates productive disorder much like the "twisted arpeggios" of the "daddy glory piano ticklers." The twisting signals the ability to move outside of, or in the breaks of time as it warps an already fractured musical chord, outside the linear, sequenced fracturing an arpeggio represents, into more of a bluesy worried state. Neal's poetics of accumulation, what Charles Rowell, in a 1974 interview with Neal refers to as "the stacking of images immediately upon each other," provides a sense of the aural outside simply the phonic, as the accumulation creates its own asymmetric cadence. Responding to Rowell's suggestion that Neal's technique stems in part from the influence of Gerard Manley Hopkins's poetry, Neal replies affirmatively, noting that "there's a certain kind of magnificence and scope in Hopkins. I just envy that scope, and I want to riff off that scope in my own Afro-American language."[33] Neal's stacking facilitates the charting of black political culture through synesthetic convergences of sound, image, and ideology, a fusion of literary tactics very much at work within his prose poem "The Summer after Malcolm":

> The Summer after Malcolm, I lost myself in a jet stream of mad words, acts, goading bits of love memory. Like that. It was a cold bitch. I mean the pain. Dig, all summer long, I could see Malcolm's face drifting with the sound of Harlem children. Old men played checkers on the blocks running between Seventh and Eight. And yes, there was a moan in the sweating night. The wine smells and hallways were screaming women. Angry the way the breeze came off from the river. Angered too, by the rustle of soft murmuring silhouettes in the dark park. Child of demon lover, I grappled with ancestral ghosts. It was Smokey Robinson's summer, the hip falsetto, the long lean lover.[34]

Neal combines the urban soundscape of Harlem with the floating, ephemeral, yet profound image of Malcolm X as a way of charting the political dimensions of the sensory moving through the fractured time of memory. The sound Neal builds through the poem is both phonic, in the flow and rhythm its sound generates, and conceptual, through Neal's nonlinear, multidimensional interweaving of images and ideas that fuse the personal and political. Neal's movement between these orientations reveals the ways in which the ideological and political value of black cultural production is embedded within the method of its expressive practices more than it is reflective of distinct, transcendent meaning.

The Acoustic Spatiality of Black Consciousness

Neal's fashioning of sound as a conduit between literary form and ideological content is intriguingly presented in his 1970 essay "New Space/The

Growth of Black Consciousness in the Sixties," included in *The Black Seventies*, a collection of essays commissioned by Floyd Barbour to examine black historical and political transitions during the progression of the 1960s into the 1970s. The logic and architecture of Barbour's anthology in many ways parallels Neal's inclination to use sound as a mode of inquiry into the shifting realities of black culture. This point of comparison emerges as Barbour, in the foreword to the anthology, explains his desire for the collection to explore relationships between the interiority of identity construction and the broader movements and trajectories of historical and political processes. Recalling his contemplation of the shape and purpose of the anthology as he expresses it in a letter to his close friend, the art historian and critic Henry Martin, Barbour points out the convergence between his vision of the anthology and the way that Federico Fellini's work interrogates the "mean and meaningful ways of the past . . . because he knows that all experience is ultimately about the human experience." Barbour points to this approach as one that allows a sense of political power through investment in the "open spaces" of narrative, rather than "rhetoric or Afro or militant stance." Barbour desires to bring together work that focuses on the deeper relationships between historical consciousness, cultural identity, and political struggle, writing that, like the films of Fellini, he "doesn't leave out the bits in order to justify a present mood."[35]

Barbour's conceptual concerns anticipate the directions of Neal's lead essay in the volume and his consideration of the sensory and political elements underlining the inchoate, yet fundamental character of black consciousness. Although Neal's essay does not overtly focus on sonic culture in the way other essays of his do, his inquiry into the substance of black consciousness is entangled within the sensory and experiential continuum he establishes as broadly moving between black expressive and political culture. This continuum, or what he refers to as an "ethos," marks the expansive sense of possibility within formations of black cultural and political life. He explains: "All the major activities that were directed towards the question of liberation and Black Power spring from an ethos, a group spirit . . . somewhere in the maw of this ethos which continuously manifests itself, are the techniques and means of our liberation . . . what we should be about is a meaningful *synthesis* of the best that our struggles have taught us. This is a more difficult task than feeling secure in our own particular, and often narrow endeavors. What we need above all, is a widening of our perceptions."[36] Neal's mapping of historical memory and its relationship to political action is the central task of his complex and at times wandering work as it revolves around his attempt to rethink the possibility for radical struggle in the face and wake of historical rupture; in this case, a chasm opened up between the assassination of Malcolm X and Neal's subsequent critical reflections on witnessing the event. His essay explores the temporal and spatial dimensions of black aesthetics as they emerge through particular historical moments and become reshaped within narrative spaces. The "new space" that Neal wishes to chart through his essay is a conceptual and multi-dimensional expanse of black radical possibility that Neal shapes through his fusion of phenomenological experience, literary aesthetics, and lived political experience.

Neal's exploration of these historical and political questions represents a critical countertradition within studies of the Black Power era, as he resists the inclination to uphold black consciousness as a stagnant, monolithic force. By recognizing the historical and temporal fluidity that sound comprises within black cultural and political expression, Neal offers a wide angle on the forces producing "all of the necessary but conflicting strands of African-American nationalism."[37] Sound, in this context, represents an alternate modality through which Neal constantly manipulates and refashions the relationship between expression and political struggle. His use of sound to articulate a critical, expansive, and nonlinear sense of historical consciousness reflects certain theoretical qualities suggested by literary theorist Raymond Williams in his rejection of fixed forms as determinate models of social and political analysis, in favor of the emergent capacity of "structures of feeling" to locate historical memory, lived experience, and cultural production within a temporally dynamic context of lived, relational perceptions and meanings. For Williams, these expressive and ideological preconditions to political formation are reflected in the shifting, unstable, and in-process interactions between imaginary, sensory, and material experience:

> We are talking about characteristic elements of impulse, restraint, and tone; specifically affective elements of consciousness and relationships: not feeling against thought, but thought as felt and feeling as thought: practical consciousness of a present kind, in a living and interrelating continuity. We are then defining these elements as a "structure": as a set, with specific internal relations, at once interlocking and in tension. Yet we are also defining a social experience which is still in *process*, often indeed not yet recognized

as social but taken to be private, idiosyncratic, and even isolating, but which in analysis (though rarely otherwise) has its emergent, connecting, and dominant characteristics, indeed its specific hierarchies. *These are often more recognizable at a later stage, when they have been (as often happens) formalized, classified, and in many cases built into institutions and formations. By that time the case is different; a new structure of feeling will usually already have begun to form, in the true social present.*[38]

The fluid, in-process nature of these structures, their existence before determinate recognition and categorization, underlines Neal's analysis of black cultural nationalism as a starting point for thinking through the breadth, rather than the monolithic character of formations of black consciousness and the creation of black aesthetics. Neal's writing bridges the critical and creative through his attention to the convergence between historical and dramatic narration within the formal structure of his essay. In the early stages Neal demonstrates this quality of expressive attunement to political analysis through the following rumination on the felt experience and critical meaning of an expanded notion of black consciousness:

> It was a squeeze really. Sometimes, in some places, it looked like we weren't gonna make it. But we squeezed through, just like we have been squeezing through for decades. Only this time there was a little more light at the end of the tunnel . . . The benevolent demon imprisoned within us broke loose and manifested itself collectively and with obvious effects everywhere throughout the country . . . One thing is clear, though. As we move into the seventies, many of the things that concerned us in the early sixties are no longer as important as we once thought they were.

Neal begins with an assumption of familiar conversation with the reader shaped by the very first sentence, sounding as if he is continuing an ongoing dialogue rather than initiating a formal essay. Inviting the reader into the narrative through a tonal familiarity and informality, Neal's framing of the squeeze allows for a vernacular, signifying reconceptualization of historical space and time. The new space is what is squeezed through and into, and the squeeze is the crucial form of historical movement itself. Neal's alternation between verb and noun senses suggests a double inscription of birth and renewal, both in squeezing through the contracting canals of history, and in unveiling the "benevolent demon" symbolizing the "Black Spirit" in search of self-determination. For Neal, this historical squeeze both reflects and refuses a seductively linear model of history, for even as it becomes clear that "the simple acquisition of those rights which abstractly belong to all citizens of the United States would in no fundamental manner alter the oppressive situation in which we found ourselves," Neal suggests that the integrationist tactics of the Civil Rights movement represent a necessary stage within a broader, "conglomerate will towards black liberation." He points to the need to recognize and hold onto the recurring and mutable techniques of liberation emerging from the "maw" of the group ethos, instead of "falling into one bag" (i.e., getting seduced by short-term goals) and re-inscribing the struggle within limited definitions of political and cultural identity. This feeling arises from a conviction that "black consciousness is necessary and good only if it allows more light, more understanding of the complex struggle in which we find ourselves."[39] Neal's examples of this productive understanding of history and political struggle are framed at different moments in the essay through an active present that hinges on evocations of particular sounds and senses enlivening the movement of the narration.

This sensibility emerges as the narrative at once narrows and ultimately dilates through his vivid memories of witnessing Malcolm X's assassination at the Audubon Ballroom in February 1965. The narration of the event is punctuated by Neal's striking attention to details, such as the foreboding absence of policemen and basic security measures at the ballroom, the abundance of children at the meeting, women with their heads wrapped, and the introductory speech on liberation movements in Africa, Asia, and Latin America given by Benjamin X. Neal then directs the narration to a more unsettling level as he recalls the particular temporal and spatial details marking the assassination as a distinct event situated in the continual present of the event Neal (re)imagines. He recalls the introduction of Malcolm X to the audience, the exchange of greetings between Malcolm X and the crowd, followed by Neal's stage directions to the readers, asking us to "count about ten beats, after the sound of the response dies down." The distillation of beats rather than seconds and Neal's ability to capture the in-process quality of experiential and historical knowledge formation spiraling outward from the resonance of the event demands a focus on the aural qualities of Neal's description:

An obvious commotion had started down in the front rows.
Malcolm was standing at a podium. He stepped from behind the
podium to quiet the commotion. He said something like, "Peace,
be cool brothers." *Then it came. The strongest possible message, direct.
The shots came rapid fire. Malcolm fell back, his arms flung outward
like wings from the impact of the bullets hitting him square in the chest.
Then there was the rumbling of scuffling feet, and chairs were overturned. After it happened there seemed to be a pause, then the fear was
everywhere. People scrambled for cover on the floor under the tables in
the back shouting. Screams came from the women and children. It
seemed like shots were coming from all over the ballroom* (a smoke
bomb in the rear, found later, didn't go off). Security guards were
trying to reach Malcolm, trying to stop the assassins who now
were safely escaping in the confusion. Ahada's daughter bolted out
of the seat beside us. Ahada managed to catch the child before she
could be trampled by the mob. A gunman ran by us, shooting and
hurdling over chairs in his way. He twisted and turned, and fired at
a knot of black men chasing him. The man was still firing as he ran
out of the door toward the 165th Street entrance. He was being
chased by several of Malcolm's men. They caught him at the top of
the steps, and he was wounded in the thigh. Another assassin left
by the side door, waving his gun, daring anyone to follow him. *The
whole room was a wailing woman. Men cried openly.*[40]

Through a careful detailing of the sounds emerging from the moment, Neal
weaves together the immediate sensory details of the event with its broader
ramifications and the extended reverberations of black historical and political chaos. A sense of fear is captured not only as emanating from the surreal
quality of undisguised black assassins delivering "the strongest possible message" of gunfire upon Malcolm X and running out of the ballroom in full
view of the crowd, but also through the resonance of historical despair
reflected in Neal's concluding sound-images of the scene: "The whole room
was a wailing woman. Men cried openly." The wails and cries reflect a collective reaction to the moment of political assassination alongside Neal's
understanding of the ability of the materiality and resonance of the sound
to convey the jagged, multiple sensibilities of loss, hope, resistance, and rage.
His focus on the wails provides a point of transition between the complexity
of the moment of Malcolm X's death to the movement, and the possibility

of translating this sentiment from the political arena to the cultural production of sonic forces occurring in the "New Music" of the time.

The articulatory force of this contingent, fluid, dynamic connectivity marks the bridging of innovative musical sound and black political consciousness that Neal outlines in a separate reflection on his 1964 encounter with the New Music of Albert Ayler in a loft at 27 Cooper Square: "Albert's music was revolutionary to us because it appeared to replicate the kind of intense attitudes we were developing towards our social and political identities . . . The complexity and cultural integrity of the new music sparked in some of us visions of alternative aesthetic and social realities. We identified the music as the consummate expression of the emerging cultural consciousness. Thus, we began to extend the "ideas" embodied in the music to the real world itself." A fusion of artistic and political meaning is generated through a convergence between music, "cultural integrity," and "alternative aesthetic and social realities." In Neal's conceptualization, sound is both vernacular in its folk manifestations and modern in its non-matrixed ability to reach forward, fulfilling "our desire for a modernist art that was rooted in the Afro-American cultural tradition."[41] His engagement with sound as a form of critical resistance offers a vision of cultural nationalism that troubles the presumptions of monolithic blackness within a framework of cultural nationalism.

Neal's bridging of the aural and ideological flexibility emerging between the innovative sounds reverberating throughout black expressive forms, and the historical terrain of post-1965 black political life, continues to be elaborated in his essay "New Space: Reactionary and Revolutionary Positions." A draft of a chapter to be included in his unfinished manuscript of essays on black culture and politics, tentatively titled "New Space," this essay extends Neal's contention that the contemporary Black Arts Movement has become ideologically defined by a "negative principle" at work in the emergence and rearticulation of black cultural nationalist thought that constructs the political through sedimented formations of African tradition imagined as distinct from the quotidian, more historically and experientially grounded rhythms of African American life. Neal calls his sense of a more desirable, less ideologically overdetermined basis for cultural nationalism a "tonal range": "More in line with the dictionary definition, we would have to agree that there is manifested in Afro-American culture an identifiable sensibility or tone. This tone may have its derivation in African modalities, but that ethos is constantly being shaped on the basis of the contemporary social environment with all of its technological implications. It is therefore in its operational characteristics different from its implicit African derivation. That does not make it inferior to the original from which it sprang, but it does make a different, subtle hybrid perhaps. Everyone knows this."[42] Truth, heard as tonal sound, functions as complementary to tradition because it begins to capture the fluidity that runs through a history of struggle against social control. Rather than rejecting claims to the utopian and inchoate, this line of thinking presented by Neal provides a way of rediscovering the diasporic and mythic traces of lived history as active presences in the concrete struggles of the present.

Neal imagines sound in his essay "New Space" through both conceptual and aesthetic registers. Sound allows Neal to situate the vernacular and ritualistic aspects of black culture in relationship to the complexity of political struggle and representation during the Black Arts Movement. Writing in response to Hoyt Fuller's 1968 Black World survey of contemporary black writers, "Black Writers' Views on Literary Lions and Values," Neal argues that black writing must emerge from and speak to a capacious, multidimensional base of folk experience and style. Neal expresses the contours of this orientation toward the creative realm by detailing the relationship between sound, experimentation, and ritualistic energy, found, for instance, in "the word-magic of James Brown, Wilson Pickett, Stevie Wonder, Sam Cooke, and Aretha Franklin." Neal asks, "Have you ever heard a black poet scream like James Brown?" and contends, "I mean, we should want to have that kind of energy in our work." On the subject of this dynamic sonic energy, he continues, "The kind of energy that informs the music of John Coltrane, Cecil Taylor, Albert Ayler, and Sun Ra—the modern equivalent of ancient ritual energy. An energy that demands to be heard, and which no one can ignore. Energy to shake us out of our lethargy and free our bodies and minds, opening us to unrealized possibilities." Through this characterization of sonic energy, Neal suggests a trajectory of folk ritual practice exemplified by the innovative sounds of Coltrane, Taylor, Ayler, and Sun Ra. Neal understands this energy not in terms of its stated political aims, but rather as it is felt through its affective qualities. Just as black artists should not be politically determined by "a matter of whether we write protest literature or not," it is crucial to recognize (for instance) the political possibility found in James Brown's vocal presence.[43] Neal maps black consciousness and cultural expression outside already recognized formal structures and into the raw expressive, critical emergence marked by the sensorium of lived experiences (how it is that historical experience gives rise to and demands articulations that might not be immediately recognizable as such). The ritualistic for Neal is an ephemeral yet foundational energy; in his words, it is "the only thing which is fundamental to good art." Its function, he explains, "is to reinforce the group's operable myths, ideals, and values" as "the energy released in the ritual act helps to clarify the mysteries of human existence."[44] Like his conceptualization of the blues, Neal's sense of the ritualistic is profound, yet difficult to neatly encapsulate in a definition. It is through the elusiveness of the concept, however, that Neal theorizes black aesthetics as expressions that delineate possibilities for cohesion out of asymmetry. Stuart Hall uses the term "articulation" to define this productive sense of difference. He explains that "an articulation is thus the form of a connection that *can* make a unity of two different elements, under certain conditions," rather than being fixed as "necessarily determined, absolute and essential for all time."[45] The articulatory aspects of black aesthetic innovation that Neal understands as central to ritualistic sonic energy open rather than foreclose the possibility for racial representation and resistance. The theoretical basis of Neal's position is underlined in Hall's explanation that articulation "enables us to think how an ideology empowers people, enabling them to begin to make some sense or intelligibility of their historical situation, without reducing those forms of intelligibility to their socio-economic or class location or social position."[46] Neal's idea of black aesthetics resists and critiques the tendency to reductively define art as a direct, over-determined reflection of black revolution.

These positions are debated in a critical dialogue between James Cunningham and Maulana (Ron) Karenga in the same issue of *Black World* that features Neal's ideas on the aesthetic relevance of ritual, energy, and sound. Without rehearsing the exchange between Cunningham and Karenga in its entirety, it is instructive to note Karenga's declarations that "art must reflect and support the Black Revolution . . . any art that does not discuss and contribute to the revolution is invalid . . . no matter how many sounds are boxed in or blown out and called music," and his subsequent claim that therefore "the blues are invalid; for they teach resignation, in a word acceptance of reality—and we have come to change reality."[47] His perspectives propose a hegemonic center to the Black Arts Movement that Cunningham critiques as ignoring the inherent diversity, dynamism, and push toward transformation already underwritten within the conditions of black artistic production. Karenga's systematized enforcing of black artistic revolutionary principles, for Cunningham, amounts to "a perfect paternalistic formula and framework for black slavery and black suicide."[48] His corrective to Karenga's programmatic ideas redirects the focus of black aesthetic inquiry toward the contingencies of the ritualistic and the possibility of a spiritual–political communion through art that Neal is invested in contemplating in his response to Hoyt Fuller. There is a continuum for Neal that bridges the ineffable nature of black sound with the ability to project political meaning from aesthetic transcendence, pushing black art outside the constricted orthodoxy of protest literature in which, as Cunningham notes, the paternalistic assumption is that "the people we are talking to do not understand the nature of their condition,"[49] into the more flexibly pluralistic notion that "the Black writer should listen first to Black people, all kinds, all classes. The initial references that inform our work should be from Black culture. It is important that the writer first understand the history of his people and the forces which produced him, that he listen to the songs and music which his culture has produced."[50] Sonic expression embodies the disruptive, collective, transcendent force that Neal feels can be gleaned from the rhythms, styles, historical memory, and quotidian experience emerging from the plurality of voices and perspectives constituting African American subjectivity.

Neal's imagining of sound as a critical opening into the political viability of black art's aesthetic complexity and openness is not only crucial for rethinking the theoretical horizons of the Black Arts Movement; his ideas also offer a bridge toward the future of black literary and cultural studies. Neal's nuanced perspective on black aesthetics from within the Black Arts Movement, outward and forward toward its correspondence with perspectives within African American literary theory offered decades later, anticipates, for instance, Barbara Christian's critical inclination against a wholesale adaptation of Eurocentric philosophy as foundational to the field in her 1987 essay "The Race for Theory." Christian, like Neal, understands the need to question the specter of Eurocentrism reflexively, so that in searching for models of artistic practice and thought that project the autonomy of black expression, one does not blindly internalize the negative aspects of Eurocentric identity politics, what Christian notes as "prescriptive" and "monologic" approaches to critical inquiry within emergent forms of black cultural nationalism. Christian speaks of her wariness of those thinkers who become seduced by broader frameworks of progress and artistic achievement, and "rather than wanting to change the whole model . . . want to be all the center." Christian specifically cites her encounters with the largely masculine

framework of the Black Arts Movement as a crucial impetus for her to propose ways of recognizing the possibilities for African American theoretical
production as an often internally generated phenomenon rather than one
imposed on the literature from an externally produced critical perspective.
Indeed, it is striking, while not entirely surprising, that Christian simultaneously critiques the Black Arts Movement as a hegemonic structure, while
articulating a critical position that resonates so strongly with writers of the
movement such as Neal, Cunningham, and Fabio. Clearly, Christian's focus
is on gender, but her position also reflects a broader tendency in African
American literary criticism to frame the Black Arts Movement through
singular rather than multidimensional frameworks. While Larry Neal may
not present a consistently outspoken counterweight to Black Arts Movement patriarchy, he is clearly invested in highlighting the levels of aesthetic
and political complexity that Christian generally finds lacking in the movement's history. Both Christian and Neal cite ritual and energy as the sublime aspects of black aesthetics that might connect aesthetics and politics
within formations of black consciousness. Christian sees the unharnessed
potential of black expression through the "hieroglyphic" force and form of
"a written figure that is both sensual and abstract, both beautiful and communicative."[51] Her framing of the hieroglyphic as an inchoate level of black
expressive culture is coded with meaning but not bound by categorization,
exemplifying the dynamic potential of Neal's orientation. Neal constructs
a fluid field of references that constantly works toward expansions of black
consciousness along a full range of lived circumstances and black experiential possibilities instead of a reduced, distilled, or frozen encapsulation that
might be more linearly offered as an unnuanced truth. Through the articulation of sound, Neal refashions racial autonomy and self-determination
as strategic, flexible hinges, rather than stagnant positions, which enable
deeper contemplations of ongoing revolutionary transformation, the simultaneity of its past, present, and futurity, through the sonorous fluidity of
black expressive culture. In the coming chapters, I will show how this charge
of Neal's is engaged with and expanded on in the writings of Toni Cade
Bambara and James Baldwin as they work to acoustically further the critical dimensions of black aesthetics and black critical thought.

CHAPTER 4

Sonic Futurity in Toni Cade Bambara's
The Salt Eaters

Temporal Rupture

In the course of independent filmmaker Louis Massiah's 1995 interview with African American writer, cultural worker, and political activist Toni Cade Bambara, he asks Bambara how and where she learned her first political lessons. She responds by sharing her memories of coming of age amid the cultural vibrancy of Harlem, and then focuses her thoughts more precisely on the lasting impact of Speakers' Corner:

> So Speakers' Corner made it easy to raise critical questions, to be concerned about what's happening locally and internationally. It shaped the political perceptions of at least three generations. It certainly shaped mine, and I miss it today. There is no Speakers' Corner where I live. There is no outdoor forum where people can not only learn the word, hear information, hear perspective, but also learn how to present information: which is also what I learned on Speakers' Corner: how to speak and leave spaces to let people in so that you get a call-and-response. You also learn how to speak outdoors, which is no small feat. You also have to learn how to not be on paper, to not have anything between you and the community that names you. So I learned a great many things and I am still grounded in orality, in call-and-response devices.[1]

Bambara's attunement to the sonic texture of Speakers' Corner is compelling in its own right, but I would like to use her recollections to begin framing several interconnected formal innovations that mark the political possibilities she pursues within her novelistic reflection on the post–Civil Rights era, *The Salt Eaters*. Bambara's response to Massiah's question reveals her attention to sound as a hinge connecting aesthetics and politics. Furthermore, her focus on the projection and communal circulation of speech on

Speakers' Corner, and to the resonance of black sound through time and space, suggests a framework for understanding her organic vision of black political culture as it is reflected within the temporal and spatial dimensions of her narrative form. Bambara's attention to the novel as a site of imaginative political analysis signals a tradition of black utopian and surrealist thought through which notions of tradition and improvisation might be perpetually expanded.[2] Her attention to the acoustic dimensions of narrative form as a means of merging aesthetics and politics place her in dialogue with Black Arts Movement writers such as Henry Dumas and Larry Neal. Although she is not considered to have been a part of the Black Arts Movement, Bambara was actively writing during the period, and her editing of the black feminist anthology *The Black Woman* (1970), during the height of the movement, suggests her central role in charting new directions in black feminist thought that are critical but not simply antagonistic in their relationships to the Black Arts and Black Power movements. For Bambara, the openness and possibility offered through the ephemeral nature of sound becomes a viable narrative tool that can simultaneously fulfill the Black Arts Movement's call for artistic expression that critically resists white supremacy, and can also reflexively map critiques of tendencies within that tradition of resistance that may rearticulate domination through patriarchal constructs.

Bambara expresses her commitment to using art as a tool of political critique by pointing out the limits of forms that claim to be universal yet offer a delimited vision of experience. In an interview with Black Arts Movement writer and critic Kalamu ya Salaam, published shortly after the publication of *The Salt Eaters*, Bambara explains how the creation of new narrative idioms reflects her understanding of historical struggle and transformation. In her response to a question from Salaam regarding her search for an alternative language through writing, she states:

> I think there have been a lot of things going on in the Black
> experience for which there are no terms, certainly not in English,
> at this moment. There are a lot of aspects of consciousness for
> which there is no vocabulary, no structure in the English language
> which would allow people to validate that experience through
> language . . . I do know that the English language that grew from
> the European languages has been systematically stripped of the
> kinds of structures and the kinds of vocabularies that allow people
> to plug into other kinds of intelligences. That's no secret. That's

part of their whole history, wherein people cannot be a higher sovereign than the state . . . I'm just trying to tell the truth, and I think in order to do that we will have to invent, in addition to new forms, new modes and new idioms. I think we will have to connect to language in that kind of way. I don't know yet what it is.[3]

Bambara speaks of silencing the unknown and often untranslatable elements of social life, and suggests the need to resist this silence through approaches to formal and idiomatic innovation. The importance of the subtle distinction she introduces between matters of form and idiom helps outline the notion of idiom as an expression of connection, diffusion, and reception. For Bambara, the political potential of idiomatic expression emerges through the exchange between the contextual elements of artistic production and the utility of its aesthetic features. This dynamic becomes a central narrative concern throughout Bambara's oeuvre, and sound presents precise experimental possibilities within *The Salt Eaters* by opening the formal and theoretical space to create outside of already established paradigms of the political imagination, or, to borrow Bambara's own phrasing, to construct a vision of political engagement "from scratch." She elaborates on this phrasing and its political weight in the conclusion to her 1970 essay "On the Issue of Roles":

> Revolution begins with the self, in the self. The individual, the basic revolutionary unit, must be purged of poison and lies that assault the ego and threaten the heart, that hazard the next larger unit—the couple or pair, that jeopardize the still larger unit—the family or cell, that put the entire movement in peril. We make many false starts because we have been programmed to depend on white models or white interpretations of non-white models, so we don't even ask the correct questions, much less begin to move in a correct direction. Perhaps we need to face the terrifying and overwhelming possibility that there are no models, that we shall have to create from scratch.[4]

In her effort to reimagine struggle Bambara designs a series of textual possibilities in and outside of recognizable temporality that are projected through her experimental deployment of sound and text. Bambara's aural reconfiguration of narrative form attends to the aesthetic processes of black radical politics outside the finished events that have been historically represented as discrete and recognizable "movements."[5]

Bambara's strategy of imagining sound as an opening for radical critique emerges alongside traditions of experimentation in black music that evolved throughout the 1960s and 1970s. Her creation of literary sound to critically reflect on the Civil Rights and Black Power historical moments, builds on the aesthetic tendency toward rupture within the musical innovations of the period. Bambara's experimental canvas of sound presents a challenge to the hegemonic regulation and reproduction of prescribed social identities being constructed through the achievements and failures of social transformation during this era.[6] Avant-garde alto saxophonist and ethnomusicologist Marion Brown, whose statements I have previously noted in this book, outlines the importance of rupture within black experimental sound by explaining the relationship between sonic awareness and free jazz improvisation. Citing the work of free jazz musician Ornette Coleman, Brown explains:

> Ornette Coleman took the art of improvisation further. Beginning where Parker left off, he showed how improvisation could be natural, and flow freely without having fixed points in space (harmony and melody), or fixed points in time (rhythm). When his music was heard for the first time, it was thought to be the end of jazz. No one liked or understood it except for those involved. When they heard everyone improvising collectively, they thought, "Chaos!" Perhaps they had forgotten (if they ever knew) that collective improvisation had been the basis of New Orleans Jazz, and that collectively is a manifestation of community.[7]

Brown's comments probe the boundaries of black experimentation. He uses the label "Chaos" to signify a level of energy that seems unrecognizable in its dissonance, yet is clearly expanding on long-standing relationships between ideas of tradition and rupture within black expressive culture. Echoing Amiri Baraka in his landmark essay "The Changing Same (R&B and the New Black Music)," Brown situates improvisation within a longer trajectory of black expressive culture, connecting the sonic impulse of free jazz to the sounds of tradition marking early New Orleans jazz. Brown describes the chaos that emerges through sound not merely as aural expression, but as a critical orientation that reflects a simultaneous commitment to cultural tradition and to the expansion of its aesthetic sensibilities.

Brown's analysis of sound as both rupture and suture, considered in concert with Bambara's post-1960s narrative construction of *The Salt Eaters*
positions the sonic as both a compositional field and a philosophical window into the nature of post–Civil Rights era black historical consciousness. Bambara, through her representations of black political culture and
collective memory, represents history and temporality as both elongated
and compressed. Her literary experimentation with sound creates representations of political resistance that encourage readers to linger within
the contingent moments of black history and politics. Representing contingency as a compositional space created in order to frame what may or
could happen, be it unforeseen or preconditioned, Bambara formally engages
with what postcolonial theorist Achille Mbembe, in attempting to complicate notions of temporality beyond simply the pre- and postcolonial, has
termed a "time of entanglement," or a nonlinear interlocking of, "presents,
pasts, and futures that retain their depths of other presents, pasts, and futures,
each age bearing, altering, and maintaining the previous ones."[8] Thus the
idea of the crossroads (which we will later see directly worked through by
Bambara in a particular scene of the novel) becomes theoretically rich as
an intersection between literary and philosophical approaches to the contours of time and history. I move between Mbembe and Bambara here to
underscore how Bambara's focus on the inner workings of textual aesthetics challenges simplified versions of late capitalist racial state formation.
Indeed, her fictional and nonfictional work, as a committed black interna-
tionalist and radical thinker, speaks to the need to absorb the complexity of
political, social, and racial formations. In this sense, much like Mbembe's
questioning of social theory's inability to "account for *time as* lived, not syn-
chronically or diachronically, but in its multiplicity and simultaneities . . .
beyond the lazy categories of permanence and change beloved by so many
historians"; and his more general questioning of linearity as a powerful but
perhaps deceptive "validation of conscious existence," Bambara's sonic expo-
sition of political life demonstrates that although historical moments may
have temporal distinction, the process of history moves and builds on itself
across time through the relative silencing of moments that destabilize traditional assumptions of subjectivity and consciousness.[9] Working within
this terrain of insurgent social theory, Bambara considers the potential of
late twentieth-century racial subjectivity to embrace the seeming chaos of
multiplicity and interconnection, not as an erosion of particular identities
and locations, but rather as a crucial starting point for the realization of the

political complexity within these racial formations. Her articulation of literary sound in *The Salt Eaters* bridges aesthetic form and political commitment in order to reimagine the years of the Civil Rights movement and its immediate wake outside of preestablished structures of bodily and sensory memory.

Acoustic Recovery

In the opening scene of *The Salt Eaters*, Bambara locates sound as a sensory framework for narrating the quotidian and inchoate aspects of struggle through the consciousness of the central character, Velma Henry. Velma, heavily burdened by her memories of the movements of the 1960s, sits in a catatonic state after attempting to take her own life, while Minnie Ransom, a widely respected local healer in the small southern city of Claybourne, faces her "humming lazily up and down the scales . . . spinning out a song . . . running its own course up under the words, up under Velma's hospital gown, notes pressing against her skin," even as Velma is "steeling herself against intrusion." Bambara positions sound as a force of confrontation and evasion moving between Velma and the healing powers of Minnie, as Velma is wary of Minnie striking "the very note that could shatter [her] bones." She wants to "resist the buzzing bee tune," "withdraw the self to a safe place," and, in a reclamation of her youth, "prop up a borderguard to negotiate with would-be intruders."[10] The opening scene clearly dispels any notion of the sonic as a straightforward pathway toward radical transformation. Bambara instead situates Velma's relationship to sound as reflective of a tension between Velma's wariness of the potential deception of appearances and the possibility of realizing deeper phenomenological modes of awareness and critique that suggest truth beyond the visual.

In the early moments of the healing, Bambara describes Minnie, "cupping gently the two stony portions of [Velma's] temporal bone," and through this description portrays memory through the specific bodily sites of aurality, in this case through the proximity and interaction of sound, mental imagery, and the body created through vibrations of bone.[11] Velma ponders her situation during the healing session and begins to place this tension in sharper relief, as her internal voicing relays, "The eyes and habits of illusion. Retinal images, bogus images, traveling to the brain. The pupils trying to tell the truth to the inner eye. The eye of the heart. The eye of the head. The eye of the mind. All seeing differently."[12] Velma's ambivalence regarding the possibility of truth emerging from the visual highlights Bambara's perspective on the stagnation of black political movements in the later years of the 1970s due to a lack of focus on the most pressing, but often overlooked aspects of social movements. Bambara sketches this atmosphere of black political defeat as an entanglement of conditions and forces, including the lack of any clear agenda to transform the state through sustained political engagement, the persistence of various forms of gender inequity within and outside of social movements, the menace of a rapidly growing nuclear industry, the depth of environmental toxification in black communities, global economic shifts that unduly affect local communities, and the continued destabilization of black movements for social justice through covert federal and state monitoring and violent repression. Indeed, part of what is at stake in the expanse of the novel is the degree to which Velma can move beyond her condition of catatonia, a personal state reflecting the broader stagnation of black struggle that largely defines the post-movement political climate.

This imbrication of the bodily, the visual, and the aural becomes a central modality through which the text operates. For example, when Velma considers a "telepathic visit with her former self" as she is poised on a stool, trying to open her eyes while they are rolling back in her head, attempting to respond to Minnie Ransom's call to "release, sweetheart. Give it all up. Forgive everyone everything. Free them. Free self," Bambara provides an extended elaboration on memory, song, and temporality as these elements mark Velma's disembodied contemplation of her attempt to take her own life:[13]

> She closed her eyes and they rolled back into her head, rolled back to the edge of the table in her kitchen, to the edge of the table in her kitchen, to the edge of the sheen—to cling there like globules of furniture oil, cling there over the drop, then hiding into the wood, cringing into the grain as the woman who was her moved from the sink to stove to countertop turning things on, turning the radio up. Opening drawers, opening things up. Her life line lying for an instant in the cradle of the scissors' X, the radio's song going on and on and no stop-notes as she leaned into the oven. The melody thickening as she was sucked into the carbon walls of the cave, then the song blending with the song of the gas.[13]

The eyes roll, literally through a continuum of body, space, and time, to end up "cringing into the grain" of the kitchen table, watching "the woman who was her" prepare to take her own life. Bambara clearly points out in this memory how Velma is relying on visual recognition and memory; first as Velma attempts to focus her eyes on Minnie, then as she channels herself back to the moment of putting her head in the gas oven. Song becomes a hinge fusing the sublime qualities of music with Velma's meditation on the terror and spectacle of death. The sensory represents a double-edged impulse in the novel: it marks the presence of temporally weighted personal reflections, and also suggests that the simultaneous seduction and paralysis felt acutely by Velma within these memories might be more broadly indicative of formations of post–Civil Rights black political culture.

The novel builds on these seemingly surrealistic interventions, moving between layers of the visual and the sonic as the kitchen memory is extended through an imagistic blend of telepathy and memory that highlights Velma's desire to both "be still" and to exist as light, outside of sound:

Looking at the glass jars thinking who-knew-what then, her mind taken over, thinking, now, that in the jars was no air, therefore no sound, for sound waves weren't all that self-sufficient, needed a material medium to transmit. But light waves need nothing to carry pictures in, to travel in, can go anywhere in the universe with their independent pictures. So there'd be things to see in the jars, were she in there sealed and unavailable to sounds, voices, cries. So she would be light. Would go back to her beginnings in the stars and be starlight, over and done with, but the flame traveling wherever it pleased. And the pictures would follow her, haunt her. Be vivid and sharp in a vacuum. To haunt her. Pictures, sounds, and bounce were everywhere, no matter what you did or where you went. Sound broke glass. Light could cut through even steel. There was no escaping the calling, the caves, the mud mothers, the others. No escape.

Velma's preference for an undisturbed interiority, a still existence contained within glass walls, a one-dimensional life awash in light without the possibility of political and material contingency, is confronted by sound's ability to break glass. Light becomes associated with an independent freedom, and sound with a lack of self-sufficiency. Yet it becomes evident to her that the two forces ultimately can't be divided, for "sound broke glass" and "light could cut through even steel," leading to a central tension being felt within the narrative—the fact that Velma wishes to become "unavailable at last" to all of that which has come to define much of her existence due to the highly organic nature of her intellectual and activist life: "To pour herself grain by grain by grain into the top globe and sift silently down into a heap in the bottom one. That was the sight she'd been on the hunt for. To lie coiled on the floor of the thing and then to bunch up with all her strength and push off from the bottom and squeeze through the waistline of the thing and tip time over for one last sandstorm and then be still, finally be still."[14] In this passage, Velma's removal from noise offers a vexing distillation of time that, on one hand, presents a direct, literal engagement with history, but also results in a stillness that avoids any sense of collective struggle emerging within her encounter with time and history. Velma's ambivalent relationship to sound reflects her wariness of its power to continue outlining the range of connections she feels have been exhausted in her life. Bambara locates sound, through its absence and through Velma's cautionary approach to it, as a way of understanding the complexity of sociopolitical forces that Velma is trying to escape from, resist, and set up a barrier against.

In her refusal of sound in favor of the stillness of death, Bambara is drawing specific attention to Velma's search for an embryonic language, an inchoate conception of radical change that begins to take shape through Minnie Ransom's close attention to the presence of sound during the healing. Bambara extends this aural dimension of the novel by fashioning relationships between the sounds emanating from the healing and the sounds defining moments of transformation in the text. Her weaving of a sonic tapestry of expressive moments emphasizes the nonlinear, multisensory composition of the political as it is constituted within Bambara's literary project. Sound operates on several levels in the narrative, not simply as the phonic matter that marks moments in the healing session, but as signposts in Velma's memory, and as a historical force helping to direct the characters toward various political possibilities.

Bambara marks the opening to the novel through her composition of alternating sensory and extrasensory duets between Velma and Minnie and between Velma and her godmother, Sophie Heywood. Bambara's narration of these duets establishes a formation of black feminist intergenerational collaboration that positions the experimental grounds of black feminist critique as a foundation within the interwoven narrative movement of the novel. Her literary expansion of black feminism works from the premise that critic Mae Henderson and others have conceptualized as the ability of black women's writing to artfully contain the multiplicity of perspective emerging at the nexus of race and gender through a "simultaneity of discourse."[15] Bambara's writing exemplifies Henderson's idea that black feminist literary representations give voice to the plurality within black women's subject positions, yet Bambara also references a broader, spiraling set of political contexts through the different connected experiences of characters that emerge through the memories of Velma, and through the proximity of various characters to her ongoing process of healing. Bambara's expansive narrative framework draws together a complex, interwoven field of memories, politics, and historical experiences through moments of sound that fluidly move between these shifting spaces, amplifying the specificity of black feminist critique as central to a post–Civil Rights context of emergent struggle.

The latter of the two duets opening the novel is central to Bambara's engagement with the convergence of sound, history, and narrative form, as Velma's refusal toward healing is critiqued by her godmother Sophie Heywood, a community activist and the coconvener of the local prayer circle known as the Master's Mind. When Sophie reflects on the scene in the infirmary, specifically Velma's resistance to recovery, she decides that Velma has become unrecognizable, she has "taken another form altogether," and Sophie leaves the treatment room to the protest of the rest of the Master's Mind. As Sophie exits, the space between her opening and closing the door is filled with "the high-pitch wail of birds overhead like whistling knives in the sky," and the buzzing of her temples, which opens onto her own memories of her son and Velma's former lover, Smitty, being crippled by the police as he attempts to blow up a Confederate statue in the town during a protest of the draft during the Vietnam War: "Smitty pulled down against the cement pedestal, slammed against the horses' hooves, dragged on his stomach to the van. A boot in the neck. Child. Four knees in his back. Son. The package ripped from his grip. The policeman racing on his own path and none other's. The man, the statue going up Pegasus. Manes, hooves, hinds, the brass head of some dead soldier and a limb of one once-live officer airborne over city hall. A flagpole buckling at the knees."[16] Bambara, through a staccato rhythm of immediate reportage, registers the deep personal and political weight of historical memory, ironically, in a modality which aesthetically echoes the snippet-like collage style of mainstream media sound bites that she signals at the beginning of Velma's orchestration of the memory through the image and sound of "a Black TV announcer misnumbering the crowd, mismatching the facts, lost to the community."[17] Yet Bambara's narration probes more deeply within that formal constraint, expanding it well beyond the limits of deception and misinformation on which the mainstream media often rely.

Bambara deftly remixes Sophie's memories of Smitty at the protest with her fragmented recollection of being beaten in a jail cell by fellow community activist Portland Edgers, who is forced to do so at police gunpoint (in a clear echo of Fannie Lou Hamer's 1963 beating in Winona, Mississippi, by the forced hands of black inmates). Through this collage of memories and thoughts, Bambara depicts Sophie Heywood comprehending state violence at an intensely felt and experiential level,[18] and registering her disappointment with Velma's restrictive focus on self, set against the sound of her closing the door when she leaves the treatment room, as "there was something in the click of it that made many of the old-timers, veterans of the incessant war—Garveyites, Southern Tenant Associates, trade unionists, Party members, Pan-Africanists—remembering night riders and day traitors and the cocking of guns, shudder."[19]

The political and historical quality of this click, the layered sense of warning drawing together the contemporary resistance and despair of Velma with the memories of elders gathered at the event, representing a broad trajectory of black struggle, continually echoes from this early formative moment in the text throughout the words, sounds, and images that move from the walls of the Southwest Community Infirmary to the bus approaching it, and through the presence and experiences of the cast of individuals helping to develop the soundscape of the text. The capaciousness of Bambara's textual sound reveals itself as the click enables the scriptural movement of time and space, pointing to the sound of Bambara's work as not only aural representation, but also as a narrative tool through its ability to signify on the connections between political ideas and historical experiences of varying density and ephemerality.

Rehearing History

Bambara configures the narrative expanse of *The Salt Eaters* into a political and historical soundscape that interrogates multiple dimensions of the Civil Rights movement and questions ideas of collective memory framing the

1960s and 1970s black public sphere. Historian Jacquelyn Dowd Hall explains the problematic nature of historical memory within conceptualizations of the Civil Rights era as follows: "Remembrance is always a form of forgetting, and the dominant narrative of the civil rights movement—distilled from history and memory, twisted by ideology and political contestation, and embedded in heritage tours, museums, public rituals, textbooks, and various artifacts of mass culture—distorts and suppresses as much as it reveals."[20] The tracks of memory, as Hall envisions them, enable a sedimentation of the political imagination by manufacturing versions of historical "truth" that obviate the complex, asynchronous nature of historical change. Bambara's intention to resist the flattening of historical memory through the imagination is also voiced by Elizabeth Alexander's thoughts on the relationship between what she refers to as the "black interior" and the possibility of "imagining the racial self unfettered, racialized but not delimited." Taking Alexander's cue to imagine black aesthetics as a creative opening offering possibilities for self-fashioning outside the external and internalized enforcement of what she terms "Negro authenticity," we can read Bambara's formal innovation as a way of accessing existence beyond "stereotypical black realism."[21] Bambara reaches past the expected and more easily recognizable sets of historical representations in order to expand the canvas of African American historical memory as more of a fractured collage than a series of linearly ordered, entirely realistic portraits. The fact that Bambara's experimentation very carefully details late 1970s intricacies of African American political economy is emphasized by a hinge-like quality operating across the temporal expanse of the text, ultimately bridging the 1960s era of political mobilization with the evolving social formations taking shape as the last quarter of the twentieth century unfolds.

The connections between Bambara's ideas of political transformation and her aesthetic practices are further elaborated in her essay "Reading the Signs, Empowering the Eye." In this critical overview of what she refers to as "the black independent cinema movement," she addresses the transformative goals of political art in a Third World, anti-imperialist context. Recalling the early 1970s efforts of black independent filmmakers to substantively break with dominant filmic conventions at the UCLA film school, she points out how these creative, political artists recognized cinema as a site of struggle: "[They were] engaged in interrogating conventions of dominant cinema, screening films of socially conscious cinema, and discussing ways to alter previous significations as they relate to Black people. In short, they were

committed to developing a film language to respectfully express cultural particularity and Black thought . . . Proponents of 'Third Cinema' around the
world were working then, as now, to advance a cinema that would prove
indigestible to the imperialist system that relentlessly promotes a consumer-
ist ethic."[22] Bambara's focus on aesthetic indigestibility as a critical foundation
for political art distinguishes her understanding of social transformation
outside more clearly recognizable theories of struggle and engagement, such
as Marxism, and, in this way, expands the constantly forming, transatlantic
body of thought that Cedric Robinson and others have conceptualized as
"the black radical tradition." Her perspective resonates with the views of
many surrealist writers and artists who emphasized the need to "deepen the
foundations of the real, to bring about an even clearer and at the same time
even more passionate consciousness of the world perceived by the senses."
André Breton, here drawing attention to the potential of the sensory to
elevate political consciousness, values the interactive and inter-animate
nature of surrealist thought and expression. Breton identifies the ability of
the sensory to question discrete barriers and definitions that mark mainstream configurations of reality, and "to avoid considering a system of
thought a refuge."[23] Surrealism, in its potential to approach political transformation through a unification of the interior and exterior dimensions
of reality, centers the aesthetic as crucial to fostering nonconformity and
disorder as the grounds for a new, enlivened sense of the real. The Mar-
tinician intellectual René Ménil, writing in the World War II–era literary
periodical *Tropiques*, builds on Breton's point, explaining that "the best
lessons about human behavior must be sought in aesthetics. It alone gives
mankind the images it deserves."[24] Ménil attests to the power of surrealist aesthetics as disruptions to the hegemonic containment of reality, and
Bambara's approach to expanding her literary aesthetics through sound
takes into account this crucial relationship between critical theories of
resistance and the texture of their deployment. The alternative sphere that
Bambara fashions through representations and ideas of sound within the
novel reflects her desire to create works of art that are, in her words, "indigestible to the imperialist system."

Bambara's narrative expansion through sound offers a formal means of
radically critiquing concepts of order and progress. Her critical perspective
extends into the thematic aspects of the text as she depicts the tensions
between alternative organizational structures and mainstream formations
of black politics. Bambara frames this dynamic through Velma's memory

as she recounts a meeting of grassroots community organizers, "a group that sometimes called itself a committee of this organization or a task force of that association or a support group of this cause or an auxiliary of that,"[25] including her sister Palma, and her godmother and elder activist, Sophie Heywood. The meeting has been called to decide if the group will support Jay Patterson, a figure clearly representing post-movement black political co-optation, in his bid for county commissioner. Velma's ambivalence regarding Patterson's candidacy gains traction as it becomes clear that he has been using Velma and the other black women organizers as workers to lay the groundwork for his campaign. Patterson attempts to take advantage of an un-formalized structure facilitating grassroots mobilization by enfolding the labor and support of the women activists within his self-serving mantle of black political leadership.

Bambara uses this window into the complexity of black political transition after the Civil Rights movement to focus on the gendered dynamics of retrenchment, cooptation, and black political hegemony. Through Velma's consciousness she points out that while the women organize the conferences, make travel arrangements, and complete large amounts of procedural duties and paperwork, they only see Patterson and his accomplices relishing in the limelight and "drinking at the bar." Velma's memories of these contentious moments are punctuated as Bambara freezes the narration on segments of Velma's speech signaling the independent position of the more radical, grassroots black women who term themselves "Women for Action," in opposition to the politically stagnant articulations of black masculinity captured by Bambara's impressionistic yet pointed questioning of the situation:

> Who's called in every time there's work to be done, coffee made, a program sold? Every time some miscellaneous nobody with a five-minute commitment and an opportunist's nose for a self-promoting break gets an idea, here we go. And we have yet to see any of you so much as roll up your sleeves to empty an ashtray. Everybody gets paid off but us. Do any of you have a grant for one of us? Any government contracts? Any no-work-all-pay posts at a college, those of you on boards? Is there ever any thing you all do on your own other than rent out the Italian restaurant on the Heights to discuss the Humphrey–Hawkins bill over wine?

Her questions build systematically to show how Patterson's political presence is connected to models of patriarchal leadership and middle-class comfort at tension with the idea of a grassroots movement. These dynamics are further highlighted when she remembers her earlier experiences during a physically taxing protest march to the state capital, and the sharp contrast between the smooth sounds and sleek appearance of the black "leader" who arrived on the scene with an entourage of limousines, and the intense fatigue and distressed state she and other activists were experiencing. Bambara narrates how the leader's arrival assaulted Velma's senses: "Exhausted, she was squinting through the dust and grit of her lashes when the limousines pulled up, eye-stinging shiny, black, sleek. And the door opened and the cool blue of the air-conditioned interior billowed out into the yellow and rust-red of the evening. Her throat was splintered wood. Then the shiny black boots stepping onto the parched grass, the knife-creased pants straightening taut, the jacket hanging straight, the blinding white shirt, the sky-blue tie." Velma's observation of the leader focuses on his manipulation of form as a strategy for accruing and maintaining power within the movement. She extends her reflections by pointing out how the leader is able to create a nonthreatening, palatable, mainstream avenue of resistance through his mastery of sound: "Some leader. He looked a bit like King, had a delivery similar to Malcolm's, dressed like Stokely, had glasses like Rap, but she'd never heard him say anything useful or offensive. But what a voice. And what a good press agent. And the people had bought him. What a disaster. But what a voice." Her analysis of the background to the leader's rise to prominence continues through Bambara's free indirect discourse, conveying the story of the literal creation of the leader by a cultural anthropologist who encounters him while engaging in ethnographic fieldwork, is struck by his voice, "and launched him into prominence."[26]

Velma's deeply critical awareness of these factors cannot, however, allay a sense of crisis that moves through the sounds and sensations of her memories. Bambara's mapping of Velma's memory in this early stage of the healing, moves between several sites: an awkward conversation in a diner booth between Velma and her husband, Obie, as their relationship is falling apart; the art gallery where Velma and Obie first meet while admiring a collage of Velma's sister Palma; the community meeting with Jay Patterson; the protest march to the state capital; and a hotel near a dilapidated tent city where Velma goes to make phone calls to assist the efforts of the suffering activists. Bambara impressionistically emphasizes these glimpses of possibility and defeat as she renders a memory occurring within her memory of the confrontational meeting over Patterson's candidacy, of journeying from the tent city to use a phone at the hotel where the leader is staying so that she might contact others to bring more support for the hungry, sick, and tired demonstrators dwelling in the tents. Bambara's interweaving of sound and memory creates a level of musicality in the prose—that is, a level of the sonic that operates compositionally in respect to expressionistic projections of sound that propel the recounting forward. Velma's voice creates this dynamic as she describes the state of the encampment: "The tents were collapsing, the bedrolls mildewed. The portable toilets had long since not worked. The children on errands in indescribable clothes and barefoot, red mud coming up between their toes like worms, and worms too. Many down with fevers. One doctor making rounds, stumbling with sleeplessness and impotence." As Velma attempts to use the telephone at the front desk of the hotel, she is physically drained and battered from the difficulty of living in the tent city, and can "barely stand up." Her body breaking down is contrasted with the "dulcet tones" of the aforementioned leader as he approaches the front desk with his coterie of "men without their sunglasses, hair glistening fresh from under stocking caps and fro cloths . . . the women clean and lean and shining, prancing like rodeo ponies . . . tossing their manes and whinnying down the corridors."[27] Velma tries to block out these images, but the mirror forces her to focus on the "red silk lounging pajamas and silver ice buckets and those women," until its stability is fractured by one of the men approaching her from behind, "crashing through the mirror to lift her, to drag her away, to hustle her out of the door." The shattered mirror not only serves as a fitting sign of breakdown and crisis brought about by this disjunctive vision of black political engagement amid luxury, excess, and removal from the masses; it also leads to Velma nearly having her neck broken by one of the leader's men as he physically removes her from the hotel. Recovering from the gravity of this confrontation, Velma finds that she cannot speak, for "the words got caught in the grind of her back teeth as she shred silk and canvas and paper and hair. The rip and shriek of silk prying her teeth apart. And it all came out a growling." The symbolic silk of the "Chinese pajamas" worn by the leader in the hotel is first referenced within the flow of Velma's memory earlier in the narrative thread when she and Obie converse in the diner. Bambara creates a chain of memory and political thought through this image and also bridges the entire section through the sound of Velma's growl that moves between her memory of the tent city, and the present of the novel, as Minnie Ransom welcomes the growling sound from Velma as a sign that she will indeed recover, thus bringing the sonority of past into the present as a transformative force of political critique and healing.[28]

Bambara's blending of sounds and images redefines the political as an act in process rather than simply a series of frozen moments. The nonlinear movement of images, ideas, and ultimately sounds reflects Velma's felt, lived experiences and her awareness of subjection moving between dimensions of race and gender. Reframing historical knowledge outside of linear narratives, and through the bodily and the sonic, allows Bambara to map critical thought as phenomenological and experiential. Instead of simply representing political co-optation, Bambara uses sound to create possibilities for black political expression that probe the interior spaces of inter- and intra-racial repression.

Acoustic Redress

As the healing progresses in the Southwest Community Infirmary, a parallel scene emerges in which the sonic dimensions of Bambara's compositional practice create space for the simultaneous consideration of seemingly disparate experiences, weaving the narration through the collective harmony and dissonance of various characters' memories. This aesthetic formalization of the sensory, enabled through the signification of actual sounds that mobilize memories, in turn provides windows into a range of political histories generated well outside of, yet in dialogue with, elements of political reflection and contingency framed by Velma's healing.

The scene in question is initiated as the middle-aged bus driver, Fred Holt, sits at a literal train crossing and the metaphorical crossroads in both his life and that of the novel, watching a "flock of birds in a low swoop over the train . . . sharply changing direction and heading back over the roadway as if pulled by an invisible hook," waiting for the train that is "taking its own sweet time" as he drives a busload of passengers to Claybourne. Listening to the women composing the Seven Sisters (a radical women of color political art troupe) discuss their plans for participating in the Claybourne Festival, he is brought into a series of thoughts and memories connected by interwoven referents, unleashed by the roar and whistle of the train. Initially, he expands on the presence of the whistle, bringing himself into a set of thoughts that recall elements of classic blues lyrics: "Hear that lonesome

whistle . . . riding the blinds . . . Please please mistuh brakeman, let a po' boy
ride yo' train . . . O the Rock Island Line is a mighty good . . . How long,
how long has the evening train been gone . . . I'm Alabamee bound." These
lyrics are given further weight when Holt refocuses on the visuals surrounding him and quickly begins to meditate on a group of hobos, "in tatters
huddled around a burning trash can . . . It could be the Depression again
he was thinking." This shift becomes an invitation for further historical
and political reflection as he provides a recounting of his childhood through
the Great Depression, specifically, how his family could only get enough to
eat due to his train worker uncle bringing "food from the dining cars wrapped
in napkins and stuffed in shoe boxes." A series of mental links between his
life and broader issues in black political economy continues and intensifies
as he bridges his memories of the Great Depression with the current conditions of inflation (which he characterizes as "the high price blues"), under-
development, and environmental destruction.[29]

Concurrently, another narrative line emerges that remixes the visual
destruction that Fred Holt is taking in within his present, against layered
visions of his own complex history. Bambara portrays this layering through
Holt's memory of his childhood home burning down due to some level of
his own complicity: "The fire this time and him leaning against the house
throwing up his insides. Trees like blazing giants with their hair aflame,
crashing down in the fields turning corn, grass, the earth black. Birds falling down out of the sky burnt and sooty like bedraggled crows. The furni-
ture blistering, crackling, like hog skins crackled on Grandaddy's birthday.
His mother dragging the mattress out sparkling and smoldering, beating it
with her slipper and the matting jumping like popcorn all over the front
yard. And her screaming at him as if she knew. And she probably did." The
blaze is unleashed in his memory, with Bambara perhaps referencing James
Baldwin's pivotal essay of the early 1960s, and also situating the importance of nausea as a reaction of Holt's that will be replayed on the bus, and
it might even suggest the specter of apocalypse. Holt extends this account
of destruction with that of the storied Pruitt–Igoe public housing project
where he later lived. He briefly depicts the aftermath of the high-rise build-
ings being blown up less than two decades after being erected, due to the
deteriorating social and physical conditions of the urban space: "And near
the crater that had been their home was the pit that had been the elevator
shaft down which he'd dropped Sen-Sen wrappers and matchbooks . . . And
down at the bottom of the shaft the other dumpage. Eleven dead bodies.

The rotted remains of bill collectors, drug dealers, wives, husbands, raped and missing girls of East St. Louis."[30] This horrific accounting of urban destruction, "renewal," violence, and loss, culminates first in Holt throwing up his lunch; a reaction that seems related to the unease he feels about wading through the memories that his senses have helped generate.[31] Then, as the bus is five minutes outside of Claybourne, Bambara describes the portentous moment following Holt telling the passengers they are approaching the town: "All conversation stopped. Mouths agape, gestures frozen, eyes locked on the driver's cap, or back, or Adam's apple, arrested, as if the announcement were extraordinary, of great import." Not only are movement and sound frozen at this point, a list is also created of where and whom the passengers could be instead, and leads to the sense that they also "might've been twenty-seven miles back in the moment of another time when Fred Holt did ram the bus through the railing and rode it into the marshes." As they are cast in this moment, "in the sinking bus trying to understand what had happened, was happening, would happen and stock still but for the straining for high thoughts to buoy them all up . . . sinking into the marshes thick with debris and intrusion," they in many ways come to symbolize the participation of helpless people in the construction of grand historical moments, not really understanding how clearly dire present situations have become. This surreal moment in the marshes flows back into the scene of healing in the Southwest Community Infirmary. All this movement and potential for existence within space and time, casts the experience as something ritualistic, a state of awareness and silent stasis being achieved by a small group, synthesized by Bambara as:

> a momentous event. But an event more massive and gripping than the spoken word or an accident. A sonic boom, a gross tampering of the weights, a shift off the axis, triggered perhaps by the diabolics at the controls, or by asteroids powerfully colliding. Earth spun off its pin, the quadrants slipping the leash, the rock plates sliding, the magnetic fields altered, and all, previously pinned to the crosses of the zodiac and lashed to the earth by the fixing laws, released. A change in the charge of the field so extreme that all things stop and are silent until the shift's complete and new radiations open the third eye.[32]

The phrasing of this particular moment is rich in its deployment of sound as an epistemological framework, starting with the fact that the sonic boom audibly marking the event is "more gripping than the spoken word," and concluding with the observation that "all things stop and are silent," before the "third eye" opens. The second to last phrase in this quote, "all things stop and are silent," alludes to how the absence of sound precedes the opening of the "third eye." If the third eye indeed signifies knowledge, wisdom, and understanding, then the period around its opening would most likely involve a deep awakening, possibly achieved through the recognition of sonic forms that precedes their categorization, within vocabularies of communal, ritualistic consciousness.

Meditations on the premusical sonic impulses of black creativity, what Nathaniel Mackey refers to elsewhere as an attempted recovery of a collective "phantom limb," are expressed by the musician JD, on his way home from prison. He links the political and spiritual awakening on board Fred Holt's bus to the sonic creativity and inspiration that has yet to be commodified in the formal vocabularies of jazz, blues, rap, or perhaps the general category of music: "His fingers splayed on the horn case, trying to connect with the music. A tune had caught him and held him in a moment when speech, movement, thought were not possible. *Something in an idiom that had to be attended to from the total interior, captured, defended.*"[33] This conception of sound as an unfettered force circulating around memory and experience becomes a framework for Velma's later thoughts regarding the sublime quality of the "terrible musicalness." Her memory details the underground life of a sonic virtuosity that creates resistance to racialized subjection out of a commitment to push the aesthetics of cultural expression beyond the knowable:

> She could dance right off the stool . . . her head thrown back and
> singing, cheering, celebrating those giants she had worshipped in
> their terrible musicalness. Giant teachers teaching through tone
> and courage and inventiveness but scorned, rebuked, beleaguered,
> trivialized, commercialized, copied, plundered, goofed on by
> half-upright pianos and droopy-drawers drums and horns too long
> in hock and spittin up rust and blood, tormented by sleazy bookers
> and takers, tone-deaf amateurs and saboteurs, underpaid and
> overworked and sideswiped by sidesaddle-riding groupies till they
> didn't know, didn't trust, wouldn't move on the wonderful gift
> given and were mute, crazy and beat-up. But standing up in their
> genius anyhow ready to speak the unpronounceable. On the stand

with no luggage and no maps and ready to go anywhere in the
universe together on just sheer holy boldness.[34]

This vision of the creative artist, harnessing the "tone and courage and
inventiveness . . . speak[ing] the unpronounceable . . . ready to go anywhere in the universe together on just sheer holy madness" proposes the
sonic as a realm through which resistance and innovation might be considered in their aesthetic and bodily registers. Velma's visions of the musicians, "those giants she had worshipped" in many ways mirror her own
trajectory as an underappreciated political organizer and artist (being a
pianist herself). As a political, aesthetic project, the ability to realize these
alternate possibilities for reflection and critique outside a linear narrative
of social movement and leadership presents a conjuncture between what
Velma, as a community worker, and Bambara, as a creative cultural worker,
are searching for.

Bambara presents an idea of musical sound here that bridges Velma's
perception of the visionary and transgressive qualities of black musicians
with Minnie Ransom's selections of jazz and blues played throughout the
healing session. As the healing builds toward its conclusion, the music ultimately becomes fused with the sounds outside the session, propelling Velma
through a kaleidoscope of psychic, imagistic, and phenomenological reflections on her political experience set within an asymmetrical continuum of
issues and individuals marking the social and political space of the town:
"The music drifted out over the trees toward the Infirmary, maqaam now
blending with the bebop of Minnie Ransom's tapes. Minnie's hand was
before her face miming 'talk, talk' graceful arcs from the wrist as though she
were spinning silk straight from her mouth. The music pressing against the
shawl draped round Velma, pressing through it against her skin, and Velma
trying to break free of her skin to flow with it, trying to lift, to sing with
it."[35] The music being discussed here is beaten out on the drums by the
"pan man in dreadlocks and knitted cap . . . trying to educate the people
about the meaning of the pan, the wisdom of the pan," and becomes a line
of interconnection between Velma's interiority and the present space of
Claybourne. Playing his drum in the Regal Theater for Miss Geula Khufu's
belly dancing class "like a man possessed," the pan man points the way
toward the memory of the marshes for Velma, where she arrives after "eavesdropping" on visions of herself and the two men most recently in her life:
Jamahl, the New Age prayer partner ("jive nigger in a loincloth and a swami

turban"), "whose so-called solutions to the so-called problem always lay in somebody else's culture"; and her husband, James (who later takes the name Obie), with whom she is "locked in a struggle that depleted and strangely renewed at the same time."[36]

As she narrates these ambivalent memories and visions, through reference to the "needle in her mind," an imagined phonograph playing the sound of her memories back to her, Velma decides to "lift the needle, to yank the arm away, to pull apart the machinery in favor of her own voice."[37] The search for this idiom of her own brings Velma to thoughts of the marshes, a landscape existing between surrealistic projection and memory, where "she waited. And it was no different from the waiting most people she knew did, waiting for a word from within, from above, from world events, from a shift in the power configurations of the globe, waiting for a new pattern to assemble itself, or a new word to be uttered from the rally podium, from a pamphlet picked up at the neighborhood bookstore. A breakthrough, a sign. Waiting. Ready. She waited as though for a battle. Or for a lover. Or for some steamy creature to arise dripping and unbelievable from the marshes. She waited for panic."[38] The stark imagery of waiting set within a landscape marked by the simultaneity of familiarity and dislocation proposes waiting as a mode for considering the dialectical emergence of possibility within a notion of defeat. The contrast between what Velma waits for compared to her sense of what most people are waiting for, turns on the point that she does not expect to have her waiting appeased by "a new pattern," "a new word," or "a pamphlet" to tell her that a goal has been achieved. Velma's waiting is instead defined by the indeterminacy of love, war, the supernatural, and the anarchic.

This innovative, fecund quality of the marshes intensifies as Velma connects the feeling of waiting for "panic" to the possible meaning intoned by sounds of the drumming of the pan man outside the infirmary,[39] as Bambara conveys her thoughts: "Panic. Pan. Pan-Africanism. All of us. Every. God. Pan. All nature. Pan. Everywhere. She was grinning, as she always grinned when she was able to dig below the barriers organized religions erected in its push toward a bogus civilization." Recognizing the marshes as a "site of metamorphosis," while hearing the "sounds surround her" amid the force of "a pulling down," Velma strives to find some way of articulating and preserving the transformative potential of this scene. She recalls the fact that her earlier visits to the marshes, "had failed to inform her days and her nights . . . had failed to inform her mind," thus setting the backdrop for the void in Velma's life leading up to her suicide attempt. Bambara uses this pivotal scene to highlight a tension between the terror of historical stagnation and the simultaneous possibility of its dilation. Although Velma never conclusively confronts the sense of terror or dread, she is able to lower her barriers to the music, allowing herself to be immersed in it through a similar sensory modality to that experienced in her meditative connections with the natural world. This particular convergence of temporality, space, and the sonic represents a potentially revolutionary movement inside narrative and historical time for Bambara. Velma's seeming inability to find words or music of change in the presence of the marshes, might be replaced by her willingness to merge with the healing sounds of Minnie in the infirmary, as the scene ends and "she shuddered and sank deeply into the music." This shuddering is a sign of self-knowledge rather than defeat as Velma realizes that the process of sonic healing represents a search for an expansion of the political that cannot simply be removed if a movement is incapacitated. Sound thus mirrors Bambara's description of Velma's perception of time "not speeding up but opening up to take her inside."[40]

It is this fusion of sensory and political possibility that marks the movement into political renewal for Velma, a renewal through forms of healing which challenge structures of Western knowledge through an eschewal of its hegemonic epistemological formations. In the portentous opening to the twelfth and final chapter, Bambara presents this convergence, as Velma enters her final stages of healing, achieving a state of being in which she is "understanding now, still and watching like a sphinx, poised, centered, music coming at her through cracks in the walls, floors, window frames." In this concluding chapter, Bambara moves between the visions of apocalypse and transformative hope as Velma becomes rejuvenated amid a dizzying set of images and comments suggesting an unknown future which exists after a yet to come shift, which may or may not be signaled by the beginning of the Claybourne spring festival reenactment of a slave uprising (occurring in real time during Velma's healing) as a stage for a post–Civil Rights era insurrection and engagement between radical, underground black activists, and elements of a retrenched U.S. police state. The music is crucial in this stage of the novel through its ability to grant Velma a level of atemporal, projective movement through imagined and real political landscapes: "A brass band coming, shiny sounds making the passageway slippery. The barrier down as promised and she can skip along now. Cymbals crashing by her ear and the leaves shuddering as the procession passes. She waits in the branches of Philo 101, time streaming along below her in the tree. Dogs caught in the shower, shiver, growl and bite the curbstones. Cats with their ears laid back hiss, seeing what the marchers will not train themselves to see."[41]

The poetic cadence and collage-like sensory depictions of Velma's vision render a scene underscored by the fact that it contains a sense of the unknown that exceeds the vision of the marchers. The concluding eruptions of sound in *The Salt Eaters*, whether they comprise song, voice, or environmental noise, are imbued with the capacity to remap the expanse of black historical resonance through the way the aurality of the textual moments fuses memory, futurity, and the present. Bambara's material literary practice can be seen as an aesthetic engagement that both grounds the local and expands the global aspects of the text. The political and formal qualities of sound emerge from its power to create and relate ideas at a more fluid, functional, and expansive level than might be encountered through a linear conception of temporality and historical narration. In this sense, the healing qualities of musical sound are layered within the momentous quality of the sonic boom that is heard as thunder, as an explosion at the Transchemical plant, and more ephemerally as the moment when Velma "started back toward life," and as a point at which several other characters become poised to recognize only years later, the political significance of this eruption. For Fred Holt, it will be "six years later when his son was finally able to reach him in the Resettlement Center." In the case of Dr. Julius Meadows, "none of it would really come together as a coherent narrative until the summer of '84 when he lunched with Mrs. Sophie Heywood and Mrs. Janice Campbell . . . and heard the younger woman hold forth on what to expect now that Pluto had moved into Scorpio for a long spell."[42] Velma's ex-husband, Obie, continues to convey a sense of temporal and phenomenological reorientation instilled by the sounds of historical and environmental rupture as he bears witness to the sonic event while preparing for a more directed series of insurgent political actions orchestrated through the Academy of the 7 Arts. This timeline of political action is reinscribed by the force of the sonic event, as Obie is, "ducking to escape whatever it was thundering towards him." His reflections on the situation are framed within the lingering aurality of the moment, what can be seen as Bambara's creation of new political space for the consideration of the unimaginable: "Stripped by lightning he would say in the days ahead, his flesh fallen away and nothing there on the back step but his soul with the stark impress of all the work done and yet to do, all the changes gone through and yet to come, all the longing and apprehension as he'd watch human beings becoming something else and wondering what it had been like for the ancestors watching the first wheel be rolled down the road."[43]

Bambara's balancing of the unknown qualities of the upheaval marked by sonic disruption against the healing renewal of Velma resists a vision of political futurity as linear progression. Working instead through the rhizomorphic qualities of sensory projections, Bambara creates a soundscape of political possibility that forces readers to focus on the contours of a political field, rather than a determinate sense of its path. This contingent quality of the sonic is elaborated by political economist Jacques Attali, who explains that the political possibility enfolded within the "immaterial production" of musical sound functions as a mirror that "relates to the structuring of theoretical paradigms, far ahead of concrete production. It is thus an immaterial recording surface for human works, the mark of something missing, a shred of utopia to decipher, information in negative, a collective *memory* allowing those who hear it to record their own personalized, specified modeled meanings."[44] Attali and Bambara agree that there is great theoretical and political value in the amorphous nature of the sonic. Understanding the capaciousness of Attali's sonic description in relationship to Bambara's novel, I argue, points to conditions of historical possibility in the text being unveiled through the blurring of sound, image, and text. Rather than looking at Bambara's project in the general tradition of African American texts borrowing from black music, or steeped within a broader tradition of postmodern literary aesthetics, I see the organization of the text as an effort to think through the political moment of the late 1970s through sound structures that envision spaces of meaning outside the boundaries of more traditionally conveyed history.[45] Bambara's artistic exploration of late twentieth-century black history might be recast on a more subliminal plane where, if we think in concert with Toni Morrison, "the underground life of a novel" is able to "link arms with the reader and facilitate making it one's own.[46] Through her aural orchestration and the acoustic dimensionality of her novel, Bambara mobilizes the capacious power of sound as a strategy for charting the bodily, psychic, and phenomenological possibilities for resistance to the segmentation of political, aesthetic, and spiritual life.

The Radical Tonality of James Baldwin's
Post–Civil Rights Blues

Critical Pitch

James Baldwin's short story "Going to Meet the Man," first published in his 1965 collection of the same title, dramatically portrays the interior tensions of a white sheriff who is committed to brutally maintaining Jim Crow apartheid in an unnamed town in the southern United States. One of Baldwin's more probing fictional examinations of the Civil Rights movement, the story is notable in its framing of the struggle for voting rights in the South through the lens of white terror—a terror that is simultaneously enforced and felt by the sheriff. The story opens with the question, "What's the matter?" posed by the sheriff's wife, Grace, to the sheriff, Jesse, as they lie in bed, following a day in which Jesse has nearly tortured a young black activist to death.[1] Grace's question to Jesse, we learn, is posed in reaction to Jesse's frustrating impotence and inability to make love to her. His conflicted attitude toward Grace reflects the various entanglements of power, race, gender, and violence that define Jesse's position as sheriff and, we later learn, that are affected by his deeply formative childhood memory of witnessing the torture and lynching of a black man. Baldwin depicts the psychological formation of Jesse's white racism as both an externally and internally projected force. He shifts this analysis of Jesse's disturbing thoughts and memories from the immediate present of the bedroom, to a broader sense of the Civil Rights–era flashpoint of an intensifying struggle for voting rights. Baldwin's frequently articulated belief that the present realities and future possibilities of white and black Americans are inextricably and tragically linked frames this narrative account of the psychic confrontation between white power and emergent expressions of black resistance. Baldwin represents Jesse's inability to fully process this tension between racist subjection and black resistance as an effect of the interminable, multidimensional haunting of race in the United States. He describes the internalized psychic costs of white racism in a 1965 address delivered at Cambridge

University, which is tightly connected to the story through Baldwin's focus on sheriff Jim Clark of Selma, Alabama, who it seems the character of Jesse is meant to invoke:

> But what happens to the poor white man's, the poor white woman's mind? It is this: they have been raised to believe, and by now they helplessly believe, that no matter what disaster overtakes them, there is one consolation like a heavenly revelation—at least they are not black. I suggest that all the terrible things that could happen to a human being that is one of the worst. I suggest that what has happened to the white southerner is in some ways much worse than what has happened to the Negroes there.
>
> Sheriff Clark in Selma, Alabama, cannot be dismissed as a total monster; I am sure he loves his wife and children and likes to get drunk. One has to assume that he is a man like me. But he does not know what drives him to use the club, to menace with the gun and to use the cattle prod. Something awful must have happened to a human being to be able to put a cattle prod against women's breasts. What happens to the women is ghastly. What happens to the man who does it is in some ways much, much worse. Their moral lives have been destroyed by the plague called color.[2]

Both Baldwin's reflections and his short story diagnose the moral fragility of white power. He uses the examples of Sheriff Clark in Selma, and Jesse (in the short story), to explore the historical reverberations of racist violence throughout the psychological dimensions of whiteness.[3]

In "Going to Meet the Man," Baldwin depicts intersections of sound and memory that amplify Jesse's relationship to the physical and psychological aspects of the racial dividing line. This acoustic dimension of the text operates most overtly through the halting vocal exchanges and moments of stillness captured in the frequent, elongated bouts of silence between Jesse and Grace. Silence allows Jesse's troubled meditations on race to unfold, and his mode of reflection serves as the winding opening to the story, prefacing the prominence of sound that marks his recollections of torturing the main black activist of the town. The sounds of Baldwin's story intensify his examination of the complex formations of white supremacy during the Civil Rights movement. He creates a synergy between the creative and the critical, the fictional and essayistic, which is forged through his ability to both represent sound and to incorporate it into the formal operations of his writing. In doing so, Baldwin outlines a transcendent quality of freedom that emerges from the blurred line between the creative and the critical, which is not contingent on the achievement of a particular end. This approach to mediating the political through works of art is discussed by philosopher Jacques Rancière as "the distribution of the sensible." Rancière understands the relationship between aesthetics and politics not simply as one in which a work of art reflects a particular political inclination or ideology; rather, he construes the relationship as a more oblique correspondence between the texture of aesthetic practices and politics as a sensory and experiential state: "Politics revolves around what is seen and what can be said about it, around who has the ability to see and the talent to speak, around the properties of spaces and the possibilities of time . . . Artistic practices are 'ways of doing and making' that intervene in the general distribution of ways of doing and making as well as in the relationships they maintain to modes of being and forms of visibility." Rancière offers an organic notion of aesthetics and politics in which artistic form fashions political force through its embodiment of "the sensible delimitation of what is common to the community."[4] The intentional breadth Rancière ascribes to the idea of community is more distinctly shaped in Baldwin's writing as a critical black radical perspective built around the realization that black liberation remains an unfinished question for the foreseeable future, even as Civil Rights legislation takes effect. Sound, then, functions as a modality through which Baldwin delineates the existential depths of subjection, containment, and division that mark American racial politics, and that must be fully understood before a vision of freedom and equality can be fully conceptualized. This chapter listens to the politics of Baldwin's post–Civil Rights era sound as that literary sound evolves between "Going to Meet the Man" and his book-length essay on the Civil Rights and Black Power eras, *No Name in the Street.*

Returning to the opening sonority of Baldwin's short story, Baldwin focalizes Jesse's perspective as he "lay there, one hand between his legs, staring at the frail sanctuary of his wife," listening to dogs "barking at each other, back and forth, insistently, as though they were agreeing to make an appointment." The sanctuary of Grace's white femininity is a crucial symbol throughout the story, one that upholds the racial dividing line through several different angles in Jesse's mind. Initially Baldwin premises the story on Jesse's understanding of Grace alongside his sense of himself as a "God-fearing man." Both Grace and God help Jesse maintain his sense of whiteness as a claim to authority that is upheld by the exercise of violent force and the power of myth. Baldwin points to a tension within Jesse's idealization of Grace, however, as Jesse moans and turns away from her, contemplating his sexual desire for black women. In his words, black women represent the "more spice" he would "pick up" or "arrest." His moan carries the additional weight of a fear he can no longer risk using black women to satisfy his sexual desires because "there was no telling what might happen when your ass was in the air."[5]

Jesse's fear reflects his perspective on blackness as unpredictable and outside rationality, a presence that moves him between desire, repulsion, and terror throughout the story. Baldwin offers a broader conceptualization of this aspect of Jesse's psyche in his essay "White Man's Guilt," in which Baldwin theorizes the existential divisions upholding and being upheld by an American color curtain: "The American curtain is color. Color. White men have used this word, this concept to justify unspeakable crimes and not only in the past but in the present. One can measure very neatly the white American's distance from his conscience—from himself—by observing the distance between white America and black America. One has only to ask oneself who established this distance, who is this distance designed to protect, and from what is this distance designed to offer protection?"[6] The complexity of the curtain is borne out as Jesse's thoughts progress into an overwhelming need to physically immerse himself within Grace "like a child, and never have to get up in the morning again and go downtown to face those faces."[7] Writing from a critical perspective that distinctly echoes the existential perspectives of W. E. B. Du Bois and Frantz Fanon, Baldwin focuses on the historical flashpoint of Civil Rights–era racial confrontation and struggle as a paradigm for considering the transition from Jim Crow white supremacy to a new period of emerging desegregation. Baldwin's depiction of Jesse and his broader analysis of race in the United States suggest that the idea of Civil Rights social transformation is perpetually challenged by the permanence of racial terror. While Baldwin is certainly making an argument about a specific region, his psychological analysis of white supremacy as a form of sexualized violence conveys his deep pessimism regarding race in America. In this framework, terror is not simply a form of violence; it persists as a fear that underlines white power. Baldwin scrutinizes the relationship between the color curtain, state violence, and white power, as the curtain becomes the "principal justification for the lives" of Harlem cops and southern sheriffs. Whiteness holds itself out, to paraphrase Baldwin, as consolation against disaster.

Baldwin's narrative composition and formal proclivities in the short story highlight the sensory dividing line upholding Jesse's construction of whiteness. His maintenance of white power is elaborated by his dramatic reflections on the phenomenological assault of blackness on his sensibilities. He desires to "never have to enter that jail house again and smell that smell and hear that singing; never again feel that filthy, kinky, greasy hair under his hand, never again watch those black breasts leap against the leaping cattle prod, never hear these moans again or watch that blood run down or the fat lips split or the sealed eyes struggle open. They were animals, they were no better than animals, what could be done with people like that?"[8] Smelling, hearing, feeling, and visualizing blackness, all inspire repulsion within Jesse. Baldwin builds on Jesse's general feeling of sensory disassociation by translating it into a more focused rejection of the sound of black voices he hears in song (as resistance) and moaning (as a response to torture) that haunt Jesse throughout the story.

Baldwin also uses sound to manipulate temporality in the narrative. He situates Jesse's memories within a present that recedes in respect to the expanses of memory bridging the recent and distant pasts. Baldwin's inclination to trouble temporality disrupts the sense of time that Jesse seeks to create through his exercise of racist violence. He introduces this dimension of his narrative approach through Jesse's lines of recollection to Grace: "There was this Nigger today." Jesse describes him as "one of the ringleaders" who is beaten and detained by the police for blocking traffic during a peaceful voting rights demonstration. Jesse describes the young man in his jail cell, "lying on the ground jerking and moaning . . . blood was coming out of his ears where Big Jim C. and his boys had whipped him." Much of what Jesse violently reacts to in this encounter is the power the young man seems to gather from the sound of protestors:

"I put the prod to him and he jerked some more and he kind of screamed—but he didn't have much voice left. 'You make them stop that singing,' I said to him, 'you hear me? You make them stop that singing.' He acted like he didn't hear me and I put it to him again, under his arms, and he just rolled around on the floor and blood started coming from his mouth. He'd pissed his pants already." He paused. His mouth felt dry and his throat was as rough

as sandpaper, as he talked, he began to hurt all over with that
peculiar excitement which refused to be released. 'You all are going
to stop your singing, I said to him.'"

Jesse's torturing of the young man intensifies until the scene is marked by
an absence of expected sound as the young man tries to scream "but the
scream did not come out, only a rattle and a moan." Baldwin emphasizes
Jesse's brutality against the sonic backdrop of other black activists singing
freedom songs outside the jail. The sound of the singing becomes the
force that Jesse reacts to as a justification for his violent outbursts. Baldwin
also maps the more ephemeral movement of the sound through Jesse's
perspective as a less linear inflection of his racist consciousness: "It was the
sound with which he was most familiar—though it was also the sound of
which he had been least conscious—and it had always contained an obscure
comfort. They were singing to God. They were singing for mercy and they
hoped to go to heaven, and he had even sometimes felt, when looking into
the eyes of some of the old women, a few of the very old men, that they
were singing for mercy for his soul too." Jesse's meditations on the sound
of black spirituality serve primarily as a means for him to articulate a vision
of interracial communion based on "rules laid down in the Bible." For Jesse,
these rules essentially concretize white supremacy as a means of maintaining a sense of shared order that Jesse, as a central arbiter of this system,
imagines as a goal of "protecting white people from the niggers, and the
niggers from themselves." The young man Jesse nearly beats to death represents the erosion of this order, as his resistance becomes an uncontrol-
lable sentiment signaling Jesse's realization that "they had not been singing
black folks into heaven, they had been singing white folks into hell."[9]

The unease Jesse expresses in deciphering this flow of black song that
has served as sonic backdrop to his life is elaborated through Baldwin bridging song in the present of the narration and the eruptions of black singing
that audibly mark Jesse's childhood memory of witnessing the lynching
and visceral torture of a black man. Baldwin frames Jesse's memory of the
lynching as an aural force that emerges, "out of the darkness of the room,
out of nowhere," through the sound of the spiritual verse "*I stepped in the
river at Jordan*," which "came flying up at him, with the melody and the beat."
The sound of the spiritual refocuses Jesse's memory back to the car ride
home from the lynching, sitting between his parents and listening to the
distant sound of black singing that Jesse's father plainly informs him must

be for the man they have just seen tortured to death. Baldwin carefully draws out the scene by then describing Jesse's restlessness in bed that night, "hearing the night sounds . . . then no sounds at all." This evacuation of sound is then contrasted with the overbearing sounds of his parents having sex, and his father's heavy breathing that "seemed to fill the world." This unsettling sonic tension within Jesse leads his mind back to the earlier horrific scene of the lynching that his parents proudly brought him into. The car ride to the picnic is sonically marked by the floating traces of black spirituals ghostly rendered as they "echoed and echoed in the graveyard silence" of a landscape which the local black community has physically evacuated in the face of white violence. When they arrive at the lynching picnic, the singing subsides and Jesse hears "sounds of laughing and cursing and wrath—and something else—roll[ing] in waves from the front of the mob to the back."[10] Baldwin's rendering of the lynching through Jesse's eyes and ears distils racial confrontation and racist violence as inchoate and, to a degree, inarticulable forces. As Jesse witnesses the elaborate torture of the black man by the white mob, he does so through an awareness of the way that sounds mark the event. He remembers the view from his father's shoulders of a white man with a knife, approaching the "hanging, gleaming body, the most beautiful and terrible object he had ever seen until then." The white man displays the black man's penis for the crowd, and as he prepares to cut it off, the black man locks eyes with Jesse, at which point "Jesse screamed, and the crowd screamed as the knife flashed, first up, then down, cutting the dreadful thing away, and the blood came roaring down. Then the crowd rushed forward, tearing at the body with their hands, with knives, with rocks, with stones, howling and cursing." Jesse's memory simultaneously reflects his terror of witnessing human destruction and his nostalgia for the white patriarchal self-possession that his father seems to embody. As his father testifies to the importance of what Jesse has witnessed with the words "I told you . . . you wasn't ever going to forget *this* picnic" against the backdrop of the completely annihilated corpse of the black man, now simply "a black charred object on the black, charred ground," Jesse is transfixed with the idea that "his father had carried him through a mighty test, had revealed to him a great secret which would be the key to his life forever." Baldwin's prose feels insufficient, as its overly linear narration of the event's impact on Jesse's consciousness too neatly attempts to draw a parallel between past, present, and future. As the memory bleeds into Jesse's present, however, and he processes this childhood memory, it becomes an incipient antidote to his sexual impotence: "Something bubbled up in him, his nature again returned to him. He thought of the boy in the cell; he thought of the man in the fire; he thought of the knife and grabbed himself and stroked himself and a terrible sound, something between a high laugh and a howl, came out of him and dragged his sleeping wife up on one elbow."[11]

Jesse's "terrible sound" is evoked in response to his memory of racial violence and impels him toward an inarticulable sexual satisfaction in the final lines of the story. Baldwin positions this moment as a concluding question: how does the sound arising from deep within Jesse reflect complex iterations of white supremacy in the United States? If, as most of Baldwin's writing suggests, we are to look beyond the legislative gains of the Civil Rights movement in order to appreciate more deeply the enduring qualities of racial antagonism, then Baldwin's rendering of Jesse's cry may offer a means of aurally troubling the deeply structured formations of white power.

Building on Baldwin's fictional engagement with sound, I turn to his later nonfiction writing as a lens through which he manipulates the aesthetics and politics of aurality in order to deepen his critical reflections on racial antagonism and resistance. His book of essays *No Name on the Street* thematically and formally incorporates sound as a means of envisioning alternative political possibilities. In it, Baldwin highlights the aurality of black expressive practices as a critical response to white supremacy. It is the sonorous formal capacity of the cry, the sentence, and the song that might create a means of accessing a renewed vision of black political futurity.

Around the time of the publication of "Going to Meet the Man," Baldwin decided to relocate from New York to Istanbul. His movement and the psychological restlessness connected to it reflected his frustration with the limitations of the Civil Rights movement. As David Leeming notes, Baldwin felt that "something new was needed, something that would speak to the disillusionment he and others felt about the commitment of white liberals and blacks who allowed themselves to be dominated by whites in the movement." This period of the late 1960s and the early 1970s represented a politically pivotal, artistically productive, yet noticeably uneasy period in James Baldwin's life and intellectual career. Moving between Turkey, France, England, and the United States, Baldwin was coping with the psychic weight of his alienation from both liberal white and militant black intellectual communities. Leeming, referencing letters Baldwin wrote to his brother, David, in 1969, captures Baldwin's unease and his sense that his ideas were too challenging within an ideological landscape "in which the whole discussion of race and America was taking place."[12] Baldwin's position was complicated, as he at once became increasingly pointed and pessimistic in his assessments of the American racial state, yet was simultaneously the target of, at times, scathing critiques from black activists and intellectuals during the 1960s. Amiri Baraka, Eldridge Cleaver, and Ishmael Reed all generally questioned Baldwin's commitment to revolutionary struggle, and in the cases of Cleaver and Reed, more openly attacked Baldwin's masculinity through homophobic rhetoric.[13] Within this vexed historical moment, however, Baldwin was undeterred in his efforts to relate to and support the new revolutionary energy of post–Civil Rights black radical activism, and of the Black Panther Party in particular. Baldwin rejected the calls of his critics as he wrote to his brother that "he had no intention of evading what he still saw as his mission."[14]

For Baldwin, this sense of responsibility was driven by his recognition of the fundamental tension emerging from, as Leeming puts it, "beings within himself—the child dancing through life, the intelligence outraged at the nature of things, the madman often blowing the house apart."[15] Baldwin's focus on the indivisibility of the personal and political during the late 1960s spoke to the need for new expressive forms that might respond to the question one of Baldwin's intellectual interlocutors, Dr. Martin Luther King, Jr., asked through the title of his 1967 book, *Where Do We Go from Here?* The tension within King's query and Baldwin's corresponding aesthetics of critical and creative dissonance defines the formal complexity and uncompromising political critique of his 1972 memoir, *No Name in the Street.*

In this impressionistic, nonlinear, recursive recounting of the Civil Rights and Black Power years, Baldwin considers the building confrontation between the energy of the black freedom struggle[16] and what Vincent Harding has termed "the limits of this country's liberal version of itself."[17] Harding, writing in the conclusion of his 1980 analysis of African American history, *The Other American Revolution*, suggests that the transition from the 1960s to the 1970s, for black activists, was an uncertain turning point marked by a weighing of the "costs of creating a just and 'beloved community' out of an unjust, racist, and deeply fearful society."[18] For Baldwin, the uncertainty underlining this turning point highlights the prospect that transforming the nation may only be possible in the most controlled and contained contexts. Grappling with the implications of this pessimistic historical reality, it is not surprising that Baldwin's awareness of the shrinking horizon of

American racial progress is evocatively reflected through the form and not merely the content of his critical meditations on the period.

Baldwin mediates the aesthetic form and political content of *No Name in the Street* through his composition of narrative sequences that critically diagnose particular existential dimensions of black life during the period. The sequencing Baldwin accomplishes occurs through extraliterary points of reference in the framing of the text, and also through the arrangement of narrative sections that are often constructed and built on one another in a nonlinear yet accumulative mode. Through his interweaving of form and content, Baldwin positions his first-person reflections on convergences of historical events, personal memories, and political thought as an opening through which he critically interrogates race and power in the United States and around the world. A distinctive feature of Baldwin's rendering of these intersections is his intense focus on the felt, at times sensory intimacy of the particular moments he is describing. Through Baldwin's focus on the sensory and phenomenological dimensions of black historical memory and experience, *No Name in the Street* projects a particular inclination toward the indeterminacy of time, historical awareness, and political conscious-ness through which the critical content of his narrative is relayed. This poetics of opposition is articulated through Baldwin's attention to the lit-erary acoustics of the text. Baldwin's attunement to a pessimistic post–Civil Rights reality that marks the latter half of the 1960s and early 1970s is dis-tinctively conveyed by his manipulation of the sound of his writing—certainly through the tonality of his critical insight, and perhaps more intriguingly, through a conceptual incorporation of sound as a literary mode and criti-cal method that pushes beyond the sedimentation of form.

There are many dimensions to Baldwin's formal articulation of sound in the essay, and perhaps the most clearly heard and critically resonant man-ifestation emerges through his orchestration of both the tonal and episte-mological registers of the blues.[19] His extension of this black musical and literary framework through nonlinear, temporally fragmented, narrative movements amplifies the distinctive critical pitch and timbre of his out-look. Baldwin's writings in the years roughly spanning the publication of *The Fire Next Time* (1963) through *No Name in the Street* (1972) reflect the convergence of his sensitivity to the registers of music and sound along-side his critical awareness of an ephemeral national commitment to racial equality.[20] This awareness is layered with the pessimism and possibility felt through Baldwin's increasingly dire outlook on the moral compass of white

America, his focus on the disturbing backlash of white racist violence and political assassinations, his hope in a renewed black revolutionary spirit manifested through the spirit of 1960s resistance movements around the world, and his understanding of a retrenched police state as a new horizon of antiblack racism.

Baldwin's formal approach through these years is signaled through a brief statement he offers on the ethical dimensions of his style in a 1962 writer's forum in the *New York Times*. Briefly reflecting on his writing of *Another Country*, Baldwin explains the connection between his method and the approach of jazz musicians, as they share the desire to express a "universal blues" pushing beyond empirical definitions of racial experience, instead "telling us something about what it is like to be alive."[21] Baldwin writes that the achievement of "writing the way they sound" reflects his understanding of Henry James's call for criticism to capture and convey "perception at the pitch of passion."[22] James's sensibility frames criticism as an art form in and of itself, one that reflects the imbrication of generalized levels of experience within a more precise, subjectively rendered perspective of the critic. This dialectical movement between "lending an ear" and projecting truth signals an improvisational movement for Baldwin, as the processing of his participation in and observation of the Civil Rights and Black Power movements becomes, by the early 1970s, only possible through his reliance on orchestrating the disjointed intersections of personal memory and collective historical consciousness. Baldwin's focus on working through the overlapping layers of temporality, subjectivity, and racial identity necessitates a different narrative pathway in engaging with these issues, one that dissects and reimagines more liberal notions of progress and universalism through not only the content, but also the texture of his prose. Baldwin's improvisational rethinking is not simply breaking with a mode of thought and creating a new reality, as was the case among many concurrent black artists who took their charge as Black Arts Movement innovators to articulate sharper breaks with previous black expressive traditions. Baldwin's approach instead explores the interstices between remembrance and futurity as a narrative state of being that critically relates known pasts and a sense of the unknown future through his aesthetic crafting of literary vignettes, which trouble these temporal and historical relationships. Baldwin expresses both the political ends of his writing and his narrative style through more inchoate formal approaches that move beyond ideas of linearity and equivalence.

Recently Magdalena Zaborowska, in her book-length study *James Bald-win's Turkish Decade: Erotics of Exile*, and Douglas Field, in his essay "James Baldwin in His Time," have both pointed to the important role of music within Baldwin's compositional process. Zaborowska, commenting on Baldwin's textual negotiation of same-sex love in *No Name in the Street*, notes his use of "the jazzlike genre improvisation that he began to embrace when he wrote *Another Country*."[23] Field similarly points to this fusion of music and the literary as formative to Baldwin's work, citing Baldwin's own description of his early sermonic practice: "I could improvise from the texts like a jazz musician improvises from a theme. I never wrote a sermon . . . You have to sense the people you're talking to. You have to respond to what they hear."[24] Building on the insights of Zaborowska and Field regarding Baldwin's attention to music as a critical and formal mode, I also want to consider how the blues, as both sonic inflection and broader cultural orientation, might offer one way of understanding the aesthetic composition of Baldwin's *No Name in the Street*. There is an important formal expressive distinction to *not* make here regarding the blues and jazz within Baldwin's understandings of the musical approaches. As we will see, the blues, for Baldwin, represent a capacious totalizing framework for black life in the United States. Not unlike Amiri Baraka, Baldwin understands blackness as a historical condition reflected in the expressive evolution and transformations of "blues people." Jazz, then, is a form stemming from the blues root, with distinctive formal properties, but not distinctive enough to rupture the horizon of blues expressive identity that stretches to contain these extensions of the root. In his short story "Sonny's Blues," for example, Baldwin brings together the two forms in the main character, Sonny, who identifies as a stridently aloof bebop jazz musician, yet most clearly realizes his ability to communicate expressively and spiritually through a concluding moment of collective jazz improvisation on blues standards. The fact that Baldwin worries any firm distinction between blues and jazz as expressive orientations and as epistemological horizons reflects his desire for black creative freedom from generic containment.

Baldwin's construction of late or post–Civil Rights blues extends the form as an expressive horizon, building on the interpretive insights of Ralph Ellison in his 1945 analysis of the work of Richard Wright. Ellison's understanding of the blues suggests a flexible expressive range encompassing "both the agony of life and the possibility of conquering it through sheer toughness of spirit."[25] At the same time, he points to the theoretical capacity of the blues to negotiate the critical tension resulting from the "thwarted ide-ational energy" in which words "are burdened with meanings they cannot convey."[26] Baldwin's writing moves in the spirit of Ellison's analysis of the blues, most pointedly, perhaps, in his later essayistic reflections on the rap-idly altering times of the 1960s, as he enters a complex political and critical space in which unburdening language, indeed, reviving it with a renewed attention to the formal and political qualities of "personal catastrophe" writ large, becomes an aesthetic and political aim for his contributions to black struggle through literary activism.

In his 1964 essay "The Uses of the Blues," Baldwin further contextual-izes the expressivity of the blues as it exceeds its musicality, providing a corrective to the inability of the national consciousness "to accept the real-ity of pain, of anguish, of ambiguity, of death."[27] As an analytical tool for Baldwin, the blues diagnose a missing orientation, a profound lack within the critical imagination of mainstream America, revealing the "very pecu-liar and sometimes monstrous" character of American identity that is shaped by a blindness to, and avoidance of, the historical and political depth of pain, loss, and ambiguity. Baldwin's use of the blues suggests formations of national and racial identity beyond recognizable lines of racial demarca-tion as the expressive and narrative capacity of the music contains a sense of joy that is unrecognizable as mere happiness; for Baldwin, the sentiment "is not a real state, and does not really exist." This ambiguous joy of the blues presents an epistemological basis for an idea of black consciousness that rejects the American tendency to ignore and forget the difficult sub-stance of lived experience and the immanence of death. Demonstrating this aesthetic and political capacity of the blues, Baldwin closely reads Bessie Smith's "Gin House Blues," pointing to, and almost riffing off, the irrever-ent, revolutionary stance of resistance she projects through the lines, "Don't try me, nobody / 'cause you will never win / I'll fight the Army and Navy / Just me and my gin." He states:

> Well, you know, that is all very accurate, all very concrete. I know,
> I watched, I was there. You've seen these black men and women,
> these boys and girls; you've seen them on the streets. But I know
> what happened to them at the factory, at work, at home, on the
> subway, what they go through in a day, and the way they sort of
> ride with it. And it's very, very tricky. It's kind of a fantastic
> tightrope. They may be very self-controlled, very civilized; I like to

think of myself as being very civilized and self-controlled, but I
know I'm not. And I know that some improbable Wednesday for
no reason whatever, the elevator man or the doorman, the policeman or the landlord, or some little boy from the Bronx will say
something, and it will be the wrong day to say it, the wrong
moment to have said it to me; and God knows what will happen.
I have seen it all, I have seen that much. What the blues are
describing comes out of all this.

Baldwin's intervention builds on an idea of political action arising out of
tragic circumstance, and in doing so, contemplates the liminal, ephemeral
quality of the "fantastic tightrope" black people are forced to walk daily. The
blues present a certain totality or horizon for black life within and beyond
its Manichean qualities that is inescapable for Baldwin. They offer a window
into the truths of experience from those most dispossessed and thus unacknowledged, reframing these testimonies as viable sociopolitical perspectives on what it means to be an American in the face of the amnesiac panic
projected through the seemingly authentic mainstream portrayals of American identity: "If you read such popular novels by John O'Hara, you can't
imagine what country he's talking about. If you read *Life* magazine, it's like
reading about the moon. Nobody lives in that country. That country does
not exist and everybody knows it. But everyone pretends it does. Now this
is panic. And this is terribly dangerous, because it means when the trouble
comes, and trouble always comes, you won't survive it." As political form,
the blues function as both indictment of the general acceptance of "the
fantastic disaster which we call American politics and which we call American foreign policy," and the possibility of correcting this blind faith by
"begin[ning] to ask ourselves very difficult questions."[28]

Baldwin's signaling of a blues epistemological framework as the meeting
point of aesthetics and politics animates works such as *Another Country*
and "Sonny's Blues," in which the narratives revolve around the relationships his characters establish and maintain with a blues sensibility. In these
cases, Baldwin calibrates the fidelity of his writing to the ways in which the
actual lyrical and structural presence of the blues is framed within the narratives. Baldwin's re-invocation and essayistic refashioning of the form, a
decade later, propels the narrative structure of *No Name in the Street* forward; he utilizes a renewed sense of the blues to chart the convergence of
time and sound as an avenue toward new forms of political articulation.[29]

One way in which the long, two-part essay engages with these temporal and sonic contingencies is reflected through Baldwin's literary incorporation of the idea of anamnesis, defined in the context of sound studies as a convergence of "sound, perception, and memory," into the narrative composition of a work. Sound theorists Jean-François Augoyard and Henry Torgue explain that the anamnesis effect "plays with time, reconnecting past mental images to present consciousness, with no will other than the free activity of association."[30] To register critical thoughts through such a nonlinear correspondence (between sentiment and historical experience) raises the stakes of Baldwin's essayistic critique of American, and more broadly Western, racial politics, as his work can not only be read as a significant memoir of his participation in the events of the Civil Rights and Black Power period, but also as a formal break with the desire to convey black political resistance through the linearity of a progressively ordered autobiographical narrative. Baldwin's break reflects a belief in the capacity of form to expand the political sphere on its own terms through the interaction between its internal temporal and imagistic rhythms and the sensibilities of the reader. Baldwin's literary improvisations enlarge the critical space of the aesthetic dimension of *No Name in the Street*. This inclination toward literary improvisation creates new critical space that is revealed through a blues understanding of the productive cracks and fissures within black historical experience. As Nathaniel Mackey stated in a 1996 interview with Peter O'Leary, "The African-American improvisational legacy in music has been instructive way beyond the confines of the venues in which it takes place and the particular musical culture in which it takes place, way beyond music itself. It's become a metaphor for all kinds of processes of cultural and social revaluation, cultural and social critique, cultural and social change."[31] Baldwin's extension of this "improvisational legacy" into the realm of the political, and his use of it as a theoretical and formal tool in assessing racial struggle and meaning in the Civil Rights and post–Civil Rights eras, is further illuminated through Derek Bailey's outlining of the distinctions between idiomatic and free improvisation: "All improvisation takes place in relation to the known whether the known is traditional or newly acquired. The only real difference lies in the opportunities for free improvisation to renew or change the known and so provoke an open-endedness which by definition is not possible in idiomatic improvisation."[32] Bailey's idea of renewing or changing the limits of knowability through the "open-endedness" of free improvisation begins to capture part of the critical and formal interplay between vernacular tradition and formal innovation that Baldwin executes in his text. Furthermore, examining Baldwin's expressive exploration of the intricacies of historical and racial consciousness amid the waning of a recognizable, organized Civil Rights and Black Power movement allows for a more nuanced inquiry into the political and aesthetic meanings of the post–Civil Rights era.

Acoustic Breaks/Narrative Fracture

The volatility and inner turmoil Baldwin felt during the late 1960s and early 1970s became increasingly heightened and reflected through his broader set of engagements with experimental aesthetic approaches across expressive forms. As both David Leeming and Magdalena Zaborowska have detailed, Baldwin's creative life in Turkey during the period in which he was completing *No Name in the Street* was shaped by his 1970 directorship of Canadian playwright John Herbert's *Fortune and Men's Eyes*, which brought together Baldwin's pressing concern regarding the growth of the prison–industrial complex with his broader philosophical critique of alienation within Western culture. Building on the confessional, psychoanalytic style of directing and staging the play, as well as the stark immediacy of the curtain-like arrangement of the prison bars dividing audience from stage, Baldwin's work on the play incorporated many elements of sound and music within the experimental production. Journalist Zeynep Oral, according to Zaborowska, "confirmed that sound was very important to Jimmy," noting that "Baldwin manipulated the stage design and props to juxtapose silence and noise." Echoing Oral's observations, Charles Adelsen, writing a story on the play for *Ebony*, describes Baldwin's use of sound in the production as a means of emphasizing the darkness and discomfort that the performance is intending to address: "Several hundred people sit in the warm darkness of a theater and wait. The house lights have been killed; not even an exit light lessens the inky darkness. The Jangling bells, a nervous drumming, sounds too loud to be heard comfortably scratch at nerve endings." The soundtrack or soundscape of the production emerged as a result of the serendipitous meeting between Baldwin and Don Cherry in Istanbul. Baldwin happened upon the Cherry family on the street and excitedly explained to his good friend, the Turkish actor Engin Cezzar, who did not recognize or know of Cherry, "This is good luck. I was wondering what we would do with the music. That's it. We've found who is going to do the music."[33] At this point, Cherry had played alongside major figures in 1950s and 1960s jazz, including John Coltrane, Archie Shepp, Albert Ayler, Sonny Rollins, and Ornette Coleman, and was particularly noteworthy, along with other new black music improvisers such as Marion Brown, for his desire to bring together world music and African American avant-garde sonic expression.[34] Engin recollected in his memoir, "We took them [the Cherry family] from the pavement, into the house, ate and drank together, and worked for fifteen days. He created wonderful music with a piano and a small trumpet."[35]

While we can't definitively hear the sonic record (Zaborowska details this fact in a footnote—to this point no publicly available or archived recording is known to exist), we can begin to capture some sense of what Cherry's sound might have added to Baldwin's staging of *Fortune* by considering the aural expansiveness of his music as it is captured in the recording of his performance with Turkish musicians Okay Temiz, Irfan Sumer, Selcuk Sun, and Maffy Falay at the U.S. embassy in Ankara in late November 1969.[36] The sound of Cherry and his ensemble confronts the listeners, and, interestingly, the live audience situated in the representative space of U.S. global power in Turkey at the time, with a distinctive sound, blending elements of free jazz improvisation, and tonality with Turkish folk melodies and musical approaches, through mostly short, expressive sonic forays dominated by the shifting timbre of Cherry's coronet. Bright, dissonant, and inclined to wander amid frequent, but not necessarily metered percussive punctuations, the music is both frenetic and bluesy. Working in an improvisational mode that recalls much of the collaborative efforts of Cherry and Ornette Coleman from the late 1950s through the mid-1960s, as well as the later contributions of Albert Ayler and John Coltrane to the ever-evolving tradition of free jazz, Cherry, in the middle of a selection titled "Ornette's Tune," breaks into a blaring and piercing sequence of notes that reject the established sensibility and compositional structure that had briefly been established. Sounds such as those created by Cherry, based on "energy playing" and acoustic effects and states such as vibration rather than the mastery of compositional form, point to a much broader continuum of black expressive expansion. The rupture projected through Cherry's sound presents a formal intervention that, in terms of its projection of dissonance, might be heard as a kind of aural corollary to Baldwin's jarringly fractured, aesthetic reconsideration of the possibilities for racial struggle and transformation in the wake of the Civil Rights movement.

Baldwin's engagement with practices of sonic experimentation and improvisation becomes highlighted in the form of *No Name in the Street* as he recasts his earlier appeals to the possibility of interracial brotherhood existing across racial lines, prominently featured in his 1963 text *The Fire Next Time*, within a much darker tonality, a critical perspective akin to the haunting sound of minor chords. This post–Civil Rights blues reflects a twinned sense of defeat and revelation in the wake of the movement, and is structured around an idea of negation, a critical focus on the dialectical complexities of historical transformation, revealing what critical theorist Max Horkheimer calls "the breach between ideas and reality."[37] In disclosing the limitations of the world's commonsense definitions of racial reality, Baldwin presents the readers of this nonfictional prose with a series of "negatives" that, in a photographic sense, present inversions and reversals, and in the sense of more experimental photography, might render the ghostly, haunting traces and vestiges of meaning and presence in the faintest, yet most compelling outlines. These negatives, rather than existing as visual sites, operate synesthetically, blending elements of sound, image, and text. Flashbacks, echoes of memory, and the reflective tone of Baldwin's prose create narrative acoustics projecting Baldwin's interrogations of a linear progression of U.S. civil rights and global racial history.

Baldwin's inquiry into the negative dimensions of this historical moment is also generated through the lingering sound of the text's title, epigraphs, and section titles. Baldwin's Christian upbringing, and his well-documented questioning and repudiation of it, lends a particular resonance to Job's search for and questioning of spiritual and ethical meaning in the pages of the Old Testament referenced in the essay's title. Baldwin's inclusion of lyrics from the spiritual "Samson and Delilah" attests to the need to "tear this building down" (lyrics we might rehear through Blind Willie Johnson's 1927 recording of the spiritual as a blues composition). Baldwin also orchestrates the two-part essay in accordance with the lyrics of the black spiritual "Take Me to the Water," as part 1 of the essay calls the song's title, and the second part of the essay invokes through its title, the desire "To Be Baptized." While we can't necessarily pinpoint the specific sonic references Baldwin may have had in mind in taking the spiritual's title as a structural marker for the essay, the fact that Baldwin admired Nina Simone, who had recorded a version of the song in 1966 on the album *High Priestess of Soul*, offers one way of thinking about a certain convergence of political commitment and spiritual searching that both artists proposed in their works.

The various movements of Baldwin's essay are also literally mapped along geographic lines within the text as the narrative shifts between New York, London, Paris, Montgomery, Los Angeles, the San Francisco Bay area, and Hamburg. Through this array of historical and geographic reference points, the text also presents an ideological mapping of the historical forces and events that have inflected Baldwin's understandings of domestic, psychic, and global processes of racial formation through the Civil Rights and post–Civil Rights eras. Baldwin creates ideological movement through dizzying, and at times dissonant representations of space and time. His approach resonates with Ralph Ellison's description in his prologue to *Invisible Man* of black consciousness emerging within "a slightly different sense of time," in which one is "never quite on the beat" but is attuned to the value of the breaks in temporality as innovative and critically useful sites of critique.[38] The value of Ellisonian invisibility, much like the Du Boisian double-consciousness that Baldwin's work embodies, lies in the insight gathered from being able to recognize the existential break represented by black humanity in the United States, and aesthetically manipulating that break in order to forge a critical perspective, which in its form and texture of presentation takes on qualities of this outsiderness.

Baldwin's narration of his evolving sense of black historical consciousness and political critique is established through the dissonance of the opening pages, as they present a collage of interwoven memories, blending fragments and traces such as the connection he remembers making between "ideas and velvet" at age five, the terror he feels regarding his father throughout his childhood and adolescence, the strong sense of solidarity with both his mother and brother in the face of "the man we called my father," and the "miraculous" quality of a newborn baby that seems to embody several levels of allegorical (national and racial) meaning. The imagery of the baby is meant to linger through the totality of the text, as Baldwin explains the complex nature of the miraculous as a certain horizon of life, through an intimate, precise, and yet depersonalized meditation on the bodily reality and existential needs of an emergent life:

A newborn baby is an extraordinary event; and I have never seen two babies who looked or even sounded remotely alike. Here it is, this breathing miracle who could not live an instant without you, with a skull more fragile than an egg, a miracle of eyes, legs, toenails, and (especially) lungs. It gropes in the light like a blind

thing—it *is*, for the moment, blind—what can it make of what
it sees? . . . Presently, it discovers it has *you*, and since it has
already decided it wants to live, it gives you a toothless smile
when you come near it, gurgles or giggles when you pick it up,
holds you tight by the thumb or the eyeball or the hair, and,
having already opted against solitude, howls when you put it
down. You begin the extraordinary journey of beginning to
know and to control this creature. You know the sound—the
meaning—of one cry from another; without knowing that you
know it. You know when it's hungry—that's one sound. You
know when it's angry. You know when it's bored. You know
when it's frightened. You know when it's suffering. You come
or you go or you sit still according to the sound the baby makes.
And you watch over it where I was born, even in your sleep,
because rats love the odor of newborn babies and are much,
much bigger.

Baldwin's attention to the sound of the baby, the formulation of its "cry" in
accordance with its various emotional states, at one level, suggests a certain calibration between sound, vitality, power, and struggle, as the sonic
is positioned as a space through which the most direct claims regarding life
and death might be signaled. Simultaneously, however, these utterances also
mark the proliferation of babies in the Baldwin family through a hopefulness
in and protection of the miracle of life, as well as an interminable chain of
responsibilities locking his mother, himself, and his siblings into a perspective on caring for new life in the face of perpetual threats to its existence, a
situation which, as Baldwin's evocative second-person prose conveys, "you
have either grown to love [it] or you have left home."[39] A level of metaphorical sound emerges in Baldwin's arrangements of his childhood memories
and reflections on his familial power dynamics as the lyricism of this rendering suggests a correlation between his critical understanding of his upbringing with the particular existential unease he feels regarding the possibility for
racial reckoning. If we are to read Baldwin's reflection as an acknowledgment
of the difficulty in maintaining the miraculous quality of life amid a delimited horizon for experience (due to both socioeconomic circumstance and
familial power dynamics), then Baldwin's flight from his father's Harlem
household may resonate with the political form of the work overall in its
initiation and recursive attention to the generation of an evolving critical

perspective on race relations that is enabled through Baldwin's mediation of expatriate flight and solidarity of return.

This opening sequence establishes a formal tone of loss, dislocation, and the attempt to suture the historical rupture brought about through the loss of a post–Civil Rights political reality, one in which, Baldwin might argue, children have been abandoned. Baldwin's narrative movement progresses as he frames the ephemerality of his early childhood memories within the narrative only to abruptly turn to the more present context of the late 1960s and early 1970s, focusing on his understanding of the ways his consciousness has been shaped by Martin Luther King, Jr.'s assassination. This new time in which "something has altered in me, something has gone away," is marked by Baldwin's loss of faith in the idea of America, as he states that "one could scarcely be deluded by Americans anymore, one scarcely dared expect anything from the great, vast, blank generality." Baldwin's sense of political estrangement is further captured by his observation that "the marchers and petitioners were forced to suppose the existence of an entity which, when the chips were down, could not be located—*i.e.*, there *are* no American people yet," other than "those descendants of a barbarous Europe who arbitrarily and arrogantly reserve the right to call themselves Americans."[40]

Baldwin's opening blends the tonality of Black Power's indictment of the U.S. racial state with a contemplative framing of American identity as more of an unfinished question. His fracturing of a distinctive, easily identifiable Black Arts Movement and Black Power critical sound stems from the fact that his position as a social critic through the 1960s was often configured in opposition to the Black Arts Movement, yet his writing in *No Name in the Street* clearly intersects with more reflective critiques emerging from that era of literary and critical production. Repositioning Baldwin's long essay within a fluid landscape of post–Civil Rights movement era black radical thought begins to more complexly render what we imagine the Black Arts Movement to have represented. For example, Larry Neal, writing in a 1966 issue of *The Liberator* (in the third of a series of essays on the role of the black writer that also addressed the writing of Richard Wright and Ralph Ellison), points out that Baldwin's role as a black writer should be understood in a dialectical rather than oppositional relationship to the efforts of Black Arts Movement writers committed to revolutionary change. Although he is critical of Baldwin as often falling back on a "supernatural kind of love," and of his "pleading with white America for the humanity of the Negro," Neal ultimately points to Baldwin's ability to "lay bare the corrupt morality of America as an essential stage in the unleashing of a dynamic new force among the younger black writers of the 1960s." Neal's claims regarding Baldwin need to be judged with the understanding that they are being offered before the writing of *No Name in the Street*, and thus might be slightly reimagined in a manner that complicates the ideological deficits that Neal is framing. Neal's discussion of Baldwin suggests that even in its perceived "limitations," Baldwin's writing charts a new path forward and demonstrates the strength of one half of the aesthetic–political synthesis Neal desires for black writing—outlined by the bringing together of Baldwin's keen social commentary with Ellison's grounding in the modalities of black cultural expression. Neal terms Baldwin's contribution to black literary political engagement as a "commitment to some kind of social dynamic," and his reflections convey a great deal of deliberation as Neal seems to intuit the complex possibility against a sense of constraint within Baldwin's writing. Neal understands that few besides Baldwin have the critical and analytical tools to diagnose racism and race relations, but that Baldwin's observations are rendered in an effort to "'save' America."[41] Hearing Baldwin on multiple frequencies enables Neal to be heard outside of the more narrow critiques of Baldwin penned by Amiri Baraka and Eldridge Cleaver, for while Neal still desires a more politically radical sensibility within new black writing in the 1960s, he is unequivocal in asserting the centrality of Baldwin's sound as a constituent aspect of a Black Arts Movement continuum of resistance-based cultural politics.

Given the fact that Neal's writing in 1966 precedes the more definitively radical contours of Baldwin's thought taking shape during the late 1960s and early 1970s, there is nonetheless a crucial connection between Neal's consistent inquiry into the intersections of political and historical consciousness and the sensory through the 1960s and 1970s, and Baldwin's focus on the specific phenomenological states created and lingering through the resonance of historical loss. Immediately after condemning the failed promise of America through the lens of King's murder, Baldwin reinvokes a notion of loss as temporal discombobulation, a blues-like sensibility containing the possibility of reassessing the political present through the memory of dislocation. The temporal dimensions of Baldwin's dislocation are notable in the way they are signaled through a specific historical event, but blend into a more diffuse sense of memory and historical consciousness: "The mind is a strange and terrible vehicle, moving according to rigorous rules of its own; and my own mind, after I had left Atlanta, began to move backward in time, to places, people, and events I thought I had forgotten. Sorrow drove it there, I think, sorrow, and a certain kind of bewilderment, triggered, perhaps, by something which happened to me in connection with Martin's funeral." Baldwin's sense of time is calibrated through the symbolic and very real presence of the suit he wore to King's funeral and vowed to never wear again. He begins unfolding his meditation through an orchestration of memory and time that follows the trajectory of racial meaning emblazoned across the suit by reflecting on his contact with an old childhood friend in need of a suit, who reads a newspaper column mentioning the fact that Baldwin will never wear this suit again. The exchange of the suit from Baldwin to his childhood friend, "drenched in the blood of all the crimes of my country," becomes a flashpoint through which Baldwin levels a harsh critique of his friend's middle-class disavowal of a critical black political consciousness, ending in Baldwin's diatribe against this friend's lack of political consciousness—most directly noted through his friend's disdain for antipoverty efforts and, most disturbingly to Baldwin, an unwillingness to condemn the American involvement in the Vietnam War.[42] This encounter ends with a sense of frozen time created when Baldwin, fed up with the friend's lack of political awareness and his assumption that he can, in his words relayed by Baldwin, "stand up and tell you what I think we're trying to do here," proclaims (a few drinks in, Baldwin admits), "You stand up, motherfucker, and I'll kick you in the ass!" The first person plural that the acquaintance speaks of and that Baldwin rejects, reflects the idea of black people having a post–Civil Rights investment in the idea of American national identity and foreign policy to the extent of supporting an imperialist aggression against darker-skinned people in Southeast Asia. This narrative space created through the temporal freezing opens onto Baldwin's critically reflective mode that adjusts the almost caricatured Black Power–inflected outburst against black people "aiding the slave master to enslave yet more millions of dark people," with an added dimension of philosophical inquiry into the scene: "For that bloody suit was *their* suit, after all, it had been bought *for* them, it had even been bought *by* them: *They* had created Martin, he had not created them, and the blood in which the fabric of that suit was stiffening was theirs."[43] Baldwin's critique of his friend's identification with an idea of middle-class American comfort is amplified through the sound of Baldwin's emphasized "*their*" and its signification of a self-serving modulation and maintenance of King's meaning and legacy. The deep resonance of Baldwin's pointed phrasing underlines the solidity of the "*their*" as an emergence of middle-class black consciousness in Civil Rights and post–Civil Rights America, and one that, as it does so, puts into greater national relief the ways King's radicalized presence in his final years has been ignored, forgotten, and cast aside as irrelevant and irritating to the construction of this mode of black middle-class affiliation.

Baldwin's critical lens dilates in several ways during the transition he orchestrates at the midpoint of his narrative, moving between his account of arriving at the Montgomery, Alabama, airport in 1957 to cover the Civil Rights movement throughout the South, and his perspective on the pivotal, later years of the 1960s, years marked for Baldwin through their revelation of the irredeemable aspects of American racial hypocrisy. This dilation is notable in the way it opens up several interrelated critical registers, pushing ideas of racial antagonism and resistance into framings that allow for further ideological expansion. In this narrative transition, Baldwin describes arriving in the airport and feeling the "concentrated, malevolent poverty of spirit" as a palpable force inhabited and wielded by the small group of local whites intent on keeping tabs on him. Baldwin's characterization of this malevolence marking the "cradle of the Confederacy" as "one of the most wretched [towns] on the face of the earth" subtly inverts Frantz Fanon's Manichean binary of the colonizer and the colonized, retroactively coloring these early experiences of Baldwin's within the Civil Rights movement. Rather than simply applying Fanon's theories to a U.S. context, as many other critical theorists of race at the time did, Baldwin instead reconfigures this binary dialectically, showing the ways in which wretchedness, as the perception of how black bodies are to be defined within contexts of colonization and segregation, can be improvised on to demonstrate the soulless character of white men, "imagining that they were holding back a flood" and policing a racial dividing line that, for Baldwin, is fungible, due to the irrefutable evidence of racial amalgamation displayed across the spectrum of black people in the South: "Girls the color of honey, men nearly the color of chalk, hair like silk, hair like cotton, hair like wire, eyes blue, grey, green, hazel, black, like the gypsy's, brown like the Arab's, narrow nostrils, thin, wide lips, thin lips, every conceivable variation struck along incredible gamuts—it was not the Southland that one could hope to keep a secret!"[44] Baldwin's observations challenge the racial dividing line by posing the visual evidence of interracial mixture and fluidity against the context of American apartheid. His blending of phenomenological and epistemological aspects of race theory builds on what Frantz Fanon, in his

close attention to the narrative elements of the struggle and refusal of hegemonic systems of colonization and racism, refers to as a "counter move," an
orientation toward reimagining possibilities for existence outside of systems
of oppression. This "counter move" echoes aspects of Baldwin's articulation
of a blues sensibility in its assertion of the knowledge that, as Fanon argues,
"we cannot go resolutely forward unless we first realize our alienation."[45]

Fanon and Baldwin both present seemingly Manichean dualities as
emergent senses of historical consciousness that reflect convergences of
the past within the present, rather than indicating "a past where [the peo-
ple] no longer exist." The temporality of revolutionary awareness is both
definitive and suggestive, as it, in the phrasing of Fanon, "will suddenly call
everything into question" within "that zone of hidden fluctuation where
the people can be found," and where "their souls are crystallized and their
perception and respiration transfigured."[46] The poetics inscribed within
Fanon's "zone" reflects an inclination to exist within and to create breaks in
time by recognizing the fluidity of historical consciousness rather than its
representation as static and temporally bounded. The contingent possibilities of the present and its futurity, as Baldwin and Fanon attest to in different
yet overlapping ways, do not simply exist on the physical level; rather, it
inflects the existential components of both white supremacy and the resistance of black subjects to it.[47] The investment in a poetics searching for possibilities of enactment through language is tied to the ability of both writers
to modulate the sound of their critical approaches. The autobiographical
register, fused within the mobilization of vignettes, creates a narrative architectonics in which the sonic is prevalent as an orientation that destabilizes
the existing claims and assumptions of the American social order. It is not
incidental that Fanon's critical intervention is framed by his engagement
with the musical poetics of Keita Fodeba's composition "African Dawn." In
providing the example of Fodeba's musical poetry, Fanon, anticipating the
epistemological grounds from which Baldwin's perspective takes shape,
highlights the use of phenomenological registers such as the sonic as tools
that enhance the organic approaches to resistance emerging from the immediacy of struggle and transformation. As Fanon states, "We should not therefore be content to delve into the people's past to find concrete examples to
counter colonialism's endeavors to distort and depreciate. We must work
and struggle in step with the people so as to shape the future and prepare
the ground where vigorous shoots are already sprouting."[48] Both as formal
orientation, in Baldwin's writing, and as site of performative resistance in

Fanon's conceptualization, ideas of blackness configured through sound, space, and time help to frame the relationship between postcolonial and diasporic subjectivity and resistance as one of interacting "structures of feeling"; that is, manifestations of black historical and political experience that emerge as ephemeral, phenomenological orientations that gather critical density through an ability to exceed more predictable lines of narration. Considering the conceptualization of sound through these interlocking levels of black critical thought diagnoses the differential temporalities of coloniality and racial segregation, as well as the need for alternate epistemologies such as the blues to resist the impositions of these master narratives.

Against this backdrop of narrative acoustics, Baldwin, following his reflection on his experiences reporting on the Civil Rights movement, transitions into the second part of *No Name in the Street* through a series of reflections on the telling linkages between domestic and international formations of neoliberal governance taking hold within the afterlives of colonialism and Jim Crow:

> Anyone . . . who has worked in, or witnessed, any of the "anti-poverty" programs in the American ghetto has an instant understanding of "foreign aid" in the "underdeveloped" nations. In both locales, the most skillful adventurers improve their material lot; the most dedicated of the natives are driven mad or inactive—or underground—by frustration; while the misery of the hapless, voiceless millions is increased—and not only that: their reaction to their misery is described to the world as criminal. Nowhere is this grisly pattern clearer than it is in America today, but what America is doing within her borders, she is doing around the world.

Baldwin suggests that the terms of black freedom must be philosophically grounded within an understanding of social transformation that moves beyond a reliance on governmental structures and mechanisms, an orientation that instead frames the cost of freedom as the continual awareness of and engagement with the depth of a certain "history of a system of thought."[49]

This point is elaborated as Baldwin recounts his 1963 encounter with Malcolm X and notes the time in the following way: "When the Black Muslims meant to the American people exactly what the Black Panthers mean today, and when they were described in exactly the same terms by that High Priest, J. Edgar Hoover, and when many of us believed or made ourselves believe that the American state still contained within itself the power of self-confrontation, the power to change itself in the direction of honor and knowledge and freedom." This critical look into the past, which draws together past and present (the "so-called Nixon administration") as well as betrayal and possibility, underlines Baldwin's skepticism in structures of American racial democracy and his desire to explore avenues and forms of redress that might mystify the disciplinary gazes of racial ordering and subjection. Baldwin's hope in the political possibilities of the post–Civil Rights years revolves around the ability of the "excluded" to "forge a new morality, to create the principles on which a new world will be built," as he suggests that the energy and attention of the nation which had been previously focused on expanding equal rights for black Americans could no longer be relied on to insure that these efforts would continue in good faith, or be furthered in the face of new forms of racial division and subjection.[50]

Increasingly, the specter of black consciousness, the "new morality" Baldwin refers to, was framed by the media as a disruptive threat to the tenuous idea of American racial inclusion. Baldwin's position reveals the fissures between equal rights and the liberal tolerance and goodwill of mainstream American values. Rather than representing an ending to an era, Baldwin's conceptualization of the idea of "post–Civil Rights" offers a flashpoint or opening into new times of struggle in which the points of engagement expand to more directly address the reformation of social inequality and interracial fear, despite the prevalence of claims regarding the reconstruction of the racial state seemingly ushered in by the Civil Rights movement. For Baldwin, the fear and misrecognition marking these new times of racial confrontation represent a "new balance" or "unprecedented inequality" of black pride in which selfhood is "no longer controlled by the white man's fantasies," as "the white man no longer knows who he is, whereas the black man knows them both."[51] The new temporality of black consciousness emerges through a recursive sense of narrative and historical time that Baldwin sutures through at once reflecting on the nearly decadelong expanse of time that has passed between his first encounter with Malcolm X and the present of his writing *No Name in the Street*, and, at the same time, showing the critical excavation of that moment's relevance to the seemingly "new times" of the present. This reconfiguration of black identity, deployed by Baldwin in the post–Civil Rights era, represents a positive fracture, a creative destruction of mind-sets that contain and constrain through physical, epistemological, and temporal force by fashioning alternate modalities of narrative time, space, and meaning.

The Sound of Poisoned Bread

Baldwin's conceptualization of a post–Civil Rights reality is further elaborated via indirect ideological meanings generated through the imagining of the sound anchoring his textual diagnosis and critique. We can hear such movement through the haunting strains of the spiritual lyrics "I told Jesus it would be all right / If He Changed my Name," which initiate the second section of the essay, titled, "To Be Baptized," as Baldwin suggests that baptism is both a spiritual and political force of reckoning. The idea of changing one's name speaks to the literal reality of such renaming by Malcolm X, and also suggests a general growth into the "new name" of a black radical consciousness that questions the possibility of achieving substantive redress and unqualified equality within the American racial state. This literary, critical soundscape within which a multiplicity of historical moments and theoretical reflections are represented is a formal tool Baldwin uses to express the simultaneity of the historical past, present, and future within his political consciousness. The sound of his prose lies, in this case, not simply in the words emerging from his narrative voice, but also in its approach to expanding sequences of narrative time, calibrating the movements of the essay with a renewed sense of freedom articulated through Baldwin's thought.

Baldwin's writing of No Name in the Street demonstrates a metaphorical relationship to sound, in that his essay helps define a tradition of black radical thought that was emerging in response to the limitations of, rather than possibilities for, racial equality in the United States. Baldwin's status within this tradition is somewhat particular and specifically noteworthy in that his deeply critical diagnosis of the U.S. racial state converges with the upsurge in late 1960s and 1970s black nationalist thought, but only as it has evolved through Baldwin's previous decades of attempting to work toward an ideal of interracial American identity (as in The Fire Next Time)—the sense that both black and white citizens, despite the historical flashpoints of racial antagonism, are ultimately bound together through a commitment (one that is, nonetheless, led by a spirit of black resistance and enlightenment) to "make America what America must become."[52] During the period in which Baldwin was composing No Name in the Street, however, the tenor of Baldwin's voice in articulating what he understood to be the central concerns facing black people in the United States, and the dispossessed of the world more broadly, exhibited a heightened sense of critical pessimism—that is, an increasing understanding of the lack of viable avenues for transforming the entrenched and recalibrated racial divisions existing both domestically and globally, yet still finding a pressing need to analyze these limits. Examples of these limits are expressed in Baldwin's 1968 essay "Black Power," signaling a fundamental inability of the nation "to do anything to make the lives of its black citizens less appalling." In cautiously assenting to the views of Stokely Carmichael (Kwame Toure), Baldwin contends that "*all* black Americans are born into a society which is determined—repeat, determined—that they shall never learn the truth about themselves or their society, which is determined that black men shall use as their only frame of reference what white Americans convey to them of their own potentialities, and of the shape, size, dimensions, and possibilities of the world."[53] Baldwin's sense of the narrative logic of racial subjection, a logic that operates both externally as violent force, and internally as psychic deficit, functions as a guiding force behind an American complex of physical, phenomenological, and psychological dimensions of racial identification, representation, and control. He elaborates on the early stages of this process of racism through historical narration in comments offered during his 1969 appearance before a House Select Subcommittee, which had convened to consider establishing a national commission on "Negro History and Culture." Baldwin testifies to the subcommittee regarding what he refers to as "the nigger we invent," a reflection of the process of miseducating black children to understand their self-definition as featuring "no past and really no present and certainly no future."[54] Furthermore, it is during this period that Baldwin speaks out publicly and unapologetically on behalf of Angela Davis and the Soledad Brothers. In his "An Open Letter to My Sister Angela Y. Davis" and his "Speech from the Soledad Rally," Baldwin clearly argues for the need to understand the possibilities of "the enormous revolution in black consciousness" signifying either "the beginning or the end of America,"[55] and the critical weight of the realization that "we are the victims and we are the results of a doctrine called white supremacy."[56] Finally, in the brief, but pivotal 1969 essay "The Price May Be Too High," Baldwin lays the anticipatory groundwork for a later intertextual linkage with No Name in the Street, as he reflects on what it means to convey "Sambo's truth": the floating, yet sedimented idea of black identity moving between the "private disaster" of black "public discontent" and "the pretension not to know the reason for Sambo's discontent" offered by the collective governmental and social sectors of the nation.[57]

The idea of "Sambo" reverberates throughout the haunting conclusion of *No Name in the Street*, as Baldwin invokes the meaning of its absence within the new times of late 1960s black consciousness. Before reflecting on the critical weight of this absence, Baldwin frames the context of uncertainty and radical possibility within this historical moment:

> In this place, and more particularly, in this time, generations appear to flower, flourish, and wither with the speed of light. I don't think that this is merely the inevitable reflection of middle age: I suspect that there really has been some radical alteration in the structure, the nature, of time. One may say that there are no clear images; everything seems superimposed on, and at war with something else. There are no clear vistas: the road that seems to pull one forward into the future is also pulling one backward into the past. I felt, anyway, kaleidoscopic, fragmented, walking through the streets of San Francisco, trying to decipher whatever it was that my own consciousness made of all the elements in which I was entangled, and which were all tangled up in me.[58]

This new, fractured sense of time, history, and consciousness becomes defined, in Baldwin's mind, through the distinctive architectonics of this remembrance of the San Francisco Bay Area in 1968 and his framing of the tension that gives rise to a present in which linear ideas of historical accounting and social transformation cease to be useful.

This sense of tension animating black historical consciousness is perhaps most clearly evident in his recall of the pre–flower children era of San Francisco and his several-page replaying of the central questions emanating from both white and black student communities. Baldwin restages the asking of these questions through the distinctive sound of their projection and conveys their ideological formation through the conditional qualities of their audition. From the white students we hear questions such as "Would black people take it amiss if the white kids came into the neighborhood, and—fraternized is probably the only word—with the kids in the pool halls, the bars, the soda fountain? Would black people take it amiss if some of them were to visit a black church? Could they invite members of the black congregation to their white churches, or would the black people feel uncomfortable? Wouldn't it be a good idea if the black and white basketball teams played each other?" Baldwin's conceptualization of late 1960s historical time and consciousness is specifically reflected in his rendering of the difficulty white liberal youth encounter in attempting to achieve a level of introspection within a historical moment in which a renewed sense of black militancy emerges. This dissonance reflects a broken "historical wheel" of racial retribution, marked by the impossible desire of "the flower children" to reject the fruits of their inheritance of white privilege, as such a legacy "could be laid down only at Sambo's feet." Baldwin remixes the historicized "coon" imagery of Sambo within a rapidly radicalizing moment of late 1960s black consciousness. He dispenses with the sound of minstrel song that might accompany a synesthetic recall of this stock racist type, in favor of a darker tonality conveying an understanding that the flower children's attempted refusal of white power cannot be so straightforwardly accomplished due to Black Power's removal of Sambo's visage and sonic presence from the racial imaginary of black youth. Baldwin's analysis of the flower children's need for Sambo, rather than simply reflecting a white reliance on racist stereotypes, more deeply signals their vexed position, posed between a genuine desire to act on "their moral obligations to the darker brother," and a reluctance to accept the broader critical standpoint arising from many of those "darker brothers" based on the fact that "the black situation in America was but one aspect of the fraudulent nature of American life."[59]

The discrepancy between black radicalism and white liberalism that Baldwin cites in this meditation is clearly frustrating, as Baldwin notes that both sides of this equation are "targets of the very same forces" (what Baldwin refers to as the Fourth Reich), yet "certainly were not together" as the black youth were "not putting their trust in flowers," due to the fact that "this troubled white person might suddenly go home."[60] The loaded narrative history of American race relations and racism seem to permanently inflect the soundscape through which new meaning is attempting to emerge. Sound is an important sensory modality through which to consider this problematic, as it begins to reflect the reverberating, resounding permanence of white fear with a more emergent sense of black refusal that, in its convergence, represents a deeper historical problem than can be addressed at a broader systemic level. What Baldwin seems to desire is a level of critical, philosophically introspective listening, which Jean-Luc Nancy describes as an inclination "toward the opening of meaning."[61] For the antagonistic force within Baldwin's heavily layered existential argument is "the fraudu-lent and expedient nature of the American innocence which has always been able to persuade itself that it does not know what it knows too well." In his diagnosis of white fear in response to the perceived threat of black revolutionary self-defense, Baldwin points out that the visceral apprehen-sion felt by many whites in respect to black people taking up arms misses the larger point that "people who treat other people as less than human must not be surprised when the bread they have cast on the waters comes float-ing back to them, poisoned."[62] The failure of American self-reflection and critical listening, a conundrum increasingly found in the critical lens of Bald-win with the 1963 publication of *The Fire Next Time*, represents a seemingly insurmountable impasse that, in *No Name in the Street*, Baldwin is only able to outline a corrective to by suggesting that the nation listen more carefully to the sound of this poisoned bread.

This sonic formation resonates through transatlantic time and space for Baldwin, marking his vision of an intensified double-consciousness reflect-ing the "two undefined and currently undefineable proper nouns," that is, Afro-American. The dissonance of the hyphenated term comes to signify an arbitrary, confused linkage that remains troubled in the sense that neo-colonial Africa represents only a "cradle and potential" as long as European exploitation persists—even in the wake of colonialism. Baldwin's unfold-ing of meaning through interlocked historical and global points of refer-ence demonstrates his particular narrative logic in projecting a revived awareness of the unending American and global crisis. His featuring of the story of his friend Tony Maynard's unjust imprisonment in a German jail while awaiting extradition to the United States to face seemingly trumped-up murder charges, creates a space to focus on black incarceration as a con-dition that may move across the Atlantic, and that, for Baldwin, seems to reflect Aimé Césaire's pointed critique of racist practices and logic as trans-historical, global, and epistemological forces emanating from the "progres-sive dehumanization" of the bourgeoisie.[63] The Maynard case puts into relief a defining factor of the post–Civil Rights era—the ways in which law enforcement and incarceration have become the new modes of racialized social control in the wake of hyper-visible Jim Crow practices of segrega-tion and racial violence. This continuity of control, management, and sub-jection is, in Baldwin's eyes, perhaps most effectively challenged by the Black Panthers' presence and their articulation of a new force, "which set itself in opposition to that force which uses people as things and which grinds down men and women and children, not only in the ghetto, into an unrecognizable powder." Baldwin is perhaps at his most hopeful in considering the possibilities of this revolutionary force, not necessarily through the specific goals it might achieve, but rather through the recognition of its potential in generating new energy that can create ruptures within teleological myths of American racial progress, moving forward instead with the understanding conveyed by "one of my brothers," that "the spirit of the South is the spirit of America." Baldwin's prophetic writing, in its utilization of sound as a critical framework, and, ultimately, in its inability to conclude—"This book is not finished—can never be finished by me"—extends the reach of the present in which he writes across multiple temporal and critical frames at once, and still may contain the analytical scope, weight, and method needed to sift through the shifting meanings of the long post–Civil Rights era we still sit within.[64]

Epilogue

Sounding the Long Civil Rights Moment

WHEN WILL IT END? Will there be a historical point at which we can mark the end of post–Civil Rights unfreedom that has persisted as an underside to the progress represented by the movement as many African Americans continue to fall outside the vision of social transformation projected by the nation? How might an analysis of post–Civil Rights black political culture account for what Adolph Reed refers to as the "reconstitution of domination" that has emerged as a self-regulating and self-disciplining force in African American sociopolitical formations?[1] This inclination toward one-dimensionality has usurped ideas of black radical possibility, allowing the terms of racial redress sanctioned by the Civil Rights–era racial state to become hegemonic boundaries that delimit ideas of freedom within these more prescribed conceptual frameworks. Gil Scott-Heron's prescient album *Free Will* aurally reflected on these queries in 1972, projecting his voice, and its capacity to open realms of the political imagination, within a liminal space between the waning Black Power era and the indeterminacy of the years to come.[2] The distinctive sonority of Heron's voice and the incredible breadth and diversity of his musical sound highlight his projection of black consciousness as both a mode of critical inquiry and a state of introspective reflection. Pointed, challenging, sardonic, tragic, and often humorous, Heron's tonal and thematic calibrations are consistently grounded in the exigencies of his non-static present. His creativity and critical thought emerge, as Fred Moten would say, "in the break." His sound explores the gaps within ideas of African American community formation. At the same time, his critical tonality questions ideas of black consciousness that rely on notions of black nationalism based on antagonism rather than on capacious ideas of self-determination. Heron's music is imminently suited to the specificity of the post–Civil Rights era—revealing its vicissitudes, pitfalls, and complexities in the wake of purportedly massive changes to the American racial state.

The distinctive two-part arrangement of Heron's album features one side of lyrically contemplative and sonically diverse compositions produced with an eight-piece band playing a mixture of jazz, funk, and blues rhythms. The second side showcases Heron's spoken-word political poetry and recalls the rhetorically strident approach of his first LP, *Small Talk at 125th and Lennox* (1970). The divergent sonic orientations marking each side of *Free Will* are often analyzed as embodying two distinct aspects of his musical career. While this is an important fact to note, I also hear a productive fusion of Heron's sonic and musical proclivities moving between the sides and highlighting his distinctive post–Civil Rights critical perspective. Through this circulation of musical sound, Heron's album critiques the permanence of racist attitudes and policies that undermine and obstruct historical transformation. At the same moment, Heron's mediation of sound reflects the indeterminacy marking the 1970s, and the shift into a sociopolitical reality no longer primarily defined through clear lines of racial antagonism. Sonically capturing and synthesizing this complex orientation, *Free Will* asserts itself as a flashpoint for considering the continued mediation of black sound, narration, and political critique.

Heron opens the musical side of the album with Hubert Laws's soulful, vibrant flute initiating an accelerated tempo that is quickly joined by drums, piano, and Heron's voice. The projection of his voice falls seamlessly within the tightly measured and subtly funky space of the composition. The synchronization between the sound of his voice, the tempo of the music, and the lyrical meaning of the song evocatively links the sonic atmosphere of the composition and Heron's political intent. His punctuated lyrical refrain, "But peace won't be still of its own free will," resonates both in its reference to an idea of self-determination framed within Western philosophical discourse and as a reminder that the potential for transformation during the Civil Rights and Black Power movements may dissipate without the energy of those committed to maintaining a state of "peace."

Heron places focused pressure on the issue of African American self-determination through the first track on the second side of the album, "The King Alfred Plan." The spoken-word selection poetically illustrates the contested nature of black space and the fear of being unduly subject to police and governmental control. Heron introduces the composition with his carefully spoken words, "It's 1972, an election year; once again, black people are running—for their lives. The reasons are things like the King Alfred Plan." Heron continues his conversational introduction, stating that "the

concentration camps . . . used during the Second World War to house ori-
ental Americans are now being refurbished to confine their new residents,
i.e., black people." The title of the "plan" is based on John A. Williams's
1967 fictional account of a U.S. government contingency plan to forcibly
detain black leaders and masses of black urban residents during a time of
protracted racial unrest. Heron's allusion to Williams's novel is less a reflection of the actual possibility of such a plan being put into action, than a
metaphor for the fracturing and continued subjection being experienced
within many African American communities. Through the lyrical emphasis of the song, Heron depicts the post–Civil Rights era as a time of "wal-
lowing in the echoes of Malcolm's words." His use of the echo form reduces
the time and space of separation between Malcolm X's presence in the early
to mid 1960s, and the contemporary moment Heron is observing. These
echoes, for Heron, reverberate with the possibility that "black unity" is not
reducible to a slogan and is instead based on "love and not hate." Love in
this formulation is revolutionary because its collective force generates the
freedom to "unite on our own" rather than out of fear of "barbed wire death."
The metaphor of containment that Heron illustrates through the idea of
the King Alfred Plan is extended through his staccato delivery of images
and ideas that highlight the visceral nature of incarceration, poverty, and
apartheid: "Locked in cages, penned, hemmed in, shoulder to shoulder,
arms out-stretched for just a crust of bread / Watermelon mirages / An
oasis that does not exist / Conjured up by the bubbling stench / Unwashed
bodies and unsanitary quarters / Concrete and barbed-wire / Babies screaming."[3] Heron's rhythmically measured delivery underlines the unresolved
echoing call of Malcolm X that represents a potential pitfall among those
who are "stumbling around in a mental circle," and have "never cared enough
to be black," set against the possibility of a hopeful post–Civil Rights futurity for those who are prepared to "unite on our own." The political dimensions of Heron's sound and lyricism amplify his desire for this call to be
taken up as a sonic pronouncement on the unfinished and undecided nature
of the post–Civil Rights era.

Heron's sound highlights the convergence of aurality, political critique,
and narration that I analyze within the wake of the Civil Rights movement.[4]
The prophetic quality of his lyricism and political analysis also reflects an
awareness of the mid to late 1970s "demise of the second reconstruction"
as an open-ended historical state that will continue to mark the sociopolitical landscape of African American activists and artists who are wary of

the thin lines between progress and alienation, equality and retrenchment, hope and failure, that continue to frame black life in the United States. Given the open-ended, largely unresolved nature of the social conditions defining the post–Civil Rights era, how can we imagine a literary genealogy of experimental African American writing that continues to assert itself through elaborations of its sonority? A majority of the connections between writing and sound that I have explored in *Imagine the Sound* have been articulated through ideas of musical experimentation and often, even when they do not expressly reference music, are clearly invested in ideas of the experimental, the surreal, or a broader sense of the avant-garde. These artistic modes were all concentrated within and around the years my study focuses on, but as the post–Civil Rights era expands temporally, the possibilities increase for sonic narration to emerge outside the heavy influence of avant-garde musical experimentation.

One such trajectory of sonic and political expansion emerges in Gloria Naylor's novel *Linden Hills* (1985), a heavily allegorical and critical portrait of African American middle-class community formation in the aftermath of the Civil Right movement. Naylor conveys the pathological self-hatred, corruption, and intra-racial subjection that occurs within a hierarchical black community tenuously built on a disingenuous idea of achieving the American dream.[5] She evocatively condenses these complex layers of race, power, and subjection through the haunting sound of a piercing scream. The scream is heard by the teenage protagonists of the novel, Willie Mason and Lester Tilson, as they sit in Lester's bedroom in his family's house, situated at the top of the concentric, ascending circles of the community. The sound travels up from the bottom of the hill, a demographic structure that has been inverted, we learn, by the founder of the community, the first Luther Nedeed, who purchased the land in 1820 (possibly with money from selling his wife and children back into slavery in Mississippi before coming north), to initiate a process of black capitalist development in the face of white power in which the bottom is the center of power. It is from this bottom level, the base of Nedeed patriarchal power, that the scream is projected and then ultimately rushes through Lester's window, "a long thin wail," ushered in on a "cold burst of wind."[6] The scream, we later learn, arises from Willa Nedeed, the estranged, captive wife of the most recent Luther Nedeed, as she holds the emaciated body of her young son who has succumbed to starvation while being imprisoned with Willa in the basement of the Nedeed house. Their captivity and torture results from the disruption that the son's too-light skin color causes within the pattern of physical replication that has symbolized the patriarchal power of the Nedeed men for over 150 years. As Naylor illustrates, the Nedeeds' power is built on a conflation of black nationalist capitalism and a veneration for white power, as the Nedeed men use their ownership and control of property to underline their belief that the ideological contours of white supremacy can be situated as the basis for African American community formation. As a constructed symbol of African American success, progress, and achievement, Naylor describes Linden Hills as a black microcosm of the emptiness of the American dream:

> Linden Hills—a place where people had worked hard, fought hard, and saved hard for the privilege to rest in the soft shadows of those heart-shaped trees. In Linden Hills they could forget that the world said you spelled black with a capital nothing. Well, they were something and there was everything around them to show it. The world hadn't given them anything but the chance to fail—and they hadn't failed, because they were in Linden Hills . . . They wanted what Luther Nedeed had, and he had shown them how to get it: Just stay right here; you step outside Linden Hills and you've stepped into history—someone else's history about what you couldn't ever do. The Nedeeds had made a history there and it spoke loudly of what blacks could do. They were never leaving Linden Hills. There was so much to be gotten.[7]

The layers of race and ideology that Naylor frames within the narrative resound through Willa's scream, but Willie and Lester can only remotely grasp at the significance of the sound before they descend into Linden Hills in search of work to help them through the winter holiday season:

> They each sat alone in the dark, trying to link some sort of human emotion to that sound because an ancient instinct told them it wasn't an animal sending out that cry into the world. They knew it didn't sound like someone in pain or danger. And it didn't echo the heightened edges of despair. Lester and Willie were totally confused, since there was really nothing that had touched their twenty years to help them locate its cause—they had not lived long enough to recognize a plea for lost time. Up from the bottom of Linden Hills, winding between bare branches, it came sliding into Lester's room

again, clear and distinct now that they had even stopped breathing to await its arrival. This time it moved across their chests, up the far wall, and over the ceiling before dying at the base of the window.[8]

The scream's purposeful movement into the aural, physical, and psychic space of the two young men propels the narrative forward through their subsequent descent into Linden Hills as cultural observers of the racial melodramas of African American middle-class pathology, duplicity and suffering. Often, the scenes and interactions they observe become surreal and colored with almost supernatural qualities because of the insular world in which they take place. At times, Willie can only translate his observations through internal quotations of poetic lyrics, and it is these renderings of an internalized sound, along with the bridging that Naylor articulates between the consciousness of Willie and Willa through dreams and thoughts that increasingly collide as the story progresses, that give voice to an emergent trajectory of resistance against the vampiric patriarchal capitalism Luther Nedeed holds up as a value of black progress.

The sound and fluidity of inchoate thoughts render the critical concerns of a narrative as impressionistic rather than definitive and linear in meaning. This literary orientation allows African American writers like Naylor to delve into the increasingly complex attitudes and circumstances of black cultural politics as the historical distance from the Civil Rights movement widens. John Edgar Wideman's *Philadelphia Fire* (1990), like Naylor's *Linden Hills*, diagnoses contradictions and self-destructive inclinations within African American social and political life during the ongoing post–Civil Rights era. Rather than signal specific sounds through which his critique might be emphasized, Wideman fashions sound as an organizing principle through which a range of narrative voices and perspectives emerge as he explores the meaning of the 1985 bombing of a West Philadelphia house communally inhabited by members of the MOVE organization. The attack on politically conscious black activists by a police department operating under the rule of a black mayor, Wilson Goode, occupies the center of Wideman's narrative, a point around which voices centripetally move in and out of modernist stream of consciousness and postmodernist self-reflexivity. Wideman's various forms and tonal dimensions of narration sprawl across the novel, and are projected in the final section of the text through the perspective of JB, a character Wideman intriguingly positions as homeless, but is more properly an urban everyman who is narrating the cityscape not

only in the wake of the MOVE attack, but also as a broader deterritorial-
ization of black space through the intensity of spectacular and structural
violence: "He thinks of young black boys shotgunning other black boys,
black girl babies raising black girl babies and the streets thick with love
and honor and duty and angry songs running along broken curbs, love and
honor and duty and nobody understands because nobody listens, can't
hear in the bloody current that courses and slops dark splashes on the
cracked cement, how desperate things have become. How straight the
choices, noble the deeds." JB's critical thoughts necessitate a sound that
Wideman establishes through ideas of rap lyricism and the ability to
quickly capture and distill images and ideas in fleeting yet resonant forms.
This aesthetic feature of Wideman's novel is itself a crucial thematic statement on the possibility that this form of urban black expression offers a
sonic epistemology for decoding the hidden and unspeakable meanings of
the post–Civil Rights era deterioration of black urban space. As we hear
the sounds spin outward, they tell several stories at once:

> *This is your rap-rap-rapcity rapper on*
> *the dial*
> *So just cool out and lissen awhile*
> *Cause if you don't dig what I'm rappin*
> *bout*
> *They'll pull your skin off, turn you inside*
> *out*
> *It's a new trickeration, a hip sensation,*
> *divine inspiration blowing cross the*
> *nation*
> *They peel your skin then you're in like*
> *Flynn*
> *Drain your brain so ain't no pain*
> *Makes you feel so real, it's a helluva deal*
> *No money down, easy credit*
> *Skin's gone, you just can't forget it.*[9]

Wideman's turn to rap announces itself as a convergence of sound and knowledge that needs to be listened to in order to avoid a condition of skinless-
ness, and being turned "inside out." The beauty of the lyrical suggestiveness
and precision of the rap lyrics allows Wideman to move between ideas of

skin being burned off by militaristic forces of the state, as in the case of the MOVE bombing, that may nonetheless be directed ultimately by the authority of black leadership, and a connected idea of losing one's skin and being turned against the interests of a broader community by the allure of hegemonically constructed black political power.

While the symmetry between JB's style of rapping and old school rap poetics is striking, Wideman also establishes a range of experimental narrative structures in the novel that connect to later aesthetic innovations in rap production and lyricism, innovations that help Wideman expand what he has called the "architectonics" of the text. In his essay "The Architectonics of Fiction" Wideman describes the connections between storytelling and the marginality of minority writers. Rather than framing marginality as a deficit, Wideman contends that "minority writers hold certain advantages in circumstances of cultural breakdown, reorientation, transition . . . Imagination has evolved as discipline, defense, coping mechanism, counterweight to the galling facts of life. We've learned to confer upon ourselves the power of making up our lives, changing them as we go along." In this context, he cites rap as a promising form of discursive resistance that can counter the "destructive definitions of the Master's tongue." It can become a "moveable feast, fluid in time, space, modality, exhibiting in theme and variations multiple relationships, including the power and independence, to change places, reverse the hierarchies, be the dominant order."[10] The reversal or replacement is not simply a reorganization of two binaries, however, because Wideman notes that the qualities that define this level of cultural expression are based on collage, mixing, blending, sampling, and fusion. Much closer to structures of feeling (to borrow from Raymond Williams), the emergent, ephemeral, and revisionary qualities of rap aesthetics are based on concepts of resistance through de- and reconstruction rather than simple replication.

While my reflections on Wideman and Naylor suggest that perhaps retrenchment has been as prevalent as progress over the past forty years, *Imagine the Sound* concludes by proposing that we find in their literary observations radical openings onto new and evolving paradigms of African American aesthetic form and critical thought. It is not despair or anger that motivates the sonically inflected texts of these writers; it is the understanding that sound, the always expanding aural dimensions of perception and experience, may best allow for creative renderings of black life that take seriously the critical possibility of literary expression to diagnose injustice and effect change.

Acknowledgments

There are many thanks to be given to all who have made this book a possibility and now a reality. Thank you to those at the end of this road: my editor, Richard Morrison, and his assistant, Erin Warholm-Wohlenhaus, and the entire staff at the University of Minnesota Press for taking on my project with such enthusiasm. Thanks as well to Joy Stoffers and Ricardo Bracho for helping me prepare the final manuscript and index. I am very grateful to the anonymous readers of my manuscript who wrote detailed, insightful, and useful reports. I hope I have been able to bring out the finer points of their suggestions in the final product.

I was fortunate to begin this project as a graduate student in the Department of African American Studies at the University of California, Berkeley. Barbara Christian was my first mentor and a cherished family friend. Her deeply nuanced understanding of literature as an imaginative tool of social critique continues to inform my thinking, writing, and teaching. Vèvè Clark taught me what it means to be an attentive interlocutor as a teacher and mentor. I thank her as well for the many dimensions she added to my thinking about African diaspora literature and theory. I am very thankful to Waldo Martin, Ula Taylor, and Robert Allen for helping me to grow as an interdisciplinary thinker. My dissertation chair, Saidiya Hartman, helped me articulate a critical vision that has grown into this book. I thank her for her dedication to this project and for her consummate grace and professionalism as a mentor.

At Rutgers, Cheryl Wall, Michelle Stephens, Evie Shockley, Marianne DeKoven, Colin Jager, Bode Iboronke, Mukti Lakhi Manghram, Stéphane Robolin, and Sarah Novacich all read and commented on portions of the manuscript, and this book has benefited greatly from their input. The English department has provided an intellectually exciting and collegial space for me to work within. Cheryl Wall has been a senior colleague par excellence. I am deeply thankful for her professional support and warmth toward my family. Many thanks to Richard Dienst, Michael McKeon, Abe

Busia, David Kurnick, Ryan Kernan, Chris Iannini, Meredith McGill, John Belton, Rebecca Walkowitz, and Elin Diamond for the support they have offered me. I am grateful to my chairs, Richard Miller, Kate Flint, Carolyn Williams, and Jonah Siegel, for guiding me through my years as a junior faculty member. I especially thank Jonah and Carolyn for their steadfast professional and financial support throughout the last stages of the publication process. I also wish to thank those at Rutgers outside my department who have reached out to me with their collegiality and friendship: Kim Butler, Nelson-Maldonado-Torres, Yolanda Martínez San Miguel, Donna Murch, and Edward Ramaswamy all deserve special mention, and I also thank all those I have had the opportunity to work with through the Center for Race and Ethnicity and the Critical Caribbean Studies Initiative.

I was fortunate to be a faculty fellow at the Rutgers Center for Cultural Analysis during the 2006–2007 seminar "Cultures of Circulation." The many conversations we had throughout the academic year helped me think through my project at an early stage. The generous Rutgers junior faculty leave policy and a NEH fellowship supported my participation in the Scholars-in-Residence Program at the Schomburg Center for Research in Black Culture. As a Scholar-in-Residence, I benefited greatly from the intensive critical discussions of work in progress. I thank all my fellow Scholars-in-Residence for their comments on the work I presented, and for creating a vibrant and rigorous intellectual community. Colin Palmer deserves special mention for his seamless leadership of these seminars. Steven Fullwood, Diana Lachatanere, and Peter Hobbs provided stellar archival assistance at the Schomburg. Evie Shockley, Anthony Foy, Laurie Woodard, Nicole Fleetwood, and I continued a series of workshops after the residency, and I thank them all for thinking along with me in great detail about my project at a crucial stage of its development.

The constant work-shopping process of what would become *Imagine the Sound* was generously facilitated by several invited talks. Minkah Makalani invited me to present an overview of my book project at the Rutgers Center for Historical Analysis Black Atlantic Seminar in 2010. Anthony Foy welcomed me to Swarthmore College in April 2011 to present a lecture based on my reading of James Baldwin's *No Name in the Street* that is the basis of chapter 5. Tsitsi Jaji brought me to the University of Pennsylvania the following year to give a talk based on my reading of John Coltrane's performance at the Olatunji Center that begins the first chapter of this book. I was also invited to participate in a roundtable on the legacy of Gil Scott-Heron at the Stoned Soul Symposium at Lincoln Center in August 2012. Portions of my remarks there became the basis for my Epilogue.

I would be remiss if I did not offer a deep thank-you to the many early mentors and more recent fellow travelers who have had a hand in this book. At points much earlier in the game, while I was an undergraduate and master's degree student, Stephen Railton, Kenneth Mostern, Janet Atwill, and George Hutchinson helped me realize that the academic profession was a possibility. Without their encouragement, I doubt I would have ever ventured down this road. Kim Benston, Margo Crawford, Aldon Nielsen, Amy Abugo Ongiri, James Smethurst, Mike Sell, Herman Beavers, Nahum Chandler, Anthony Bogues, Wahneema Lubiano, Leigh Raiford-Cohen, John Jackson, Mercy Romero, Sarah Jane Cervenak, Jennifer Stoever-Ackerman, Jonathan Sterne, Scott Trudell, Tsitsi Jaji, Anthony Reed, Emily Lordi, Edwin Hill, David Scott, Avery Gordon, Jeremy Glick, and Kevin Bell have either directly or indirectly provided advice and/or inspiration. Daphne Brooks, Fred Moten, and Brent Edwards have been incredibly generous with their time and support. I have had the benefit of working with Brent as a departmental colleague, interlocutor in the field, mentor, and friend. His commitment to helping so many scholars who are going through the tenure and first-book process is a beautiful model of selfless academic work that I hope to model.

I must also thank my closest comrades along the way: Dennis Childs and Lisa Ze-Winters. It's been a long road, and one I couldn't have remained relatively sane traveling along without your love, humor, and unconditional support!

This book would not have been possible without the assistance of Loretta Dumas, Evelyn Neal, Amiri Baraka, Oliver Lake, A. B. Spellman, Eugene Redmond, James Spadey, Charles Fuller, Ted Wilson, Billy Taylor, Henry English, Diane Moser, Hollis King, and Bernard Drayton. Their willingness to share their thoughts and memories about different individuals explored in *Imagine the Sound* has certainly made the book stronger. I thank them for teaching me a great deal and reminding me of the importance of knowledge that lies outside the "official" archives.

There have been many colleagues and peers outside, or on the fringes of, the academy whose impact on me as a thinker, writer, and researcher have been crucial. A sincere and heartfelt thanks to Dave Tompkins, Heather Dobbins, Ras Sydney DaSilva, Sharon Chacko, Swithin Wilmot, Giovanni Singleton, Karim Fairmon, Ras Tree, Marta Lucia Vargas, Chike McLoyd, Pharoahe Monch, David Dodson, and Nyota Shy.

A massive thank-you to my family for their patience, time, and understanding throughout a process that must have seemed like it would never end. My children, Samantha Ashley, Malik Zion, Meridian Virginia, Judiah-Amilcar, and Juniper Nyabinghi, have sustained me with their brilliance, humor, and love. I am constantly learning from each of you! My parents, John and Virginia Mathes, have been incredibly supportive of my work and have helped me in innumerable ways during the writing of this book. I couldn't have done this without you. Thank you to Virginia Skeens for all her love and generosity. Thanks as well to Bill Anderson for his support over the years.

I have the highest thanks for all that my partner in life, Shannon Lee Mathes, has done for me while I have worked on this book. She reads everything I write, and her discerning critical eye, artistic vision, and beautiful spirit inspire me. I dedicate this work to her with love and eternal gratitude.

Notes

Introduction

1. Because this incident and the subsequent trials of Assata Shakur were generally covered as sensationalistic events in which her guilt was generally assumed (she was, after all, "guilty" of being a member of the Black Liberation Army in the court of public opinion), there has never been a comprehensive reconstruction of the details of the Turnpike shootings entered into the public record. During the murder trial, Trooper Harper admitted to lying during his previous grand jury testimony about key details of the Turnpike incident (such as Shakur exiting the car and firing a gun at him). This is but one troubling element that raises many questions about the guilty verdict (as accomplice to the murder of Foerster and for the attempted murder of Harper) ultimately imposed on Shakur. For an overview of the circumstances surrounding Shakur's trial and the prejudicial treatment of her defense team by the courts, see Lennox Hinds's foreword to her autobiography. For the fullest accounting of the physical and circumstantial evidence connected to the Turnpike shooting, see the in-depth analysis included in Evelyn Williams's *Inadmissible Evidence: The Story of the African-American Trial Lawyer Who Defended the Black Liberation Army* (New York: Lawrence Hill, 1993).

2. Assata Shakur, *Assata: An Autobiography* (Chicago: Lawrence Hill, 1987), 3.

3. Ibid., 5.

4. Mladen Dolar, *A Voice and Nothing More* (Cambridge, Mass.: MIT Press, 2006), 52.

5. Fred Moten, *In the Break: The Aesthetics of the Black Radical Tradition* (Minneapolis: University of Minnesota Press, 2003), 216.

6. For more detailed examinations of COINTELPRO domestic state repression, see Ward Churchill and Jim Vander Wall, *The COINTELPRO Papers: Documents from the FBI's Secret War against Dissent in the United States* (Boston: South End Press, 2001); and Kenneth O'Reilly, *"Racial Matters": The FBI's Secret File on Black America, 1960–1972* (New York: Free Press, 1991).

7. Shakur, *Assata*, 234.

8. Ibid., 239.

9. Jonathan Sterne, "Hearing, Listening, Deafness," in *The Sound Studies Reader*, ed. Jonathan Sterne (New York: Routledge, 2012), 20.

10. See Aldon Nielsen, *Black Chant: Languages of African-American Postmodernism* (Cambridge: Cambridge University Press, 1997); Madhu Dubey, *Signs and Cities: Black Literary Postmodernism* (Chicago: University of Chicago Press, 2003); and Wahneema Lubiano, "Shuckin' Off the African-American Native Other: What's 'Po-Mo' Got to Do with It?" *Cultural Critique* 18 (Spring 1991): 149–86.

11. Jacques Attali, *Noise: The Political Economy of Music*, trans. Brian Massumi (Minneapolis: University of Minnesota Press, 1985), 7. For more on sonic surveillance, and state intelligence/military uses of sound technology, see Steve Goodman, *Sonic Warfare: Sound, Affect, and the Ecology of Fear* (Cambridge, Mass.: MIT Press, 2009); and Dave Tompkins, *How to Wreck a Nice Beach: The Vocoder from World War II to Hip-Hop, The Machine Speaks* (Chicago: Stop Smiling Books, 2009).

12. Attali, *Noise*, 4.

13. Fredric Jameson, *The Political Unconscious: Narrative as a Socially Symbolic Act* (Ithaca, N.Y.: Cornell University Press, 1981), 102.

14. This level of sonic black resistance that merges the quotidian and networks of local, national, and global power is a hallmark of much conscious rap, and can be heard in the work of the producer and lyricist Robert Diggs, known as the RZA (a formative member of the Wu-Tang Clan). For example, in the first verse of "Daily Routine," the final cut from his 1998 album *Bobby Digital*, he cites convergences between daily life in the projects, the global span of black historical experience, and the technological and cosmological as battlegrounds for humanity. The RZA, as he does in much of his work as a producer, creates a tonally sophisticated, ambient soundscape for the track. The relationship between the narrative and critical power of rap and the sonic dimensions of its production is certainly a topic related to this study and one that demands more attention within the always rapidly growing field of rap and hip-hop studies.

15. The descriptor "white," which I will frequently use throughout this book, is not primarily intended as a delimited phenotypical description of a group of people or particular individuals. Whiteness is intended, rather, to mark a particular proprietary, philosophical, and legally bound investment in the U.S. racial state. Proceeding from the contention that the United States was founded on and continues to hold at its foundation (in increasingly diffuse ways) the logic of white supremacy, whiteness needs to be understood as a critical term of art that often intersects with a commonsense notion of "people." It is not, however, intended as simplistic shorthand hinging on an inversion of Eurocentric identity politics.

16. My thoughts on the subject of U.S. global imperialism and domestic race relations have been informed by many academic and nonacademic works. The most formative would include Thomas Borstelmann, *The Cold War and the Color Line: American Race Relations in the Global Arena* (Cambridge, Mass.: Harvard University Press, 2003); Roderick Bush, *The End of White World Supremacy: Black Internationalism and the Problem of the Color Line* (Philadelphia: Temple University

Press, 2009); and Sohail Daulatzai, *Black Star, Crescent Moon: The Muslim International and Black Freedom Beyond America* (Minneapolis: University of Minnesota Press, 2012). The speeches of Martin Luther King, Jr., and Malcolm X, ironically, in the years immediately preceding their assassinations, represent crucial foundations in late/post–Civil Rights critical reflections on the topic. See, for example, King's "Beyond Vietnam: A Time to Break the Silence" (delivered April 4, 1967, at Riverside Church, New York); and Malcolm X's "The Worldwide Revolution" (delivered December 13, 1964, at the Audubon Ballroom, New York).

17. David Theo Goldberg, *The Racial State* (Malden, Mass.: Blackwell, 2002), 30.

18. Ibid., 107–8.

19. Cedric Robinson, *Black Marxism: The Making of the Black Radical Tradition* (1983; repr., Chapel Hill: University of North Carolina Press, 2000), 187.

20. Ibid., 190.

21. Terry Eagleton, *The Ideology of the Aesthetic* (Oxford: Blackwell, 1990), 196–233.

22. W. E. B. Du Bois, *The Souls of Black Folk* (1903; repr., New York: Penguin, 1989), 207.

23. Herbert Marcuse, *An Essay on Liberation* (Boston: Beacon, 1969), 27.

24. Marcuse serves as an important interlocutor throughout the expanse of this work, as his critical reflections on the broader conditions of one-dimensionality and aesthetic transformation underline the context of black political and artistic revolution in relationship to many of the writers examined in this book. Marcuse's place as a prescient social theorist of political repression, revolution, and counterrevolution in post–World War II industrialized societies (particularly in the 1960s United States) makes his relevance to this study pronounced.

25. Du Bois, *The Souls of Black Folk*, 204.

26. The term is taken from Amilcar Cabral's January 1966 address to the first Tricontinental Congress of the peoples of Asia, Africa, and Latin America held in Havana, Cuba. The text of the speech can be found in *Revolution in Guinea: An African People's Struggle* (London: Stage 1, 1969), 73–90.

27. Du Bois, *The Souls of Black Folk*, 122.

28. Saidiya Hartman, *Scenes of Subjection: Terror, Slavery, and Self-Making in Nineteenth-Century America* (New York: Oxford University Press, 1997), 125.

29. Du Bois, *The Souls of Black Folk*, 205.

30. Ibid., 205–6.

31. Ibid., 215, 214.

32. Zora Neale Hurston, "Spirituals and Neo-spirituals," in *The Sanctified Church* (New York: Marlowe, 1981), 81.

33. Ibid., 80.

34. Hurston's importance to theorizing black sonic expression has been noted by other critics, most notably Cheryl Wall. See her indispensable chapter on Hurston, "Zora Neale Hurston's Traveling Blues," included in her book *Women of the Harlem*

Renaissance (Bloomington: Indiana University Press, 1998); as well as her treatment of Hurston that focuses more specifically on Hurston as a sonic theorist, "Zora Neale Hurston's Essays: On Art and Such," *The Scholar and Feminist Online* 3, no. 2 (2005): http://sfonline.barnard.edu/hurston/wall_01.htm.

35. Hurston, "Spirituals and Neo-spirituals," 80, 79.

36. Ibid., 80, 82.

37. Cecil Taylor, *Unit Structures*, recorded May 19, 1966, Blue Note, 1966, liner notes.

38. Ibid.

39. Charles Lloyd, cited in "Editor's Note," in *Moment's Notice: Jazz in Poetry and Prose* (Minneapolis: Coffee House Press, 1993).

40. Larry Neal, "And Shine Swam On," in *Black Fire: An Anthology of Afro-American Writing*, ed. LeRoi Jones and Larry Neal (New York: William Morrow, 1968), 646.

41. Ibid., 653.

1. The Sonic Field of Resistance

1. John Coltrane, *The Olatunji Concert: The Last Live Recording*, recorded April 23, 1967, Impulse, 2001, liner notes.

2. The quality of smoothness I am attributing to Western modernity is artifice. It is a *projection* of linearity, order, and progress rather than disjuncture, super-exploitation, and terror that constructions of Western modernity propose as their philosophical grounding. The *reality* underlying this construction is much of what black radical thought attempts to diagnose, but doing so becomes a task loaded with the weight of a position perpetually marked as irrational. Robinson's *Black Marxism* (1983 [2000]) is a foundational text that inquires into this tension between European models of historical consciousness, philosophy, and social theory, and the evolving contours of a black radical tradition. As Robinson states, "The Black radical tradition cast doubt on the extent to which capitalism penetrated and re-formed social life and on its ability to create entirely new categories of human experience stripped bare of the historical consciousness embedded in culture. It gave them cause to question the authority of a radical intelligentsia drawn by its own analyses from marginal and ambiguous social strata to construct an adequate manifestation of proletarian power. And it drew them more and more toward the actual discourse of revolutionary masses, the impulse to make history in their own terms. And finally, the Black radical tradition forced them to reevaluate the nature and historical roles of ideology and consciousness" (179).

3. Anthony Bogues, *Black Heretics, Black Prophets: Radical Political Intellectuals* (New York: Routledge, 2003), 10.

4. Ibid., 14–15, 19.

5. Kofi Agawu, *Music as Discourse: Semiotic Adventures in Romantic Music* (New York: Oxford University Press, 2009), 104. For an example of a more elaborated analysis of semiotic approaches to musical narrativity, see Naomi Cummings, *The Sonic Self: Musical Subjectivity and Signification* (Bloomington: Indiana University Press, 2000). Other important statements in this subfield of musicology include Jean-Jacques Nattiez, *Music as Discourse: Toward a Semiology of Music* (Princeton, N.J.: Princeton University Press, 1990); and Susan McClary, *Conventional Wisdom: The Content of Musical Form* (Berkeley: University of California Press, 2000).

6. Billy Taylor, qtd. in Lewis Porter, *John Coltrane: His Life and Music* (Ann Arbor: University of Michigan Press, 1999), 288.

7. Babatunde Olatunji, "John Coltrane: My Impressions and Recollections," n.d., Institute for Jazz Studies, Rutgers University, Newark, New Jersey, 28.

8. Babatunde Olatunji with Robert Atkinson, *The Beat of My Drum: An Autobiography* (Philadelphia: Temple University Press, 2005), 150.

9. Ibid., 155.

10. Ibid., 199.

11. Archie Shepp, "Musicians Talk about John Coltrane," *DownBeat*, July 12, 1979, 20.

12. Ekkehard Jost, *Free Jazz* (1975; repr., New York: Da Capo, 1994), 100–101.

13. Charles Keil and Steven Feld, *Music Grooves* (Chicago: University of Chicago Press, 1994), 22. For a different, yet related take on the importance of "grooves" to understandings of black sonic expression, see Alexander G. Weheliye's *Phonographies: Grooves in Sonic Afro-Modernity* (Durham, N.C.: Duke University Press, 2005). Weheliye's brilliant study most directly addresses the groove as a concept that allows for consideration of the convergence of sound, race, history, and technology. He describes grooves as they mark phonography, "suggesting a different form of writing than the fraught domain of alphabetic script, one that makes black sounds mechanically repeatable" (81).

14. Sun Ra and His Afro Infinity Arkestra, *Atlantis*, recorded 1967–69, Impulse, 1969.

15. Olatunji, "John Coltrane," 28, 29. It should be noted that Olatunji's recall and rendering of Coltrane's comments are not specifically verifiable by others who might have been present. Yusef Lateef and Billy Taylor have, however, both commented more generally on the connections between Olatunji and Coltrane.

16. Leonard Brown, "Conversation with Yusef Lateef," in *John Coltrane and Black America's Quest for Freedom: Spirituality and the Music*, ed. Leonard Brown (New York: Oxford University Press, 2010), 195.

17. Ibid., 195–96, 215.

18. Frank Kofsky, *Black Nationalism and the Revolution in Music* (New York: Pathfinder, 1970), 227.

19. A. B. Spellman, "Revolution in Sound," in *The Black Revolution: An Ebony Special Issue* (Chicago: Johnson, 1970), 82–83.

20. Interestingly, Alice Coltrane on piano and Jimmy Garrison on bass are only clearly heard twice, in separate solo passages, throughout the recorded set.

21. Sandra T. Barnes, *Africa's Ogun: Old World and New* (Bloomington: Indiana University Press, 1997), 2. Barnes's text offers a thorough, enlightening, and conceptually rich study of Ogun's presence in West African as well as Afro-American cultures

22. Olatunji, *The Beat of My Drum*, 33.

23. The Alice Coltrane statements are taken from a September 21, 1984, feature and partial interview with her by Robert Palmer in the *New York Times*, to preview a concert she was to perform that evening at Carnegie Hall.

24. For a related discussion regarding the status of "tradition" within African diasporic cultural practices, see David Scott, "That Event, This Memory: Notes on the Anthropology of African Diasporas in the New World," *Diaspora: A Journal of Transnational Studies* 1, no. 3 (1991): 261–84.

25. John Coltrane, *Interstellar Space*, recorded February 22, 1967, Impulse, 2000, compact disc, liner notes.

26. Bernard Drayton, conversation with author, March 2009. Billy Taylor, in a separate conversation with the author (April 2009), remembers the crowd at the Olatunji performance as "black, white, all kinds of people. It was a Coltrane crowd."

27. Coltrane's attention to the relationship between his sound and his intensifying focus on the spiritual and ethical realms of existence as the 1960s progressed is covered extensively in much biographical, journalistic, and critical writing about Coltrane. See, for example, the works of Jack Cooke, "Late Trane," *Jazz Monthly*, January 1970, 2–6; Kofsky, *Black Nationalism and the Revolution in Music*; J. C. Thomas, *Chasin' the Trane: The Music and Mystique of John Coltrane* (Garden City, N.Y.: Doubleday, 1975); Bill Cole, *John Coltrane* (New York: Schirmer, 1976); Porter, *John Coltrane*; and the collection of essays edited by Leonard Brown, *John Coltrane and Black America's Quest for Freedom*.

28. Tynan's comments are reprinted in Don DeMichael's subsequent creation of a critical platform (also in the pages of *DownBeat)* from which Coltrane and Dolphy could respond to these charges, "John Coltrane and Eric Dolphy Answer the Jazz Critics," April 12, 1962, 16.

29. Ibid., 52.

30. Ibid.

31. James Stewart, "Introduction to Black Aesthetics in Music," in *The Black Aesthetic*, ed. Addison Gayle, Jr. (Garden City, N.Y.: Doubleday, 1971), 90, 87.

32. Attali's perspective is useful to an extent and largely echoes much critical writing in the pages of periodicals that often published work focusing on the possibility of free jazz disrupting the means of cultural production and consumption.

33. James Snead, "On Repetition in Black Culture," *Black American Literature Forum* 15, no. 4 (1981): 150.

34. Keith Knox, "Sounds from the Avant Garde: The Aesthetic Problem," *Jazz Monthly*, February 1967, 11.

35. Nathaniel Mackey, *Bedouin Hornbook* (Los Angeles: Sun & Moon, 1997), 21–22.

36. Mackey also explores Zuckerkandl's phenomenological and epistemological inquiry into the possibilities of dynamic tonality in his touchstone essay on music and creative writing, "Sound and Sentiment, Sound and Symbol," in *Discrepant Engagement: Dissonance, Cross-Culturality, and Experimental Writing* (Tuscaloosa: University of Alabama Press, 1993), 231–59.

37. Clearly, this correspondence between shifting sociopolitical conditions and experimental approaches to black musical expression not only reflects the discord marking the post–Civil Rights period, but is also embedded within a broader historical trajectory of American interracial antagonism in which the presence of blackness has been cast as abject.

38. Jonathan Sterne, *The Audible Past: Cultural Origins of Sound Reproduction* (Durham, N.C.: Duke University Press, 2003), 343.

39. Jean-Luc Nancy, *Listening*, trans. Charlotte Madell (New York: Fordham University Press, 2007), 16, 7, 40, 41.

40. John Coltrane, *Ascension*, recorded June 28, 1965, Impulse, 2000, compact disc, liner notes.

41. Valerie Wilmer, *As Serious as Your Life: John Coltrane and Beyond* (1977; repr., New York: Serpent's Tail, 1992), 34.

42. Porter, *John Coltrane*, 234.

43. "Pharoah Sanders: A Philosophical Conversation with Elisasbeth van der Mei," *Coda*, June–July 1967, 4.

44. This represents the opening of a tectonic question regarding black cultural studies and studies of black music. In some ways a corollary of the intersection between theories of race and anthropological inquiry in the first half of the twentieth century, the question arises as to what degree one might consider the conceptual solidity of the category black, or African American music. This is often posed as a debate between positions represented by, for instance, Ronald Radano, *Lying Up a Nation: Race and Black Music* (Chicago: University of Chicago Press, 2003); Paul Gilroy, *The Black Atlantic: Modernity and Double Consciousness* (Cambridge, Mass.: Harvard University Press, 1993); LeRoi Jones (Amiri Baraka), *Blues People* (New York: William Morrow, 1963); and Sterling Stuckey, *Slave Culture: Nationalist Theory and the Foundations of Black America* (New York: Oxford University Press, 1987). Baraka and Stuckey both make claims to definable African presences that underline the expressive patterns within black music. Baraka's claims are oriented around a broad tapestry of American social, economic, and political history through which he charts a genealogy of black musical expression that is always emerging from particular historical environments and conditions

throughout the nineteenth and first half of the twentieth century. Stuckey's book more specifically takes up the evolution and persistence of the ring shout as a syncretic Africanized cultural form of the nineteenth-century Americas, with longitudinal effects on black performance and improvisation into the twentieth century. Gilroy's well-rehearsed point of departure is to imbue black music with a transfigurative power that carries forward the sublime terror and unsayability of the Middle Passage and enslavement. Radano critiques what he sees as the general premise of essentialism operating throughout black cultural studies as a given. He denies the autonomy of black music, and in a true Ellisonian move, makes a series of claims for the Americanness of black music. In some ways Radano may be too polemical to realize the proximity of his own desire to the positions expressed by many of those he criticizes, for it is not at all clear that making a claim to the blackness of music is making the claim that it is therefore one thing or monolithic.

45. Valerie Wilmer, *As Serious as Your Life: John Coltrane and Beyond* (1977; repr., New York: Serpent's Tail, 1992), 60, 65.

46. Don Ihde, *Listening and Voice: A Phenomenology of Sound* (Athens: Ohio University Press, 1976), 81.

47. Ibid., 76.

48. Anthony Braxton, *Tri-axium Writings*, vol. 1 (Hanover, N.H.: Frog Peak Music, 1985), 267.

49. Graham Lock, *Forces in Motion: The Music and Thought of Anthony Braxton* (New York: Da Capo, 1988), 282.

50. Braxton, *Tri-axium Writings*, 267–69.

51. Ibid., 276.

52. Ibid.

53. Henry English, *You See What I'm Trying to Say* (NYU Summer Motion Picture Workshop, 1967), 16mm film, 8:46, http://vimeo.com/19619667.

54. For a first-person reflection on the process of collaborating with Brown on this film project, see Henry English, "About YOU SEE WHAT I'M TRYING TO SAY," n.d., https://docs.google.com/file/d/oB4fnIgyuRZhlNWIyZDMoZDAtM TMwNiooZDRlLWFhNWItYTAxOWYzOGJiZmJh/edit?hl=en&pli=1.

55. English, *You See What I'm Trying to Say*.

56. Henry English, e-mail message to author, August 18, 2012.

57. This point builds on Eric Porter's important work on Marion Brown as a theorist of improvisation, included in his monograph *What Is This Thing Called Jazz? African-American Musicians as Artists, Critics, and Activists* (Berkeley: University of California Press, 2002). See especially pp. 249–53.

58. Marion Brown, "The Relationship between Language and Texts and Language and Music in Afro-American Songs," in *Recollections: Essays, Drawings, Miscellanea*

(Frankfurt: JAS, 1984), 155; Brown, "Improvisation and the Aural Tradition in Afro-American Music," *Black World*, November 1973, 16.

59. Marion Brown, "A Love Supreme: The Spiritual Awakening of John Coltrane," in *Recollections*, 149, 133, 131.

60. Marion Brown, "The Beauty of the Sound," in *Recollections*, 53.

61. Marion Brown, "On the Other Side of Everybody's River," in *Recollections*, 199–200.

62. Marion Brown, *Afternoon of a Georgia Faun: Views and Reviews* (N.p.: Nia Music, 1973), 21.

63. Jason Weiss, *Always in Trouble: An Oral History of ESP-Disk', the Most Outrageous Record Label in America* (Middletown, Conn.: Wesleyan University Press, 2012), 145–46.

64. Amiri Baraka, "You Think This Is about You," liner notes, Albert Ayler, *Holy Ghost: Rare and Unissued Recordings (1962–1970)*, Revenant, 2004, 38.

65. LeRoi Jones (Amiri Baraka), *Black Music* (New York: William Morrow, 1968), 188.

66. Ibid., 126.

67. LeRoi Jones (Amiri Baraka), "Black Art," in *Black Fire*, ed. Jones and Neal, 302, 303.

68. Iain Anderson, *This Is Our Music: Free Jazz, the Sixties, and American Culture* (Philadelphia: University of Pennsylvania Press, 2007), 120; Benjamin Piekut, *Experimentalism Otherwise: The New York Avant-Garde and Its Limits* (Berkeley: University of California Press, 2011), 119–20.

2. Apocalyptic Soundscapes

1. Henry Dumas, letter to Larry and Evelyn Neal, March 20, 1967, TS, Box 2, Folder 1, Larry Neal Papers, Schomburg Center for Research in Black Culture, New York Public Library (hereafter cited as the Larry Neal Papers), 1.

2. Larry Neal, "The Black Arts Movement," *Drama Review* 12, no. 4 (1968): 29.

3. For more critical analyses of the aesthetics and politics of literary modernism as they relate to race, see Houston Baker, *Modernism and the Harlem Renaissance* (Chicago: University of Chicago Press, 1989); Michael North, *The Dialect of Modernism: Race, Language, and Twentieth-Century Literature* (New York: Oxford University Press, 1998); Lorenzo Thomas, *Extraordinary Measures: Afrocentric Modernism and Twentieth-Century American Poetry* (Tuscaloosa: University of Alabama Press, 2000); Nicholas Brown, *Utopian Generations: The Political Horizon of Twentieth-Century Literature* (Princeton, N.J.: Princeton University Press, 2005); and Kevin Bell, *Ashes Taken for Fire: Aesthetic Modernism and the Critique of Identity* (Minneapolis: University of Minnesota Press, 2007).

4. R. Murray Schafer, *The Soundscape: Our Sonic Environment and the Tuning of the World* (1977; repr., Rochester, Vt.: Destiny, 1994). Ari Kelman provides a thorough analysis of the soundscape concept and of the ways he feels that many contemporary writers within sound studies who utilize the concept "either misapply it or redefine it to fit their needs." Kelman provides a very useful intellectual genealogy of Schafer's concept, but his critique of studies that he feels do not engage substantively enough with Schafer's original framing of it, such as John Picker's *Victorian Soundscapes* (New York: Oxford University Press, 2003); Charles Hirschkind's *The Ethical Soundscape: Cassette Sermons and Islamic Counterpublics* (New York: Columbia University Press, 2006); and Fiona Richards's edited volume *The Soundscapes of Australia* (Hampshire, U.K.: Ashgate, 2007), seems to be overly focused on his own specific reading of Schafer and his reluctance to grant any degree of separation between Schafer's very broad, encompassing definition of soundscapes (as I have cited in the body of my text) and Kelman's contention that Schafer's text is a prescriptive valuing of natural sounds over those produced through the "cacophonies of modern life." Kelman is right about the larger context of *The Soundscape*, but the fact remains that Schafer's work is both prescriptive—in the arc and full critical context of its argumentation—and suggestive in his actual specific, close definition of the term. Counter to Kelman, I would argue that it is possible to engage with Schafer's specific definitional engagement with soundscapes, and to apply that broad categorization, even extending it critically, within various methodologies in sound studies. This is not to discount the crucial political work that Schafer intended the term to accomplish for his study; it is simply to point out that his text contains more than one avenue of interpretation. See Kelman, "Rethinking the Soundscape: A Critical Genealogy of a Key Term in Sound Studies," *The Senses and Society* 5, no. 2 (2010): 212–34.

5. Schafer, *The Soundscape*, 7.

6. Jameson, *The Political Unconscious*, 79.

7. Eugene Redmond, ed., "Henry Dumas Issue," *Black American Literature Forum* 22, no. 2 (Summer 1988). The details surrounding Dumas's tragic death remain murky. What is known is that an altercation of some sort ensued between Dumas and at least one other individual in the 135th Street New York City subway station just outside the Schomburg Center for Research in Black Culture in Harlem, and a transit policeman reportedly shot Dumas in a case of mistaken identity during, or in the wake of, this altercation. For more details on the incident and its aftermath, see, Jeffrey Leak's biography, *Visible Man: The Life of Henry Dumas* (Athens: University of Georgia Press, 2014). Leak's biography was published just as I was completing the copyedits for this book, thus I was not able to include any references beyond this one to his invaluable work.

8. Gwendolyn Brooks, "Henry Dumas: Perceptiveness and Zeal," and Margaret Walker Alexander, "Goodbye Sweetwater," in ibid., 177, 155.

9. Amiri Baraka, "Henry Dumas: Afro-Surreal Expressionist," in ibid., 164.

10. I am deriving these thoughts on the formal and thematic aspects of "Saba: Black Paladins" from its inclusion in *Knees of a Natural Man: The Selected Poetry of Henry Dumas* (New York: Thunder's Mouth Press, 1989), in which the editor, Eugene Redmond, groups it along with twenty-two other poems titled "Saba." The poems are not dated.

11. Henry Dumas, "Saba: Black Paladins," in ibid., 128. Used by permission of the Henry Dumas Estate–Loretta Dumas and Eugene B. Redmond. Originally published by Southern Illinois University Press in 1970.

12. These comments are taken from an interview of Jarman conducted by Ted Panken on a WKCR five-hour retrospective of his music in 1987. See http://tedpanken .wordpress.com/2011/09/14/in-honor-of-joseph-jarmans-74th-birthday-a-wkcr -interview-from-1987 for the transcript.

13. On the relationship between Dumas and Sun Ra, see John Wright's most recent introduction to *Echo Tree: The Collected Short Fiction of Henry Dumas* (Minneapolis: Coffee House Press, 2003), xxvii–xxxi; and especially the sound recording *The Ark and the Ankh: Sun Ra/Henry Dumas in Conversation, 1966, Slug's Saloon NYC*, Ikef Records, 2001. For earlier references to this connection, see Larry Neal, "The Social Background of the Black Arts Movement," *The Black Scholar*, January–February 1987; and Clyde Taylor's "Henry Dumas: Legacy of a Long Breath Singer" *Black American Literature Forum* 22, no. 2 (1988): 353–64, in which he mentions how "another strand in Dumas' myth is a space motif, doubtless influenced by his study with Sun-Ra, space musician, poet, gnostic, and teacher." Other works that are equally helpful and instructive on a range of ideas related to Sun Ra's commitment to artistic and metaphysical innovation, while not specifically asserting any direct claims about these possible influences and exchanges between Ra and Dumas, include Valerie Wilmer, *As Serious as Your Life* (London: Quartet, 1977); Brent Edwards, "The Race for Space: Sun Ra's Poetry," in *The World in Time and Space: Towards a History of Innovative American Poetry in Our Time*, ed. Edward Foster and Joe Donahue (Jersey City, N.J.: Talisman House, 2002), 609–35; Graham Locke's *Blutopia: Visions of the Future and Revisions of the Past in the Works of Sun Ra, Duke Ellington, and Anthony Braxton* (Durham, N.C.: Duke University Press, 1999); and John Szwed's indispensable biography of Sun Ra, *Space Is the Place: The Lives and Times of Sun Ra* (New York: Da Capo, 1998).

14. Szwed, *Space Is the Place*, 223.

15. Locke, *Blutopia*, 51.

16. Sun Ra and his Myth Science Arkestra, *Cosmic Tones for Mental Therapy*, Saturn, 1967, vinyl. The tracks were recorded in late 1963 according to Szwed. The break in time between the conceptualizing and recording of the album, and its release four years later is not specifically detailed in any discographies or accounts of Sun Ra's career that I have encountered.

17. Sun Ra, "My Music Is Words," *The Cricket* 1 (1968): 8.

18. The logic behind the difference in the rendering of "Sunra" instead of "Sun Ra" in Dumas's story is not entirely clear. The title of the story contains both formations of the name, "The Metagenesis of Sunra (to Sun Ra and His ARKestra)," but, not having seen the original manuscript of the story, and without any evidence in the text to clearly support a reason behind Dumas's renderings of the name, I can only speculate that perhaps "Sunra" is written in this fashion by Dumas in order to emphasize a certain sonority and fluidity (in terms of phonics and meaning) to its vocal invocation (projected as speech, or internally configured in one's mind as they read it). Try saying both out loud, and note the difference in how the "Ra" becomes less of an individuated factor in speech and thought due to its enjambment with "Sun." For Dumas, it may be the case that the symbology of the sun was most pertinent to his meditations on the meaning of Sun Ra, and his rendering of the name is intended to reflect this epistemological standpoint.

19. Henry Dumas, "The Metagenesis of Sunra (to Sun Ra and His ARKestra)," in *Echo Tree*, 345, 346–49.

20. Ibid., 349–50.

21. Hortense Spillers, "Mama's Baby, Papa's Maybe: An American Grammar Book," *Diacritics* 17, no. 2 (1987): 80.

22. Dumas, "Metagenesis," 351, 352, 360.

23. Steve Goodman, *Sonic Warfare: Sound, Affect, and the Ecology of Fear* (Cambridge, Mass.: MIT Press, 2010), 65.

24. Larry Neal, "The Social Background of the Black Arts Movement" *The Black Scholar*, January–February 1987, 22. This essay was originally presented as a lecture at the University of Iowa Afro-American Studies Program summer institute for college and university teachers titled "Black Culture in the Second Renaissance: A Study of Afro-American Thought and Experience, 1954–1970."

25. For a firsthand account of this period and the opening of the Black Arts Repertory Theater and School in Harlem, see Amiri Baraka, *The Autobiography of LeRoi Jones/Amiri Baraka* (New York: Freundlich, 1984), 200–229.

26. Henry Dumas, "Will the Circle Be Unbroken?" in *Echo Tree*, 105.

27. Ibid., 106.

28. Jan's character seems to have been written in the obvious shadow of Norman Mailer's analysis of the relationship between white countercultural formations and Civil Rights–era black culture, "The White Negro: Superficial Reflections on the Hipster," *Dissent* 4, no. 3 (1957): 276–93.

29. Dumas, "Will the Circle Be Unbroken?" 106–8.

30. Ibid., 108.

31. Nathaniel Mackey, *Djbot Baghistus's Run* (Los Angeles: Sun & Moon, 1993), 8.

32. Dumas, "Will the Circle Be Unbroken?" 108–9.

33. Ibid., 109.

34. Ibid., 109–10.

35. Jay Wright, introduction to *Play Ebony Play Ivory* by Henry Dumas (New York: Random House, 1974), xx–xxi.

36. Brandon LaBelle, *Acoustic Territories: Sound Culture and Everyday Life* (New York: Continuum, 2010), 40.

37. Michael Veal, *Dub: Soundscapes and Shattered Songs in Jamaican Reggae* (Middletown, Conn.: Wesleyan University Press, 2007), 198.

38. Henry Dumas, "Echo Tree," in *Echo Tree*, 23.

39. Ibid.

40. A sense of the political also extends into the realization that "Echo Tree" is one of many short stories written by Dumas set within temporally unspecified, yet generally understood spaces of the post–World War II southern United States. The backgrounds in these stories are partly defined by the presence of terror—lynched bodies turning up in rivers, a dead brother, the fear of families wondering when and if their young men will return from a walk in the countryside—and the need to find alternative spaces for existence that challenge the hegemony of apartheid terror.

41. Dumas, "Echo Tree," 24.

42. Robert Farris Thompson, *Flash of the Spirit: African and Afro-American Art and Philosophy* (New York: Vintage, 1983), 144.

43. Robert Farris Thompson, *Face of the Gods: Art and Altars of Africa and the African Americans* (Munich: Prestel, 1993), 84.

44. Dumas, "Echo Tree," 24–25.

45. Herbert Marcuse, *One-Dimensional Man: Studies in the Ideology of Advanced Industrial Society* (1964; repr., Boston: Beacon, 1991), 1.

46. Michael Hardt and Antonio Negri, *Multitude: War and Democracy in the Age of Empire* (New York: Penguin, 2004), 7.

47. Marcuse, *One-Dimensional Man*, 4.

48. Dumas, "Echo Tree," 24.

49. Schafer, *The Soundscape*, 9, 43.

50. Dumas, "Echo Tree," 22.

51. Ibid., 26.

52. Ibid., 23.

53. This type of communion might speak to the possibility of politically imagining the African diaspora in a way which seeks to envision cultural dialogues and exchanges between the transforming realities of Africa and the Americas, responding to massive attempts at cultural erasure, and fighting for the promise of transformative existence in the face of these destructive forces. Nathaniel Mackey suggestively notes such a phenomenon as the (dis)articulation of a "phantom limb." He

states, "The phantom limb haunts or critiques a condition in which feeling, consciousness itself, would seem to have been cut off." See Nathaniel Mackey, "Sound and Sentiment, Sound and Symbol," in *Discrepant Engagement: Dissonance, Cross-culturality, and Experimental Writing* (Tuscaloosa: University of Alabama Press, 1993), 235.

54. Goodman, *Sonic Warfare*, 81–84.

55. Dumas, "Echo Tree," 30.

56. In early 2014, the United States Supreme Court heard a challenge to section 5 of the Voting Rights Act of 1965, often referred to as the "preclearance requirement" by which jurisdictions with a history of voting discrimination must argue their reasoning before a three-judge panel before any changes to voting qualifications can be made. At an early stage in the oral arguments, Antonin Scalia, one of the more politically conservative justices, made the statement that reauthorizing the Voting Rights Act in 2006 amounted to the "perpetuation of a racial entitlement." Shelby County, Alabama v. Eric H. Holder, Jr., Supreme Court case no. 12-96 (2013), transcript p. 47, ll. 7–8. Original transcript can be found at http://www.supremecourt.gov/oral_arguments/argument_transcripts.aspx. In many ways his statement reiterates the epistemological basis of segregationist belief that guided the resistance to and retrenchment against the Civil Rights movement. Scalia's rhetorical articulation of this standpoint, some fifty years after the Voting Rights Act, is a stark reminder of the open, enduring, and unfinished aspects of the Civil Rights historical moment.

57. The Goldwater quote is taken from Katherine Beckett's remarkable study of the problematic rise of a law and order state during the 1960s, *Making Crime Pay: Law and Order in Contemporary American Politics* (New York: Oxford University Press, 1999), 35. Beckett closely analyzes governmental crime policy and its shifting contours in relationship to discursive claims made in the political and popular arenas during the 1960s. Beckett shows the earlier genesis of "law and order" that many attribute to Richard Nixon's late 1960s and early 1970s legislative agenda, directing our attention back to 1964 and the conservative ideology, articulated largely through the voice of Barry Goldwater during the presidential campaign, linking the government's provision of social welfare to the production of illegality among its beneficiaries. Listen as well to the rather unsettling, stunning tone of Barry Goldwater's campaign trail stump speech: "It is on our streets that we see the final, terrible proof of a sickness which not all the social theories of a thousand social experiments has even begun to touch. Crime grows faster than population, while those who break the law are accorded more consideration than those who try to enforce the law. Law enforcement agencies—the police, the sheriffs, the FBI—are attacked for doing their jobs. Law breakers are defended. Our wives, all women, feel unsafe on our streets." Barry Goldwater, "Peace through Strength: Private Property, Free Competition, Hard Work," delivered at Prescott, Arizona, September 3, 1964.

58. Henry Dumas, "Strike and Fade," in *Echo Tree*, 111.

59. Ibid.

60. Walter Rodney, *The Groundings with My Brothers* (London: Bogle-L'Ouverture, 1969), 17.

61. Stokely Carmichael (Kwame Ture), quoted in Robert Allen, *Black Awakening in Capitalist America* (Garden City, N.Y.: Anchor Books, 1969), 7.

62. Dumas, "Strike and Fade," 111.

63. Ibid., 111–13.

64. Ibid., 113–14.

65. For various perspectives on the idea of black international consciousness, see for example Richard Wright, *White Man Listen!* (1957; repr., New York: HarperCollins, 1995); Rodney, *Groundings with My Brothers*; Robin D. G. Kelley and Sidney Lemelle, eds., *Imagining Home: Class, Culture, and Nationalism in the African Diaspora* (London: Verso, 1995); and Robin D. G. Kelley, *Freedom Dreams: The Black Radical Imagination* (Boston: Beacon Press, 2002).

66. Dumas, "Strike and Fade," 115.

67. Gwendolyn Brooks, "The Womanhood," in *Selected Poems by Gwendolyn Brooks* (New York: Harper & Row, 1963), 54.

68. Dumas, "Strike and Fade," 115.

69. Robert Levin, "Sunny Murray: The Continuous Cracking of Glass," in *Black Giants*, ed. Pauline Rivelli and Robert Levin (New York: World Publishing Company, 1970), 57–58.

3. Peering into the Maw

1. Evie Shockley, *Renegade Poetics: Black Aesthetics and Formal Innovation in African American Poetry* (Iowa City: University of Iowa Press, 2011), 4–5, 9.

2. James G. Spady, *Larry Neal: Liberated Black Philly Poet with a Blues Streak of Mellow Wisdom* (Philadelphia: PC International Press, 1989), 10.

3. In addition to Spady, James Smethurst in his book *The Black Arts Movement: Literary Nationalism in the 1960s and 1970s* (Chapel Hill: University of North Carolina Press, 2005); and Mike Sell, *Avant-Garde Performance and the Limits of Criticism: Approaching the Living Theatre, Happenings/Fluxus, and the Black Arts Movement* (Ann Arbor: University of Michigan Press, 2005), both address the Muntu background of the Black Arts Movement.

4. James G. Spady, "Muntu–Kuntu and the Philly Origins of the Black Arts Movement," *Philadelphia New Observer*, July 24, 1996.

5. James Stewart, "Just Intonation and the New Black Revolutionary Music," *The Cricket* 2 (1968): 14.

6. Charles Fuller, qtd. in Spady, *Larry Neal*, 15–16.

7. Larry Neal to Amiri Baraka, n.d., Box 2, Larry Neal Papers, 1. The type-script consists of two pages, numbered 1 and 3. The second page is missing from the archived collection of Neal's papers.

8. Herbert Marcuse, *The Aesthetic Dimension: Toward a Theory of Marxist Aesthetics* (Boston: Beacon Press, 1978), 31.

9. Neal to Baraka, n.d., 1.

10. Marcuse, *The Aesthetic Dimension*, ix.

11. Neal to Baraka, n.d., 1.

12. Larry Neal, "The Black Writer's Role, II: Ellison's Zoot Suit," in *Visions of a Liberated Future: Black Arts Movement Writings by Larry Neal*, ed. Michael Schwartz (New York: Thunder's Mouth Press, 1989), 49. The essay originally appeared as "Ellison's Zoot Suit," *Black World*, December 1970, 31–52. The quote of Ellison's is taken from *Shadow and Act* (1964; repr., New York: Quality Paperback Book Club, 1994), 78–79.

13. Neal, "The Black Writer's Role, II," 30.

14. Ibid.

15. Ibid., 32. The Wright quote is taken from his foreword to George Padmore's, *Pan-Africanism or Communism?* (1956; repr., New York: Doubleday, 1971), xiii.

16. Neal, "The Black Writer's Role, II," 41, 38.

17. Erica Edwards terms this dynamic "the epistemological violence of struc-turing knowledge of black political subjectivity and movement within a gendered hierarchy of political value that grants uninterrogated power to normative mascu-linity." *Charisma and the Fictions of Black Leadership* (Minneapolis: University of Minnesota Press, 2012), xv.

18. Sarah Webster Fabio, "Tripping with Black Writing," in *The Black Aesthetic*, ed. Addison Gayle, Jr. (Garden City, N.Y.: Anchor Books, 1971), 180.

19. Neal, "The Black Writer's Role, II," 41, 44.

20. Hortense Spillers, "Ellison's 'Usable Past': Toward a Theory of Myth," in *Black, White, and in Color: Essays on American Literature and Culture* (Chicago: University of Chicago Press, 2003), 67. It should be noted that the first publica-tion of this essay in 1977 might allow for the placement of this piece in a closer proximity to the Black Arts Movement.

21. Larry Neal, "Black American Music," TS, Box 21, Folder 7, Larry Neal Papers, i–vi. This page of Neal's manuscript is actually handwritten without clear pagination. My pagination reflects the fact that earlier pages in the introduction are numbered sequentially with roman numerals.

22. Ibid., 186–87.

23. Kimberly Benston, *Performing Blackness: Enactments of African-American Modernism* (New York: Routledge, 2000), 29.

24. Larry Neal, "The Black Arts Movement," *The Drama Review* 12 (Summer 1968): 29–30.

25. Ibid., 36–37, 30.

26. The argument I am making here deserves a fuller treatment through an essay devoted to a literary–historical resituation of the Black Arts Movement that would encourage readings of its theoretical principles in more proximate relationship to western European as well as African diasporic and Third World critical theories of resistance. I suggest this approach at different points throughout this study—most consistently in respect to the Frankfurt School social theory of Herbert Marcuse. Creating a more extensive and systematic genealogy of the critical exchanges between western European critical theory and black radical formulations of black aesthetics and cultural nationalism would help scholars of twentieth-century literature understand the Black Arts Movement period as a more multifaceted and dynamic critical and creative moment rather than a reductive symbol of black identity politics.

27. Neal, "The Black Arts Movement," 29, 31.

28. Larry Neal, *Black Boogaloo (Notes on Black Liberation)* (San Francisco: Journal of Black Poetry Press, 1969), n.p.

29. Amiri Baraka, "Sound for Sounding," introduction to ibid., i.

30. My reading of the poem focuses on the slightly amended and updated version Neal included five years later in *Hoodoo Hollerin' Bebop Ghosts* (Washington, D.C.: Howard University Press, 1974), 19–23. The differences between the two versions are primarily spatial in that the later version is more consistently and tightly marked by indentations and stanza breaks. For the extract quoted here, see pp. 20–21.

31. Ibid.

32. Ralph Ellison, *Invisible Man* (1952; repr., New York: Random House, 1980), 8.

33. Charles H. Rowell, "An Interview with Larry Neal," *Callaloo* 8, no. 1 (1985): 13.

34. Neal, *Hoodoo Hollerin' Bebop Ghosts*, 70.

35. Floyd Barbour, foreword to *The Black Seventies*, ed. Floyd Barbour (Boston: Porter Sargent Publishers, 1970), viii.

36. Larry Neal, "New Space/The Growth of Black Consciousness in the Sixties," in *The Black Seventies*, ed. Barbour, 9.

37. Ibid., 17.

38. Raymond Williams, *Marxism and Literature* (London: Oxford University Press, 1977), 132. The first italics are in original text; the second are from my perspective.

39. Neal, "New Space," 9, 10, 12.

40. Ibid., 26; emphasis added.

41. Larry Neal, "Spirits Rejoice: The Lower East Side and Black Art," TS, Box 7, Folder 20, Larry Neal Papers, 1–2.

42. Larry Neal, "New Space: Revolutionary and Reactionary Positions—Literary Criticism," TS, Box 21, folder 5, Larry Neal Papers, 7.

43. Larry Neal, contribution to "Black Writers' Views on Literary Lions and Values," *Black World*, January 1968, 81.

44. Ibid., 35.

45. "On Postmodernism and Articulation: An Interview with Stuart Hall," in *Stuart Hall: Critical Dialogues in Cultural Studies*, ed. David Morley and Kuan-Hsing Chen (New York: Routledge, 1996), 141.

46. Ibid., 142.

47. Ron Karenga, "Ron Karenga and Black Cultural Nationalism," *Black World*, January 1968, 5, 9.

48. James Cunningham, "Ron Karenga and Black Cultural Nationalism," *Black World*, January 1968, 80.

49. Ibid.

50. Neal, "Black Writers' Views," 83.

51. Barbara Christian, "The Race for Theory," *Cultural Critique* 6 (Spring 1987): 61, 52.

4. Sonic Futurity in Toni Cade Bambara's *The Salt Eaters*

1. Toni Cade Bambara, "How She Came by Her Name: An Interview with Louis Massiah," in *Deep Sightings and Rescue Missions: Fiction, Essays, and Conversations*, ed. Toni Morrison (New York: Pantheon, 1996), 215.

2. Since the 1980 publication of *The Salt Eaters*, there have been several waves and permutations of critical studies on the novel, and on Bambara's intellectual contributions to black aesthetics and radical thought. Key early works include Gloria Hull's "What It Is I Think She's Doing Anyhow: A Reading of Toni Cade Bambara's *The Salt Eaters*," in *Home Girls: A Black Feminist Anthology*, ed. Barbara Smith (New York: Kitchen Table: Women of Color Press, 1983), 124–44; Eleanor Traylor, "Music as Theme: The Jazz Mode in the Works of Toni Cade Bambara," in *Black Women Writers (1950–1980): A Critical Evaluation*, ed. Mari Evans (Garden City, N.Y.: Anchor Doubleday, 1984), 58–70; and Susan Willis, "Problematizing the Individual: Toni Cade Bambara's Stories for the Revolution," in *Specifying: Black Women Writing the American Experience* (Madison: University of Wisconsin Press, 1987), 129–49. The 1990s witnessed a refocusing on Bambara's writing from a variety of critical perspectives, as seen in the following essays: Derek Alwes, "The Burden of Liberty: Choice in Toni Morrison's *Jazz* and Toni Cade Bambara's *The Salt Eaters*," *African American Review* 30, no. 3 (1996): 353–66; Janelle Collins, "Generating Power: Fission, Fusion, and Postmodern Politics in Bambara's *The Salt Eaters*," *Melus* 21, no. 2 (1996): 35–48; and Margot Anne Kelley, "'Damballah Is the First Law of Thermodynamics': Modes of Access to Toni Cade Bambara's

The Salt Eaters," *African American Review* 27, no. 3 (1993): 479–93. Most recently, the volume edited by Linda Janet Holmes and Cheryl Wall, *Savoring the Salt: The Legacy of Toni Cade Bambara* (Philadelphia: Temple University Press, 2008) collects a range of critical perspectives, reaching back into the 1970s and 1980s, but also offers several newly penned treatments of Bambara's artistic and political work. On this latter note, see especially the contributions of Cheryl Wall, Salamishah Tillet, Farah Jasmine Griffin, Rebecca Wanzo, and Avery Gordon.

3. Kalamu ya Salaam, "Searching for the Mother Tongue: An Interview with Toni Cade Bambara," in *Savoring the Salt: The Legacy of Toni Cade Bambara,* ed. Janet Holmes and Cheryl A. Wall (Philadelphia: Temple University Press, 2008), 58.

4. Toni Cade Bambara, "On the Issue of Roles," in *The Black Woman,* ed. Toni Cade Bambara (New York: Mentor, 1970), 109.

5. Bambara's experimental aesthetics suggest a meta-commentary on the interaction between the dominant trends in Western Marxism and traditions of black radicalism expressed through the possibilities of innovative literary form. I am calling attention to the possibility that when Raymond Williams refers to the fixed nature of the category of "the social" being set against the "effective presence" of lived and felt material reality, his formulation might shed some inadvertent light on the vexed relationship between black radical thought and Western Marxism. This contradiction is discussed by Cedric Robinson as a by-product of Marx's underestimation, as a theorist of labor, of "the actual terms" of the humanity of African slaves. Robinson points out how African labor was not simply labor, but "also contained African cultures, critical mixes and admixtures of language and thought, of cosmology and metaphysics, of habits, beliefs, and morality." Raymond Williams's idea of "effective presence," extended aesthetically by Bambara, might begin to approximate expressions of black radicalism in relationship to the objective category of the social posed by many renderings of Western Marxist theory. See Raymond Williams, *Marxism and Literature* (London: Oxford University Press, 1977), 128–35; and Cedric Robinson, *Black Marxism: The Making of the Black Radical Tradition* (Chapel Hill: University of North Carolina Press, 2000), 121.

6. The wealth of writing on this topic is large. The works most formative to my thinking on this topic include Manning Marable, *Race, Reform, and Rebellion: The Second Reconstruction in Black America, 1945–1990* (Jackson: University Press of Mississippi, 1991); Vincent Harding, *The Other American Revolution* (Los Angeles: UCLA Center for Afro-American Studies, 1980); Martin Luther King, Jr., *Where Do We Go from Here: Chaos or Community?* (Boston: Beacon Press, 1967); Robert Allen, *Black Awakening in Capitalist America* (New York: Doubleday, 1970); Komozi Woodard, *A Nation within a Nation: Amiri Baraka (LeRoi Jones) and Black Power Politics* (Chapel Hill: University of North Carolina Press, 1999); and Nikhil Singh's *Black Is a Country: Race and the Unfinished Struggle for Democracy* (Cambridge, Mass.: Harvard University Press, 2004).

7. Marion Brown, "Improvisation and the Aural Tradition in Afro-American Music," *Black World*, November 1973, 19.

8. Achille Mbembe, *On the Postcolony* (Berkeley: University of California Press, 2001), 16.

9. Ibid., 14, 17. Here I would also like to point to the way that the conversation with Mbembe's text, regarding time/temporality and black consciousness, could also be clearly extended to include Paul Gilroy's *The Black Atlantic: Modernity and Double Consciousness* (Cambridge, Mass.: Harvard University Press, 1993); David Scott's *Conscripts of Modernity: The Tragedy of Colonial Enlightenment* (Durham, N.C.: Duke University Press, 2004); and Brent Edwards's *The Practice of Diaspora: Literature, Translation, and the Rise of Black Internationalism* (Cambridge, Mass.: Harvard University Press, 2003).

10. Toni Cade Bambara, *The Salt Eaters* (New York: Random House, 1980), 3–5.

11. Bambara's reference to the temporal bone signals her finer attention to the physiological dimensions of Velma's sonic healing. The specific reference to the temporal bone contains a wealth of potential thematic lines that are touched on throughout the novel. For example, the two sections of the temporal bone are situated at the lower portions of the skull, and in surrounding each ear not only situate these hearing organs, but also encompasses the vestibular labyrinth in its petrous portion. This portion of the inner ear regulates one's sense of equilibrium and balance—physiological processes that Bambara often invokes to describe the nexus of the political, personal, and spiritual dimensions of experience and consciousness. For contemporary critical approaches very much in line with Bambara's consideration of the bodily and the sonic, see, for example, Douglas Kahn, *Noise, Water, Meat: A History of Sound in the Arts* (Cambridge, Mass.: MIT Press, 2001); as well as Michael Bull and Les Black, eds., *The Auditory Culture Reader* (New York: Berg, 2003).

12. Bambara, *The Salt Eaters*, 6–7.

13. Ibid., 18.

14. Ibid., 19–20.

15. Mae G. Henderson, "Speaking in Tongues: Dialogics, Dialectics, and the Black Woman Writer's Literary Tradition," in *Changing Our Own Words: Essays on Criticism, Theory, and Writing by Black Women*, ed. Cheryl A. Wall (New Brunswick, N.J.: Rutgers University Press, 1989) 20.

16. Bambara, *The Salt Eaters*, 15.

17. Ibid., 14.

18. Hamer's August 22, 1964, testimony before the Credentials Committee at the Democratic Party National Convention in Atlantic City, New Jersey, recounts this brutal experience as enacted and choreographed by Mississippi law enforcement officials. Her reframing of this scene is instructive not only for its documentation

of state violence, but also in the way that she focuses on the sounds of terror to help her narrate this situation within a continuum that might recall apocryphal scenes of subjection under slavery such as Frederick Douglass's aural witnessing of his Aunt Hester's torture. Here are Hamer's words: "And June the 9th, 1963, I had attended a voter registration workshop; was returning back to Mississippi. Ten of us was traveling by the Continental Trailway bus. When we got to Winona, Mississippi, which is Montgomery County, four of the people got off to use the washroom, and two of the people—to use the restaurant—two of the people wanted to use the washroom. The four people that had gone in to use the restaurant was ordered out. During this time I was on the bus. But when I looked through the window and saw they had rushed out I got off of the bus to see what had happened. And one of the ladies said, 'It was a State Highway Patrolman and a Chief of Police ordered us out.' I got back on the bus and one of the persons had used the washroom got back on the bus, too. As soon as I was seated on the bus, I saw when they began to get the five people in a highway patrolman's car. I stepped off of the bus to see what was happening and somebody screamed from the car that the five workers was in and said, 'Get that one there.' When I went to get in the car, when the man told me I was under arrest, he kicked me. I was carried to the county jail and put in the booking room. They left some of the people in the booking room and began to place us in cells. I was placed in a cell with a young woman called Miss Ivesta Simpson. After I was placed in the cell I began to hear sounds of licks and screams, I could hear the sounds of licks and horrible screams. And I could hear somebody say, 'Can you say, "yes, sir," nigger? Can you say "yes, sir"?' And they would say other horrible names. She would say, 'Yes, I can say "yes, sir."' 'So, well, say it.' She said, 'I don't know you well enough.' They beat her, I don't know how long. And after a while she began to pray, and asked God to have mercy on those people. And it wasn't too long before three white men came to my cell. One of these men was a State Highway Patrolman and he asked me where I was from. I told him Ruleville and he said, 'We are going to check this.' They left my cell and it wasn't too long before they came back. He said, 'You are from Ruleville all right,' and he used a curse word. And he said, 'We are going to make you wish you was dead.' I was carried out of that cell into another cell where they had two Negro prisoners. The State Highway Patrolmen ordered the first Negro to take the blackjack. The first Negro prisoner ordered me, by orders from the State Highway Patrolman, for me to lay down on a bunk bed on my face. I laid on my face and the first Negro began to beat. I was beat by the first Negro until he was exhausted. I was holding my hands behind me at that time on my left side, because I suffered from polio when I was six years old. After the first Negro had beat until he was exhausted, the State Highway Patrolman ordered the second Negro to take the blackjack. The second Negro began to beat and I began to work my feet, and the State Highway Patrolman ordered the first Negro who had beat me to sit on my feet—to keep me from working my feet. I began to scream and one white man got up and began to beat me in my head and tell me to hush. One white man—my dress had worked up high—he walked over and pulled my dress—I pulled my dress down and he pulled my dress back up. I was in jail when Medgar Evers was murdered. All of this is on account of we want to register, to become first-class citizens. And if the Freedom Democratic Party is not seated now, I question America. Is this America, the land of the free and the home of the brave, where we have to sleep with our telephones off the hooks because our lives be threatened daily, because we want to live as decent human beings, in America? Thank you." The transcript and audio of speech can be found on the American Radio Works website, *Say It Plain: A Century of Great African American Speeches*: http://americanradioworks .publicradio.org/features/sayitplain/flhamer.html.

19. Bambara, *The Salt Eaters*, 15.

20. Jacquelyn Dowd Hall, "The Long Civil Rights Movement and the Political Uses of the Past," *Journal of American History* 91, no. 4 (2005): 1233.

21. Elizabeth Alexander, *The Black Interior* (Saint Paul, Minn.: Graywolf Press, 2004), 5, 7.

22. Toni Cade Bambara, "Reading the Signs, Empowering the Eye: *Daughters of the Dust* and the Black Independent Cinema Movement," in *Deep Sightings and Rescue Missions*, ed. Morrison, 92–93.

23. Andre Breton, *What Is Surrealism? Selected Writings* (New York: Pathfinder, 1978), 155–56.

24. René Ménil, "Introduction to the Marvellous," in *Refusal of the Shadow: Surrealism and the Caribbean*, ed. Michael Richardson, trans. Michael Richardson and Krzysztof Fijalkowski (London: Verso, 1996), 90.

25. Bambara, *The Salt Eaters*, 28.

26. Ibid., 35–37.

27. Ibid., 38–39. Bambara's specific use of equine female imagery resonates strongly with an account of King's extramarital affairs provided by an unnamed King associate, quoted by David Garrow: "He loved beautiful women . . . the girls he 'dated' were just like models . . . the girls were tall stallions, all usually were very fair, never dark." *Bearing the Cross: Martin Luther King, Jr., and the Southern Christian Leadership Conference* (New York: Vintage, 1988), 375.

28. Ibid., 39–41.

29. Ibid., 69–70.

30. Ibid., 83, 73.

31. There is clearly a way in which Fred Holt might invoke the Yoruba figure of Eshu–Elegba, or Legba, particularly through Bambara's invocation of the crossroads to begin the scene, and possibly reflected in Holt's nausea as symbolic of the physical reactions to forms of spiritual initiation or possession. See, for example, the work of Robert Farris Thompson in *Flash of the Spirit*.

32. Ibid., 86–87

33. Ibid., 87; emphasis added.

34. Ibid., 265.

35. Ibid., 168.

36. Ibid., 168–69.

37. Ibid., 168. Separate critical attention should be dedicated to thinking about Bambara's engagement with the phonograph and psychic space alongside Ellison's prologue to *Invisible Man.*

38. Bambara, *The Salt Eaters,* 170.

39. The "pan man in dreadlocks" who pays close attention to the possibilities of "Word-Sound-Power" and the oneness of life (Jah), seemingly represents a Rastafarian presence in the text, thus expanding the diasporic scope of Bambara's spiritual/political lens on black life.

40. Ibid., 170–72.

41. Ibid., 251.

42. Ibid., 278–79.

43. Ibid., 291–92.

44. Attali, *Noise,* 9.

45. The sense of a space–time continuum that Bambara's use of textual sound explores and reconfigures, does speak to an effort at epistemological disruption of the kind formulated through surrealists in the first half of the twentieth century, and theorized by writers such as Herbert Marcuse and Frantz Fanon in the 1960s. Across these efforts, intellectuals share a commitment to eroding the maintenance of hierarchies of reason, difference, and social stratification.

46. Toni Morrison, "Unspeakable Things Unspoken: The Afro-American Presence in American Literature," *Michigan Quarterly Review* 28, no. 1 (1989): 32.

5. The Radical Tonality of James Baldwin's Post–Civil Rights Blues

1. James Baldwin, "Going to Meet the Man," in *Going to Meet the Man* (New York: Dell, 1965), 198.

2. James Baldwin, "The American Dream and the American Negro," in *The Price of the Ticket: Collected Nonfiction, 1948–1985* (New York: St. Martin's Press, 1985), 405. Originally delivered as address at the Cambridge Union Society of Cambridge University, February 1965. Subsequently published in the *New York Times Magazine,* March 7, 1965.

3. Baldwin's short story provides a creative window that anticipates a field of theoretical investigation now referred to as "critical whiteness studies." A signal and early formative text that bridges the deep psychological inquiry into whiteness offered by Baldwin, and the eventual formation of critical whiteness studies, is Joel Kovel's heavily psychoanalytic study *White Racism: A Psychohistory* (1970;

repr., New York: Columbia University Press, 1984). Kovel's preface to the second edition, published in 1984, is interesting in itself as a commentary on the question of a post–Civil Rights era. Writing amid the continuing retrenchment against the Civil Rights gains of the 1960s that was occurring during the first term of the Reagan administration, Kovel argues that "no responsible person would claim today that the racial breakthroughs of the sixties have even held their own, much less advanced beyond the modest proportions won during that period of hectic struggle" (xix).

4. Jacques Rancière, *The Politics of Aesthetics: The Distribution of the Sensible*, trans. Gabriel Rockhill (2000; repr., New York: Continuum, 2004), 12, 18.

5. Baldwin, "Going to Meet the Man," 198–99.

6. James Baldwin, "White Man's Guilt," in *The Price of the Ticket*, 412. Originally published in *Ebony*, August 1965.

7. Baldwin, "Going to Meet the Man," 199–200.

8. Ibid., 200.

9. Ibid., 200–205.

10. Ibid., 207–14. For a thorough account of the "cultural logic" of lynching in the United States, see Jacqueline Goldsby, *A Spectacular Secret: Lynching in American Life and Literature* (Chicago: University of Chicago Press, 2006).

11. Baldwin, "Going to Meet the Man," 216–17.

12. David Leeming, *James Baldwin: A Biography* (New York: Henry Holt, 1994), 256, 304.

13. The central issue of Baldwin's homosexuality and its relationship to his intellectual production has now been addressed rather extensively from a variety of critical positions. See, for example, Magdalena Zaborowska, *James Baldwin: Erotics of Exile* (Durham, N.C.: Duke University Press, 2009); Fred Moten, *In the Break: The Aesthetics of the Black Radical Tradition* (Minneapolis: University of Minnesota Press, 2003); Maurice Wallace, *Constructing the Black Masculine: Identity and Ideology in African American Men's Literature and Culture, 1775–1995* (Durham, N.C.: Duke University Press, 2002); and Marlon Ross, "White Fantasies of Desire: Baldwin and the Racial Identities of Sexuality," in *James Baldwin Now*, ed. Dwight McBride (New York: NYU Press, 1999), 13–55.

14. Leeming, *James Baldwin*, 304.

15. Ibid.

16. I use the term "black freedom struggle" to denote an historical perspective in which the expanse of Civil Rights movement organizations and Black Power–influenced formations are considered as part of a broader continuum, rather than as discrete historical stages. Such a perspective is crucial in assessing the contributions of Baldwin during this period, as his writing and activism allowed for more ideological fluidity within this continuum, and, arguably, did not depend on him having to reconstruct his stances in order to appreciate and connect with various political points within such a continuum.

17. Vincent Harding, *The Other American Revolution* (Los Angeles and Atlanta: Center for Afro-American Studies, University of California, Los Angeles, and Institute of the Black World, 1980), 212.

18. Ibid.

19. By "blues epistemology," I am referring to the long tradition of black critical inquiry into the various meanings of the blues. This tradition encompasses, but is certainly not limited to, perspectives on the distinctive musicological and thematic qualities of the blues provided by Zora Neale Hurston, Sterling Brown, Ralph Ellison, Albert Murray, Gayl Jones, Langston Hughes, Amiri Baraka, Sherley Anne Williams, Houston Baker, and August Wilson. These writers all share an appreciation for the expressive power of the form and its ability to convey various intricacies of black historical consciousness.

20. Although many critics have commented in passing, or in part, on Baldwin's attention to music (indeed it is inescapable), there are relatively few studies that singularly treat this aspect of his intellectual background and approach outside of close readings of specific creative works. The studies that seem most oriented in this direction of theorizing the various conceptual aspects of Baldwin's relationship to black music are D. Quentin Miller, "Using the Blues: James Baldwin and Music," in *A Historical Guide to James Baldwin*, ed. Douglas Field (New York: Oxford University Press, 2009), 83–110; Walton Muyumba, *The Shadow and the Act: Black Intellectual Practice, Jazz Improvisation, and Philosophical Pragmatism* (Chicago: University of Chicago Press, 2009); Moten, *In the Break*; and Josh Kun, "Life According to the Beat: James Baldwin, Bessie Smith, and the Perilous Sounds of Love," in *James Baldwin Now*, ed. McBride.

21. James Baldwin, "What's the Reason Why? A Symposium by Best-Selling Authors," *New York Times*, December 2, 1962.

22. The reference to Henry James is from the essay "Criticism," included in the volume *Essays in London and Elsewhere* (1893).

23. Magdalena Zaborowska, *James Baldwin's Turkish Decade: Erotics of Exile* (Durham, N.C.: Duke University Press, 2009), 212.

24. Douglass Field, "James Baldwin in His Time," in *Critical Insights: James Baldwin*, ed. Morris Dickstein (Ipswich, Mass.: Salem Press, 2009), 26.

25. Ralph Ellison, "Richard Wright's Blues," in *Shadow and Act* (New York: Quality Paperback Book Club, 1964), 94.

26. Ibid., 89.

27. James Baldwin, "The Uses of the Blues," in *The Cross of Redemption: Uncollected Writings*, ed. Randall Kenan (New York: Pantheon, 2010), 64. It should be noted that Leeming points to Baldwin's early relationship with Beauford Delaney as a formative aspect of his blues sensibility. Leeming writes, "For the first time, under Beauford's guidance, he began to undergo the 'religious' experience of jazz and blues. Beauford played Ella Fitzgerald, Ma Rainey, Louis Armstrong, Bessie

Smith, Ethel Waters, Paul Robeson, Lena Horne, and Fats Waller. And he talked about them in the soft caressing voice to which Baldwin would turn for comfort in the darkest moments of years to come." *James Baldwin*, 33.

28. Baldwin, "The Uses of the Blues," 57–66.

29. The 1960s were a flashpoint for reconsiderations of the social, historical, and political contexts of the blues. Baldwin's essayistic inquiry into the meaning and uses of the blues can also be understood in the literary historical context of LeRoi Jones's social and political history of black music, *Blues People*, published one year prior, as well as Ellison's somewhat scathing review of Jones's work.

30. Jean-François Augoyard and Henry Torgue, eds., *Sonic Experience: A Guide to Everyday Sounds*, trans. Andrea McCartney and David Paquette (Montreal: McGill-Queen's University Press, 2005), 21.

31. Nathaniel Mackey, *Paracritical Hinge: Essays, Talks, Notes, Interviews* (Madison: University of Wisconsin Press, 2005), 290.

32. Derek Bailey, *Improvisation: Its Nature and Practice in Music* (New York: Da Capo, 1993), 142.

33. Zaborowska, *James Baldwin's Turkish Decade*, 180, 189, 178.

34. For more details on Cherry's music and his place within free jazz, see Ekkehard Jost, *Free Jazz* (New York: Da Capo, 1974); and Valerie Wilmer's *As Serious as Your Life: John Coltrane and Beyond* (1977; repr., New York: Serpent's Tail, 1992).

35. Zaborowska, *James Baldwin's Turkish Decade*, 179.

36. This performance was originally released as an LP in 1978, on the Sonet label, under the title *Live Ankara*. It has subsequently been rereleased as part of a double album titled *The Sonet Recordings: Eternal Now/Live Ankara* by Verve in 1996.

37. Max Horkheimer, *Eclipse of Reason* (New York: Continuum, 1974), 182.

38. Ellison, *Invisible Man*, 8.

39. James Baldwin, *No Name in the Street* (New York: Dial, 1972), 3–7.

40. Ibid., 10.

41. Larry Neal, "The Black Writer's Role, III: James Baldwin," in *Visions of a Liberated Future*, ed. Schwartz, 59–61.

42. Baldwin, *No Name in the Street*, 10–11, 14. The fact that this childhood friend of Baldwin's remains nameless in the account is perhaps significant in the way it becomes another point of thematic interplay with the title of the work—as the "no name" or nameless quality of the acquaintance helps put into relief that fact that the individual here is more broadly representative of a national and racial set of conditions that have shaped the dynamics of the moment.

43. Ibid., 19–21.

44. Ibid., 78–79.

45. Frantz Fanon, *The Wretched of the Earth*, trans. Richard Philcox (1961; repr., New York: Grove Press, 2004), 163.

46. Ibid. Reading Fanon and Baldwin together opens up an unending series of questions and observations regarding critical race theory and narrative aesthetics. One particularly interesting level of this convergence in terms of Fanon's work is the way his poetic phrasing has been translated by different individuals, and in different historical moments. For instance, the 1966 edition of *Wretched of the Earth*, translated by Constance Farrington, renders the phrase I have drawn on, "zone of hidden fluctuation," as "zone of occult instability." For more on the issue of Fanon and translation, see Robert J. C. Young's essay "Frantz Fanon and the Enigma of Cultural Translation," *Translation: A Transdisciplinary Journal* 1 (2012): 91–100.

47. This point regarding the epistemological issues of racial consciousness and resistance emerges from both a long and contemporary tradition of writing on race and philosophy. Building on the work of these intellectuals and scholars in today's academy, my critical viewpoint is that understanding the philosophical substance of racial consciousness is relevant not only to mapping the different contours of how ideas of race have functioned within a black critical tradition, but also that such an orientation allows for a specific engagement with the much-debated question of identity politics. Once one begins to chart the depth and richness of black philosophical discourse through the past two centuries of American life (and this is not to limit the scope of the enterprise geographically, for as all scholars of the African diaspora realize, addressing the cultural and critical manifestations of black thought within any location within the diaspora can never be limited entirely by that particular black space, as the spatiality of black freedom transcends national lines and moves much more enticingly and ephemerally through diasporic space), it becomes increasingly clear that the various articulations of black national and Pan-African consciousness that move through these years are often as much tied to contemporaneous discussions of matters of essence, phenomenology, identity, and expression within broader Western philosophical discourse, as they are reflective of any sense of ethnic and racial particularity.

48. Frantz Fanon, *The Wretched of the Earth*, trans. Richard Philcox (1961; repr., New York: Grove Press, 2004), 168.

49. Baldwin, *No Name in the Street*, 86–87.

50. Ibid., 92, 90.

51. Ibid., 190.

52. James Baldwin, *The Fire Next Time* (1963; repr., New York: Random House, 1993), 10.

53. James Baldwin, "Black Power," in *The Cross of Redemption*, ed. Kenan, 82–83.

54. James Baldwin, "The Nigger We Invent," in *The Cross of Redemption*, ed. Kenan, 90.

55. James Baldwin, "An Open Letter to My Sister Angela Y. Davis," in *The Cross of Redemption*, ed. Kenan, 211.

56. James Baldwin, "Speech at the Soledad Rally," in *The Cross of Redemption*, ed. Kenan, 101.

57. James Baldwin, "The Price May Be Too High," in *The Cross of Redemption*, ed. Kenan, 87.

58. Baldwin, *No Name in the Street*, 178–79.

59. Ibid., 179–85.

60. Ibid., 188.

61. Jean-Luc Nancy, *Listening*, trans. Charlotte Mandell (New York: Fordham University Press, 2007), 27.

62. Baldwin, *No Name in the Street*, 188, 192.

63. Aimé Césaire, *Discourse on Colonialism*, trans. Joan Pinkham (1955; repr., New York: Monthly Review Press, 2000), 68.

64. Ibid., 192, 166, 164, 196.

Epilogue

1. Adolph Reed, "The 'Black Revolution' and the Reconstitution of Domination," in *Race, Politics, Culture: Critical Essays on the Radicalism of the 1960s*, ed. Adolph Reed (Westport, Conn.: Greenwood, 1986), 63.

2. Gil Scott-Heron, *Free Will*, recorded March 2–3, 1972, RCA, 1972. *Free Will* was the third release in Heron's over four-decade career—a career that included not only twenty-five albums, but two novels, a master's thesis completed for an MFA at Johns Hopkins, at least one volume of poetry, and a film collaboration with Robert Mugge, *Black Wax* (in which concert footage is intermixed with Heron "waxing" poetic about the political situation in the 1970s, sometimes to a wax figure of Uncle Sam).

3. While it is fairly common for critics to point to Heron as a "godfather of rap," he never completely embraced the label. It is true that his late 1960s spoken-word style did formally prefigure early rap music; the political content of his lyrics sets a path for the political use of rhyme and flow most obviously demonstrated by artists such as Public Enemy and KRS-One.

4. Heron actually intersects in several direct and indirect ways with several figures I cover in this book. His love of John Coltrane is reflected on the last track of *Free Will*, a spoken-word composition dedicated to Coltrane's *A Love Supreme* titled, "... And Then He Wrote Meditations." He also worked closely with producer Bob Thiele, who produced Coltrane's later work on the Impulse label. Heron, like Larry Neal, attended Lincoln University, the famed institution of African American higher learning with a list of notable alumni including Langston Hughes, Cab Calloway, Melvin Tolson, and Kwame Nkrumah. Also, at the "No Nukes" concert at Madison Square Garden in 1979, Heron performed the song "South Carolina (Barnwell)," which sonically converges with Toni Cade Bambara's commentary on the threat posed by the nuclear industry to black communities in the South.

5. Naylor states in a 1997 interview, "*Linden Hills* is about the black upper class and their morals. However, there is no simple answer. Black folks were so eager to integrate into the white world so they could make believe that their good work would make them colorless. After all that's what America is all about." Ethel Morgan Smith, "An Interview with Gloria Naylor," *Callaloo* 23, no. 4 (2000): 1431.

6. Gloria Naylor, *Linden Hills* (New York: Penguin, 1985), 60.

7. Ibid., 16.

8. Ibid., 60.

9. John Edgar Wideman, *Philadelphia Fire* (New York: Henry Holt, 1990), 158.

10. John Edgar Wideman, "The Architectonics of Fiction," *Callaloo* 13, no. 1 (1990): 43–45.

Index

accumulation, 29, 111, 120–21; framework of, 83; poetics of, 121

Acoli, Sundiata, 1

acoustics, 10, 15, 41, 64, 66, 83, 87; literary, 94, 168; narrative, 5, 176, 184

activist, 103, 133, 141–43, 160; elder, 146; veteran, 21; young, 159

Adderley, Cannonball, 28

Adelsen, Charles, 174

Adorno, Theodor, 105–6

Africa, 12, 125; neocolonial, 190, 207n26, 217–18n53

African diaspora, 33, 87, 217n53; scholars of, 231n47

Afro-Atlantic cultural production, 59

Afternoon of a Georgia Faun, 52–53

Alexander, Elizabeth, 144

Ali, Rashied, 23, 32, 35

alienation, 64, 83, 86, 89; critique of, 84, 174; progress and, 202; psychic weight of, 146

alterity, 24, 38, 78, 90

ambivalence, 33, 55, 138, 146

American Radio Works, 225–26n18

Americas, the, 59, 211–12n44

amplification, 33, 87

analyses, 213n3; musicological, 18; verbal, 94

Anderson, Iain, 58

"And Shine Swam On," 22

Ankara, 175

anticapitalist, 31

apartheid, 159, 182, 195, 217n40

arc, 43, 66, 89, 214

armed struggle, 5

Armstrong, Louis, 120

arpeggio, 120

Art Blakey's Jazz Messengers, 28

articulation, 108, 129, 183, 190, 218n56; (dis)articulation, 217–18n53, 231n47; political, 172; predetermination and, 11; racial state and, 9; rearticulation, 35, 74, 127; struggle and, 99; sound and, 20, 85, 131, 138, 168; stagnation and, 146; transgressive forms of, 5, 31

artifice, 81, 208n2

Ascension, 24, 43, 49, 51

Asia, 125

assassinations, 24, 169, 206–7n16

As Serious as Your Life: John Coltrane and Beyond, 44

asymmetry, 6, 113, 129; cohesion out of, 129; difference and, 6, 129

Atkins, Russell, 62

Atlanta, 52

Atlantic City, 224–25n18

"Atlantis," 29

atmosphere, 56, 105, 139; sonic, 194

Attali, Jacques, 7, 38–39, 157

Audubon Ballroom, 125

Augoyard, Jean-François, 173

CARTER MATHES is associate professor of English at Rutgers University, where he teaches African American literature, twentieth-century music and literature, literature of the African diaspora, and experimental writing.